Taking Stands

Maureen G. Reed

Taking Stands:
Gender and the Sustainability
of Rural Communities

UBCPress · Vancouver · Toronto

© UBC Press 2003

All rights reserved. No part of this publication may be reproduced, stored in a retrieval system, or transmitted, in any form or by any means, without prior written permission of the publisher, or, in Canada, in the case of photocopying or other reprographic copying, a licence from CANCOPY (Canadian Copyright Licensing Agency), www.cancopy.com.

09 08 07 06 05 04 03   5 4 3 2 1

Printed in Canada on acid-free paper that is 100% post-consumer recycled, processed chlorine-free, and printed with vegetable-based, low-VOC inks.

National Library of Canada Cataloguing in Publication Data

Reed, Maureen Gail, 1961-

Taking stands : gender and the sustainability of rural communities / Maureen G. Reed.

   Includes bibliographical references and index.
   ISBN 0-7748-1017-3 (bound). – ISBN 0-7748-1018-1 (pbk.)

   1. Women in rural development – British Columbia. 2. Rural development – British Columbia. 3. Sustainable forestry – British Columbia. I. Title.
   HQ1240.5.C3R43 2003   307.72'09711   C2003-910355-2

Canadä

UBC Press gratefully acknowledges the financial support for our publishing program of the Government of Canada through the Book Publishing Industry Development Program (BPIDP), and of the Canada Council for the Arts, and the British Columbia Arts Council.

This book has been published with the help of a grant from the Humanities and Social Sciences Federation of Canada, using funds provided by the Social Sciences and Humanities Research Council of Canada.

Printed and bound in Canada by Friesens
Set in Stone by Brenda and Neil West, BN Typographics West
Copy editor: Dallas Harrison
Proofreader: Janet Dimond
Indexer: Noeline Bridge

UBC Press
The University of British Columbia
2029 West Mall
Vancouver, BC V6T 1Z2
604-822-5959 / Fax: 604-822-6083
www.ubcpress.ca

To my father:
You never doubted that I could complete this task if I believed in myself; you taught me my place in the world and that "real-life stories" are even more dramatic than fiction;

To my mother:
You taught me to be compassionate toward others, to be tenacious in (re)quilting and (re)writing, and to celebrate the perfection of everyday life;

And, especially, to my sons, Michael and Louis, and my life partner Bruce: You are the place where my politics begin and my heart rests; may we work together for a world of equality, justice, and good, plain fun.

Contents

Preface / ix

Acknowledgments / xi

Abbreviations / xiii

1 Introduction: Seeing the Trees among Women in Forestry Communities / 3

2 Transition and Social Marginalization of Forestry Communities / 25

3 Policy and Structural Change in Rural British Columbia / 57

4 Women and Woods Work: The Gender of Forestry Jobs / 79

5 Women's Lives, Husbands' Wives: "Managing" Forestry Communities / 117

6 Communities Confront Outsiders / 159

7 Fitting In: Making a Place for Gender in Environmental and Land Use Planning / 189

8 Social Sustainability and the Renewal of Research Agendas / 217

Epilogue / 231

Appendix: Describing and Reflecting on Research Methods / 233

Notes / 253

References / 261

Index / 275

Preface

> A man in the wilderness
>   asked this of me,
> How many strawberries
>   grow in the sea.
> I answered him,
>   as I thought good,
> As many red herrings
>   as swim in the wood.[1]

This book is primarily concerned with exploring the lives and perspectives of women who resist new environmental regulations affecting logging in the temperate rainforests of British Columbia, Canada. The research has been guided by the question "Should women who resist new environmental regulations be considered part of feminist struggles for environmental sustainability and social justice, or are they part of the problem of resolving them?" Drawing on geographic and feminist theory, and on rural and environmental studies, I consider how recent environmental priorities, as expressed through the environmental movement and policy practices, are viewed by, and affect, the social lives of women living in forestry communities. These women pose a paradox. In research about gender and environmental activism, women are usually depicted as protectors of the natural environment; in research about gender and labour activism in rural/resource communities, women are viewed as defenders of workers and communities. When forestry is both the target of environmental activism and the source of livelihood and community struggles, these depictions fall short. These images are, as the poem above suggests, red herrings in the woods.

In this book, I relate stories about forestry-town women. I consider women's lives within diverse and changing aspects of social life in forestry communities. I discuss their attachments to forestry and endeavour to explain their perspectives and activism during times of transition, in both public policy and land use. In a study focused on women's experiences, I make observations about gender and gender relations, recognizing that stories about gender relations require explanations of the lives of both men and women. As I write about the lives of these women, I consider how they are situated in relation to changes in government policies and practices, systems of economic relations, prescribed gender behaviours within local communities, and specific (paid and unpaid) labour practices. I argue that women's experiences have been dramatically shaped by their relation to men and masculinist institutions associated with forestry.

My objective, then, is to discuss women in relation to men and to study feminine and feminist institutions in relation to male and masculinist institutions – that is, to explore gendered relations. In forestry communities of Canada's West Coast, the relations between women and men, women and forestry, women and women, and women and place are intertwined with a particular history of resource extraction and dependency. Furthermore, these relations are punctuated by a specific present characterized by the region's geographic and social location in the provincial and, indeed, national and international political economies.

My choice to speak from the experiences of forestry-town women is a personal one. It is not born of the idea that women are the only or most important component of forestry debates. Neither is it born of a belief that all women in forestry communities share the same experiences or perspectives. Rather, I believe that the voices of women have been muted within the institutions that shape public policy making and that their stories are legitimate ones. My interest in activism is strategic. I deliberately go beyond the front lines of political protest and enter the communities, the homes, and the personal lives of forestry-town women whose stories have yet to be told.

In keeping with other feminist geographies, this study is a multiscale analysis. It establishes links between macroscale processes associated with economic practices and public policy making affecting the environment and development; the mesoscale of action in the workplace and household; and the microscale of personal perspectives and values where individuals' actions, behaviours, and meanings are revealed and their implications are assessed. By doing so, I extend ideas about what constitutes activism and link relations in the home and workplace to an agenda of publicly observed protest.

During this research project, I was frequently asked why I wanted to focus attention on women's anti-environmental activism. It is a central thesis of this book that environmentalism is an important social challenge, and social considerations must accompany demands for changes in human-ecological relations. By considering forestry issues from the perspective of women who live in forestry communities, I hope to dispense with the dichotomies of "pro" and "anti" that currently polarize environmental debates. By examining how women's experiences are shaped through historical, environmental, social, economic, and political changes, it is possible to understand how women interpret these changes and organize to take action within the larger society. Only through a heightened understanding of these processes can we address problems of mutual concern that link a politics favouring environmental protection with a politics that supports social justice.

Acknowledgments

The research for this book was funded by a grant from Forest Renewal BC, administered by the Science Council of BC. The techniques used in this project were possible because of the generous allowances provided under this program. In addition, the seeds of this research were sown by virtue of a scholar-in-residence position that I held at the Centre for Research in Women's Studies and Gender Relations at the University of British Columbia in 1996. Although I was new to gender studies at that time, I was welcomed by all those at the centre. Thank you for the refuge that you provided.

While we complain about the loneliness of writing, we sometimes forget the supports on which we draw. I owe much gratitude to Randy Schmidt, my editor at UBC Press, who believed that this book was possible and who, along with Jean Wilson, indeed demonstrated that the press was a "kinder, gentler" group with whom to work. Dallas Harrison provided a careful and constructive copy edit and Darcy Cullen oversaw the production of the book. Two anonymous reviewers offered generous comments and constructive advice for improving the manuscript.

In addition, Paul Jance (University of British Columbia), and Keith Bigelow and Elise Pietroniro (University of Saskatchewan), completed maps and provided other technical assistance. Maija Heimo, Janice May, and Mary Pullen were UBC graduate student research assistants on the project. Cathie Williamson undertook transcribing. Parts of this book were read by many people, including Gerry Pratt (who encouraged me to speak out), Elizabeth Bronson, Rose Klinkenberg, Maija Heimo, Scott Prudham, and Juanita Sundberg. Greg Halseth badgered me every so often to get that "often talked about but never seen" book finished. Bruce Mitchell, always ready to lend support, helped me to become a better scholar throughout this project. His leadership and friendship have served me long after his "statutory obligations" were fulfilled. He offered logistical and practical assistance as well as solid advice. Rhonda Koster, Lesley McBain, and Sharmalene Mendis helped me in the final year of editing after I had moved to the University of Saskatchewan. Terry Rolfe gave me a great deal of support when my energies flagged and provided editorial assistance toward the end.

While at UBC, I was fortunate to count my colleagues as friends. Many people heard half-baked ideas and computer woes and offered support, including Trevor Barnes, Rosemary Cann, Lorna Chan, Elaine Cho, Michael Church, Derek Gregory, Dan Hiebert, Brian Klinkenberg, Sandy Lapsky, Les Lavkulich, Geraldine Pratt, Olav Slaymaker, John Stager, Graeme Wynn, and Jeanne Yang. Alison Gill at Simon Fraser University has remained a steadfast friend.

Since moving to the University of Saskatchewan, I have been surrounded by a small but welcoming group of women, both in the Department of Geography and the Department of Women's and Gender Studies. Lesley Biggs, Pamela Downe, Diane Martz, Lesley McBain, Evelyn Peters, and Colleen Youngs have all provided ideas and encouragement. Beyond individual places, many people have had to listen to me "preach" parts of this book during conferences, special presentations, and classes. I thank them for their indulgence, sharp questions, and opportunities to refine my argument. I also acknowledge the late Suzanne MacKenzie, whose scholarship, integrity, compassion, and good humour I still attempt to model.

Of course, this book would not have been possible without the women of Vancouver Island. Women on northern Vancouver Island gave up their time for interviews, focus groups, and community meetings. Women researchers on the North Island undertook some of the interviews and participated in an initial interpretive workshop. The women whom I encountered were courageous, warm, funny, and smart. Thank you for letting me into your lives. In addition, I thank the organization North Island Women for its faith in me by allowing me to give the keynote address at their inaugural celebration in April 1999. This invitation remains one of the personal highlights of my career. I thank Fiona for her friendship.

Finally, I owe a very personal debt to my family, near and far. My siblings, Kathi, Don, and Nancy, and my parents have been my champions for so many years. Long after everyone else was bored by my work, they continued to ask how it was going. I know that my dad will read every word, including the endnotes. That means a lot to me. Please don't tell me if you find any typos. My mom and I will continue to share our writing and quilting frustrations. It helps to know that I'm not the only one who has to rip things out. I know that it's worth it to get it right. My immediate family members – Bruce, my life partner, Louis and Michael, my sons – have put up with my obsession with this project for years. They first taught me that family is an appropriate site of radical and ongoing political action. I promise that I will clean up the dining table as soon as I'm finished with this book.

Abbreviations

BCRTEE	British Columbia Round Table on the Environment and the Economy
The Charter	Land Use Charter
The Code	Forest Practices Code
CORE	Commission on Resources and Environment
CRB	community resources board
CWIT	Canadian Women in Timber
ENGOs	environmental nongovernmental organizations
FRBC	Forest Renewal British Columbia
IUCN	World Conservation Union (formerly known as the International Union for the Conservation of Nature and Natural Resources)
IWA	International Woodworkers of America
LRMP	land and resource management plans
MOF	Ministry of Forests (also called the Forest Service)
MWRD	Mount Waddington Regional District
PAS	Protected Areas Strategy
SHARE	generic abbreviation for numerous groups who seek to "share" resources between environmental and industrial interests. SHARE groups are called "wise use" groups in the United States. On northern Vancouver Island, the name of the specific SHARE group is the Coalition for Shared Resources on Northern Vancouver Island.
SSHRC	Social Sciences and Humanties Research Council
VICORE	Vancouver Island CORE process

Taking Stands

Forestry families unite in protest at the BC Legislature against the Vancouver Island Land Use Plan. *Courtesy John Yanyshyn/Vancouver Sun*

1
Introduction: Seeing the Trees among Women in Forestry Communities

> A lot of people that I know that aren't involved in the [forest] industry ... said they didn't realize there was another point of view.
>
> – Interviewee, 1997

"Other" Women's Environmental Activism

On 13 January 1993, a full-page advertisement, paid for by eight major international environmental organizations, appeared in the *New York Times*, with the question "Will Canada do nothing to save Clayoquot Sound, one of the last great temperate rainforests in the world?" Since the 1970s, several attempts to determine the fate of forestry in the region had failed. During this time period, environmental nongovernmental organizations (ENGOs) became more politically astute, professionally organized, and internationally recognized. Perhaps the best-known environmental actions were the mass demonstrations in the summer of 1993. During that long, hot summer on Canada's West Coast, a "Clayoquot Sound Peace Camp" became the focal point for civil disobedience. The camp and associated protests made nightly headline news in Canada, captured worldwide attention, drew visitors and protesters from around the world, and resulted in the arrest of over 800 people. A representative of the Sierra Club of Western Canada was quoted as saying, "Clayoquot Sound does not just belong to the Alberni-Clayoquot District anymore. It belongs to the whole world" (cited in Dearden and Mitchell 1997, 502).

Since that time, the valour of these protesters, and the women in particular, have been celebrated by environmental organizations and the popular media. The peace camp was deemed a site of ecofeminist activism by its organizers and even the popular press (Bell 1993). Indeed, this action is now part of a larger popular and academic celebration of women's environmental activism. Several sites on the World Wide Web, books, articles, a documentary film, and even academic theses have highlighted and applauded the roles that women play as moral and logistical leaders in social protest and nature protection (e.g., Berman et al. 1994; Boucher 1998; Mellor 1997; Merchant 1995; Shiva 1989; Warren, K.J. 1987, 1990; Wine 1998). This rich concentration of academic and popular work has contributed to an international recognition of the importance of Canada's

West Coast to the long-term protection of globally significant, ecologically sensitive, increasingly endangered, even sacred, temperate rainforest ecosystems.[1] It has also highlighted the important moral and political contributions that women make to these struggles for environmental sustainability.

Other stories, however, remain untold. On the other side of the issue, women who stood in support of industrial forestry also attended the peace camp in Clayoquot Sound. They stood on the opposite side of the road, wearing yellow ribbons, nervously eyeing their "sisters" (perhaps their daughters or their mothers, certainly their opponents), and occasionally throwing out comments across the way.[2] In contrast to the broad interest in the environmental protesters, the international media did not turn their lenses and microphones toward these "other" women. Consequently, we know little about the women who supported the forest industry.

We do know that these women have shown up in other places and contexts. For example, a long-awaited land use plan for Vancouver Island proposed in February 1994, by the newly created Commission on Resources and Environment (CORE), recommended reducing a proportion of the island's land base devoted to timber harvesting and placing it into parks, reserves, and other special management zones. The commissioner, Steven Owen, estimated that these recommendations would result in the loss of hundreds of direct jobs in forestry, and at least as many indirect jobs, with associated local dislocations and impacts (CORE 1994a, 195). In March 1994, 15,000 forest workers and their families congregated at the legislature to denounce the plan and demand the resignation of the commissioner (see Figure 1.1). One of the theme speakers that day was the wife of a forester. Visibly pregnant, she overcame her nervousness to speak out for the protection of forestry communities. Other protests throughout the province have also "used" women to relate threats to themselves, their families, and their communities stemming from the demands for more lands to be allocated to wilderness protection.

These other women do not fit easily within our prevailing notions about women, activism, and environmental protection. They are sometimes referred to as forestry-town women, or loggers' wives, terms that suggest a collective identity, a singularity of purpose, position, situation, perspective, and activism. In the limited research and public representations made about these women, they have been depicted primarily in terms of their dependence on men's incomes and jobs, materialistic support of industrial practices, misguided conservatism, and/or maternalistic attachments to their families. They have frequently been viewed as unworthy, irrelevant, or regressive actors in environmental debates, or, more charitably perhaps, they have been classified as victims of an exploitative system who are unable to overcome the contradictions in their lives (e.g., Boucher 1994). Mostly, these women have simply been ignored, their own struggles effectively erased. Through labelling, there has been a tendency to marginalize and silence the concerns of these women within the public land use debates that have rocked the temperate rainforest along Canada's West Coast.

For activists and scholars alike, forging a link between environmentalism and social justice in the context of forestry debates on Canada's West Coast is relatively new. A few BC ENGOs have begun to address the social implications of their environmental advocacy (David Suzuki Foundation 1999; Schoonmaker, von Hagen, and Wolf 1997). Similarly, with the exception of ecofeminism, feminist scholars have just begun to consider seriously how environmental problems can inform and be informed by feminist theory (Eichler 1995). Yet feminist researchers have a rich history in theory and method that seeks to achieve engagement with and understanding of their research subjects (England 1994). In keeping with these approaches, I seek here to provide an accurate, yet sensitive, portrayal of women's support for the forest industry and, by doing so, to broaden the basis for understanding social dimensions of sustainability.

My effort is born of the belief that feminist environmentalists must seriously engage other women to understand the bases of different perspectives and to advocate for practical mechanisms and policy alternatives that incorporate, rather than marginalize, their voices. My starting point is to encourage us to see the trees among women living in forestry communities, to see their lives and perspectives as varied, nuanced, and worthy. I have situated women's perspectives and activism within a framework that includes land use change and changing public policies, labour market participation, household dynamics, as well as rural lifestyles and gender identities. By doing so, I challenge the assumption that environmental politics and policy making should begin as a public policy debate over human-ecological relations and suggest that household, workplace, and community relations are important concerns for a socially informed and ultimately successful environmental politics. By doing so, I also seek to contribute to an environmental movement that is sensitive to differences among us, seeks solutions that are socially and environmentally sound, and devises strategies of sustainability that serve the needs of all people living in rural resource communities.

The Need for New Theories
There are at least three challenges for conducting research about gender and activism in rural resource communities. The first challenge is that there remains a rather dated and incomplete picture of the lives of women in forestry towns. The classic Canadian study in forestry in which gender is given some prominence is *Green Gold: The Forest Industry in British Columbia*, written by Patricia Marchak in 1983 and based on data and

theoretical developments of the late 1970s. Consequently, it reflects both feminist thought and economic and social conditions of that time. Societal expectations about gender relations and femininity have changed since that book was written. In addition, changes in the forestry economy have affected women's home and work lives as well as their "rightful" place in society. In short, we need new empirical descriptions to reflect these changing circumstances. We also need new theories.

The second challenge relates to how researchers develop their explanations of social life. The cultural turn in the social sciences has implications for researchers in both feminist and rural studies. Researchers now point out that previously given categories and dichotomies such as "rural/urban" and "masculinity/femininity" are not fixed or uniform but constructed through social and cultural practices that have given them meaning (Cloke and Little 1997; McDowell 1997; Parr 1990; Philo 1992; Whatmore, Marsden, and Lowe 1994). Even actions taken to "preserve" and to "use" the environment can be interpreted differently depending on the context and the positions of different actors (Di Chiro 1995; Pulido 1996). In this vein, the dichotomy of "pro-environmental/anti-environmental" may not be appropriate for classifying women's actions. Human geographers, among other social scientists, are now challenged to be more sensitive to differences among social groups, to consider multiple social divisions and identities (e.g., gender, class, and ethnicity), and to attend to the experiences of marginalized others (e.g., women, children, the elderly, and lesbians and gay men) (Hughes 1997; Little and Austin 1996; McDowell 1993a; Philo 1992; Pratt and Hanson 1994; Valentine 1997). This focus on difference is also emerging as an important element of environmental management (Jakes and Anderson 2000; Kellert et al. 2000; Moote et al. 2001). In the context of this study, such sensitivity would suggest a need to explain the experiences of women in their diversity and richness.

Similarly, debates in feminist theory about difference and identity politics have had repercussions for research strategies and theoretical understandings (Gibson-Graham 1994) as well as for public policy debates (Cloke and Little 1997). For example, Julie-Katherine Gibson-Graham (1994) described the problems of undertaking an action-based research project about mining-town women at precisely the moment when feminist researchers began to discard unified determinations of "women's identities" and "women's experiences" in favour of multiple and rich, possibly conflicting, descriptions of women's identities and experiences. This focus on difference is more than an academic exercise. Representations have significance both for the places depicted and for the people who live and work in them. An uncritical embrace of a local community can hide local variability and exacerbate existing social, economic, and even environmental inequalities in these localities (Braun 1998; Reed 1995, 1997a).

The third challenge is that contemporary feminist theorists have attempted to redefine public and private domains. For example, feminist political economists have illustrated the importance of household dynamics in understanding the "public" economic domain (Gibson-Graham 1996; Maroney and Luxton 1997). The family and household may be considered important sites for an understanding of activism – both as catalysts for activism outside the home and as sites themselves for the transformation of social relations (Gibson-Graham 1996; Maroney and Luxton 1997; Littig 2001; Staeheli 1996). Considering research in gender and politics, then, it follows that household and community conditions are important constituents in the environmental policy domain, and these conditions should be taken into consideration when environmental policy decisions are made. This theoretical argument legitimates the voices of women from forestry communities in the arena of environmental politics and sustainability. This is not an argument for simply grafting women onto our discussions; rather, we must consider the extent to which gendered aspects of social life dealing with family, household, paid employment, and community shape contemporary discourses of environmentalism. How, then, can we *see the trees* among forestry-town women? Below I provide working definitions of terms used in the book and explain the choices that I made about my entry into, and analysis of, the lives of forestry-town women.

Coming to Terms

Forestry Communities as Rural Communities

The notion of "forestry community" binds together three related ideas: territory, interest, and attachment. Territorial or place-based communities are drawn by political and sometimes physical boundaries such as mountains or rivers. In practice, rural and resource geographers have tended to define their study areas by territorial boundaries. Such definition assists in data collection, aggregation, comparison, and analysis. Territorial communities may also be imposed by the state. For example, the state has created territorial communities by establishing "reserves" to delineate spaces for First Nations, by developing systems of municipal zoning, and by establishing public land use planning designations outside municipal areas. Territorial definitions of community based on watersheds have also been advocated more recently in resource management to promote management practices and lifestyles that are more in synch with natural ecosystem processes.

Beyond territories, sociologists have offered sociopsychological views of community in which "community involves a limited number of people in a somewhat restricted social space or network held together by shared understandings and a sense of obligation" (Bender 1978, 7-8). These networks may be developed within or without territorial boundaries. "Interest communities," identified by Graham Crowe and Graham Allan (1994), may be considered local social systems in which links are established on the basis of ethnic origin, religion, occupation, leisure interests, and so on. For many researchers, forestry is a mobile community where those engaged in waged or salaried employment are on the move in search of new opportunities or promotions (Halseth 1999). But the shared interests in forestry as an occupation and a way of life remain strong.

Last, the notion of "community of attachment" is expressed in forms of collective association and action that take place within communities. Members of territorial and interest communities may be included in some forms of collective activity and excluded from others. Communities of attachment may also include attachment to elements of nonhuman nature. This definition also includes a variety of ways in which people attach themselves to each other and to the land (Carroll 1995; White 1995). This affiliation is important since it is frequently cited by environmentalists to explain their pro-environmental activism. Yet such attachments to nature are also expressed by those who work in nature and choose to make their livings away from the pace and scale of city life. In her research about rural communities in New York state, Janet Fitchen found that a "description of physical landscape elides into a statement of socially valued attributes of the space in which they [residents] live" (e.g., it is clean, peaceful, etc.) (1991, 250). A community of attachment based on an affiliation to nature is an important one, yet rural people may see this association in differing ways from their environmental counterparts in the city. Rural residents may also question the "legitimacy" of this attachment for nonrural residents and question the actions that urbanites take to express their own associations with nature.

In the research reported here, I extend the notion of "occupational community" developed by sociologist Matthew Carroll (1995). Whereas he examined this notion for male loggers, here I examine the extent to which attachments to the dominant occupational community of logging/forestry are made by women, either as direct participants and workers in the industry or as partners of men who work in the industry. Through these associations, women come to share and express like interests in communities of attachment.

Ideas of community have also been advanced by feminist theorist Iris Marion Young (1990), although she prefers the term "social group" over "community." She argues that the former term avoids the potentially static geographical definition or the reifying and romantic notions often attributed to the latter term.[3] She defines a social group as "a collective of persons differentiated from at least one other group by cultural forms, practices, or way of life" (43). Thus, a social group is defined "not primarily by a set of shared attributes, but by a sense of identity ... [, by] its identification with a certain social status, the common history that social status produces, and self-identification that define the group as a group" (44). This notion of community or group identity is reinforced by Fitchen, who suggests that "the deeper meaning of community, while locality-connected, is of the mind: the ideational or symbolic sense of community, of belonging not only *to* a place but *in* its institutions and *with* its people" (1991, 253).

Groups can also be identified in relation to other groups. Sometimes group status is assigned by others outside the group; sometimes it is self-identified. Naming a group may be a way for that group to draw on a common purpose for positive change, or it may be a way to stereotype and set others aside from that group. This issue is taken up in Chapters 2 and 6 when I discuss moral exclusion.

These three elements of community – territory, interest, and attachment – come together in complex and even contradictory ways. Crowe and Allan (1994) remind us of four cautions as researchers approach the topic of community from the "outside." First, physical proximity does not necessarily lead people to establish social relations with one another. However, localities that have a sense of shared history and long-standing roots and relationships are more likely to develop community than are mobile and heterogeneous localities. Second, boundaries are not fixed but fluid. For example, geographical mobility may result in a reworking of insider/outsider divisions, which frequently characterize small towns. In addition, social strife within communities may also challenge long-standing designations of insider and outsider (e.g., Beckley 1995; Parr 1990). Third, communities are not necessarily freely chosen or voluntary but are influenced by a number of social and structural processes that happen within and upon them. And fourth, the bounds of community may be more visible to insiders than to outsiders. Residents of a community may show only those elements that they want to make visible to those on the outside. As outside researchers, academics may easily "miss the point."

In this book, I use the term "forestry communities" to denote this multilayered concept. I consider forestry communities within the broader rubric of rural communities, partly because this term has been chosen by people who live in these places during policy and planning debates (CORE 1994b) and partly because people living in forestry communities share common elements and concerns with residents of other rural places who rely on extraction and/or processing of natural resources for their livelihoods (e.g., mining, fishing, and agricultural communities). When I refer solely to a territorial definition of forestry communities, I use the more restricted term "forestry towns."

Forestry-Town Women

Women living in forestry towns are sometimes called forestry-town women or loggers' wives. These terms have been used loosely both by academics and by residents. The conflation of forestry-town women with loggers' wives assumes that most women living in these communities are married to loggers. In this context, the term "loggers" loosely refers to those people with an occupation in the forestry sector. Thus, both waged and salaried workers may be called loggers in the local vernacular. The terms "forestry-town women" and "loggers' wives" suggest a collective identity, a singularity of purpose, position, situation, perspective, and activism.

Women described as forestry-town women or loggers' wives have been viewed as the obverse of women involved in environmental campaigns. They have been characterized as traditional, dependent, conservative, maternalistic, regressive, or simply victims of their exploitation within systemic power relations (Boucher 1994; Warren 1992). These portrayals are contrary to the now prevailing determination that women's identities are (or at least should be) primarily pro-environmental, within biological or socialized expectations of gender (e.g., Merchant 1995; Nesmith and Wright 1995). These themes are examined in later chapters.

In this study, I use the term "workers' wives" when I draw on literature that reports on places outside forestry communities (e.g., mining communities). "Forestry-town women" is my term to describe all women living in these places. I use the term "loggers' wives" to consider those women specifically in relationships with men in the forestry sector. In keeping with the local understanding, loggers' wives may be related to actual loggers or to people who work for companies or the government in other forestry-related occupations. Women who work in forestry may also be classified as loggers' wives in this context. This is not a clean classification. I will take up some of the issues of classification in Chapter 4.

Theoretical Underpinnings

I undertook this study using different theoretical and policy entry points. Here I explain how gender and activism have been conceptualized in rural resource communities and in feminist theory more broadly to set the context for this study.

Gender and Activism in Rural Resource Communities

There is a long tradition of examining the lives of women and gender relations in rural resource communities in Western industrialized contexts (Ali 1986; Boulding 1981; Davis and Nadel-Klein 1991; Gibson 1992; Gibson-Graham 1994, 1995, 1996; Gill 1990; Little 1986, 1987, 1994; Maggard 1990; Murray 1995; Porter 1985, 1987; Sachs 1996; Whatmore, Marsden, and Lowe 1994; Wright 2001). Yet, to date, little research has focused on gender and forestry (see Beckley 1995; Brown 1995; Carroll 1995; Egan and Klausen 1998; Warren 1992).

According to this broad literature, traditional conceptions of femininity and masculinity are strong in rural resource communities where women are seen as the primary caregivers and nurturers and men as the providers and decision makers (Gibson 1992). These conceptions are reinforced by a dominant ideology that locates women's "rightful" place in the home and contributes to a relative lack of employment prospects for women outside the home. Women's community involvement has been characterized as an extension of this dominant ideology and practical work constraints (Cloke and Little 1990; Gibson 1992; Little 1987; Marchak 1983; Seitz 1995; Warren 1992). Alienation from the centres of corporate and government decision making is a key theme in both long-standing and contemporary debates about rural resource communities (e.g., Bradbury 1988; Egan and Klausen 1998; Matthews 1983; Randall and Ironside 1996). Thus, women are often viewed as being in a "double bind": both marginalized in their own communities and isolated from the sites of political and economic power.

In literature on rural and industrial restructuring, two subject positions have predominated in descriptions of workers' wives and their associations.[4] Some researchers have portrayed these women as conservative, ambivalent, passive, or apathetic and/or as victims of their physical and social environments. In this literature, the impacts of geographic and social isolation, the lack of employment opportunities, financial and emotional dependence on spouses, company domination of social life, and limited social services have generally had greater negative effects for women than for men (e.g., National Film Board 1979; Warren 1992).[5] In contrast, a body of research has situated women as victors over their circumstances.[6] This work has focused on women's roles in industrial disputes affecting resource towns. These women have been seen as active on the basis of their class affiliation, joining "their men" in working-class struggles to retain male employment, family incomes, and ways of life (e.g., Ali 1986; Maggard 1990).

From the perspective of my own research, both subject positions are problematic. Women's activism in both cases is viewed in relation to their dependence on the means of production: that is, their reliance on men's income and employment. The conceptualization of workers' wives has been connected "with essentialist notions of women as less political animals ... whose strategic vision is myopic, individualistic or family centered" (Gibson 1992, 30). In addition, gender roles and relations have frequently been viewed as solid and unchanging.[7] Such stark depictions provide fertile ground for challenge. As discussed later, within broader feminist research agendas, fixed conceptions of gender roles and relations have now dissolved in favour of emphases on difference, performance, and mobility in the construction and maintenance of gender identity. My search for an improved theoretical understanding of women's perspectives must evidently go beyond the existing confines of research about gender relations in rural resource communities.

Toward Feminist Environmentalism

My first attempt was to examine literature related to ecofeminism, yet I found this work unsatisfying. In North America at least, ecofeminism originated from a focus on the cultural-symbolic links between women and nonhuman nature (e.g., Salleh 1984). Early work celebrated women's "rightful" position closer to nature than that of men (King 1990; Salleh 1984), either because of women's biological and essentially nurturing character, or because of parallels that theorists identified between the dual domination and exploitation of women and nonhuman nature within patriarchal societal structures (Warren, K.J. 1987, 1990). While some theorists have attempted to overcome this early bias on the "essential" nature of women's relationship to the nonhuman environment (e.g., Eckersley 1992; Plumwood 1991, 1993), contemporary empirical research on women and environmental activism has largely maintained that women have a unified and universally progressive voice on environmental issues. Even those who resist essentializing women's experiences still argue that women's social location does transcend boundaries of race, ethnicity, and class to favour environmental protection (e.g., Merchant 1995; Seager 1996; Sturgeon 1997). In contrast, I agree with Bina Agarwal that ecofeminism has largely "failed to differentiate among women by class, race, ethnicity, geographic location, etc. It [has] also failed to connect the domination of women and nature with other social, economic, and political structures and institutions that reinforce or alleviate this dominance" (1992, 122-23).

Hence, I came to favour Agarwal's conception of "feminist environmentalism." In her research about the lives and activism of women in India, Agarwal (1992) argues that studies of women and the environment should examine how women's social relations to the environment are made and reinforced through their daily activities in specific localities. Consequently, women do not share similar relations to their environments because of their essential biological functions; instead, women's relations to their environments vary across socially constructed categories of gender, ethnicity, culture, and class (see also Di Chiro 1995). Furthermore, these relations are made and reinforced through women's daily activities in specific localities. By using the term "feminist environmentalism," Agarwal emphasizes that social relations to the environment are materially based, socially constructed, culturally embedded, and locally specific.

In contrast to ecofeminism, feminist environmentalism does not privilege women as caretakers or nurturers of the environment (whether by biology or socialization). It does not assume that all women will take a singular position or that those whose actions do not support environmental protection are somehow "fallen" from grace or in denial of their essential selves. Instead, feminist environmentalism supports the broader feminist insight that both the environment and gender are historical, mutable sets of forms and patterns that alter one another (Mackenzie 1986). This approach shares much in common with research in feminist development studies (e.g., Marchand and Parpart 1995a, 1995b) and feminist political ecology or environmental justice (Di Chiro 1995, 1998; Rocheleau, Thomas-Slayter, and Wangari 1996). So far, however, researchers have focused on urban and/or industrial examples in North America and Europe and on rural and/or agrarian cases from Africa, Asia, and Latin America. Where the gender/development theories have been applied in North American contexts, they have focused on women's activism within social institutions that exclude environmental concerns (Seitz 1995).

Feminist environmentalism encourages one to make links between the household, the community, and other political levels to understand the intersections of gender, environments, and public policy. Within material realities and identity perspectives, women's relation and resistance to environmental decisions can also be understood in terms of the contested and heterogeneous everyday lives of women. Therefore, women's perspectives and choices cannot be considered essential, singular, or fixed. They are necessarily partial and situated, opening a range of possible social actions (Feldman and Welsh 1995; Haraway 1991; Sachs 1994; Whatmore, Marsden, and Lowe 1994). Emphasis shifts from simple configurations such as "victims" and "victors" toward a consideration of women as purposeful agents who represent a multiplicity of perspectives (Kettle 1995). Consistencies as well as contradictions in women's situations produce both opportunities and constraints for choice and agency (after Gibson-Graham 1995; and Liepins 1998).

Locating Activism in Forestry Towns
How, then, might one conceptualize both the consistencies and the contradictions in women's situations? Drawing on insights from feminist scholarship in other contexts, I began by "locating" activism in both public and private places and by "embedding" it within social contexts. I remain open to women's multiple situations by emphasizing how environmental perspectives and positions are embedded within broader social, political, and economic conditions. If we consider feminist environmentalism as well as its attendant repercussions as a social phenomenon rather than an ecological imperative, then the "responses" of residents to protect

their way of life can be classified not by the dichotomy of "anti" and "pro" environmentalism but as a social phenomenon that is more plural and complex. Advocacy, in turn, can be viewed as a multifaceted concept rather than strictly an anti-environmental position.

A central component of feminist theory has been to interrogate the public/private divide of people's lives. Feminists have argued that issues in which men have dominated politically have been narrowly conceived as public, whereas issues affecting women's lives have been considered private and therefore not part of the political domain. Early research about women's political activism challenged this separation and argued that many matters of household and community are legitimate areas for political attention and scholarship.

More specifically, Western feminists argued that gender interests could be classified into practical and strategic interests. Practical gender interests focused on the private domain, with specific demands linked to women's ascribed domestic roles. In contrast, strategic issues were considered part of the public domain, where demands are made for legal or structural change to overcome gender inequality (Brownhill and Halford 1990; Kofman and Peake 1990). Feminist researchers observed that women tended to mobilize around practical-domestic demands that affected families and communities. The nature and effects of their activism were attributed to their roles and relations as housewives, mothers, and community caregivers (Neal and Phillips 1990; Sachs 1994; West and Blumberg 1990).

Maria Garcia-Guadilla (1995) discussed the gendered aspects of environmental activism according to a similar breakdown. She theorized that strategic environmental issues and problems were those that gained attention in political arenas and the public eye through the media. Men were more likely to gain this attention and to assure the "strategic" value of their concerns. Women, who frequently mobilized around "domestic" or "community" issues, were less likely to draw media attention and consequent political action to address their concerns.[8] For women, the problem in gaining a public profile can be further exacerbated by the fact that strategic problems are frequently newsworthy, capturing short-term media attention, while domestic and community-based problems are endemic and thus viewed as commonplace and less newsworthy. Garcia-Guadilla's empirical work, however, focused on women in South America. In the North American context, environmental politics is still frequently separated from concerns about domestic lives, households, local gender politics, and gender relations.[9] My own research challenges this separation.

In this book, I use the term "activism" broadly to include mobilization by groups or individuals as a political means of challenging or actively affirming the status quo (after West and Blumberg 1990). This definition includes activities that have conventionally been seen as "voluntary," "communal," and "self-help." These activities are considered political as well as moral (West and Blumberg 1990). The term also includes various institutions outside public policy arenas as sites for activism: for example, schools, churches, social welfare agencies, as well as service and/or labour organizations. In addition, it considers the family and household as important sites for activism – both as originators of and catalysts for activism outside the home (Gibson-Graham 1996; Maroney and Luxton 1997). Finally, I include activities geared to retaining the status quo in the face of changing societal conditions. This inclusion may seem counterintuitive at first since the greatest attention to social protest and activism is usually placed around movement toward some "progressive" end. However, where contemporary lives are threatened, this definition implies that affirmation of the status quo is an important political act.[10]

Theoretical Openings: The Embeddedness of Women's Activism
I propose using a conceptualization of "embeddedness" as one alternative for theorizing women's activism. Human geographers believe that social relations create and are created by the peculiarities of particular places. In this context, embeddedness pays attention to who is linked in social relations as well as where the links are made. For example, Susan Hanson and Geraldine Pratt (1995) suggested that embeddedness had a spatial connotation of being rooted in place and in social life. They argued that embeddedness implies more than simply opportunities and constraints in women's lives; it also "opens the recognition that gendered identities, including aspirations and desires, *are fully embedded in* – and indeed inconceivable apart from – place and that different gender identities are shaped through different places" (18; emphasis added). Similarly, Elizabeth Teather (1996, 1997) studied the meaning of rural women's voluntary networks by considering how networks form and operate in light of *how places and people develop together*. While she did not use the terminology of embeddedness, she did affirm the connection between social and spatial relations. Other feminist scholars have also illustrated how women's subject identities are shaped by their notions of rurality, nature, and locally constituted gender relations (e.g., Gibson 1992; Gibson-Graham 1994, 1996; Hughes 1997; Liepins 1998; Little 1997; Teather 1996, 1997).

The idea of embeddedness within specificities of place and social relations may bridge the gap between feminists primarily concerned with women's connections to economic and social life (e.g., labour studies students) and feminists concerned with women's connections to their nonhuman environments (e.g., ecofeminist researchers). For example, Mary Mellor (1997), an ecofeminist, argued that women's experiences of environmental changes are embodied by *and embedded within* historical and material relations of society and their nonhuman environments. If gender identities are shaped by and embedded within material and cultural conditions, then we might anticipate that gender practices are played out in different ways in different places (Pratt and Hanson 1994). For example, one might anticipate different forms of femininity and activism to be played out in forestry towns and in urban settings. This idea is useful and guides my interpretation of women's perspectives and activism as embedded within reciprocal relationships among women's actions and public policies, labour market participation, and household and community norms. I consider each dimension as both a source and a site of women's activism.

With this conceptualization, it is possible to consider women's multiple subject positions, contrary motivations, and actions without dichotomizing women and their activist choices into "progressive" and "conservative" camps. Feminist work outside environmental studies offers many openings in this regard. For example, Lynn Staeheli's (1996) work on women's political activism argued for separate consideration of the contents of actions from the spaces in which such actions are taken. This distinction opens up a diversity of sites such as household, family, and community for women's activism as well as a range of activities within and across these sites. In the context of environmental activism, this is important because it challenges the public policy focus of environmental debates and opens up a more nuanced reading of motivation, perspective, and activity.

I locate women's activism within the changing social contexts of forested rural landscapes. I do so by considering labour market participation, household dynamics, gender identities, and lifestyles as relevant to women's responses to changes in environmental and land use policy. I also view these factors as sites both of perspectives and of activism. For example, the paid work site may be a location where women identify the needs of their community. Alternatively, women's work experiences may grant them authority to speak out in land use debates. For other women, the workplace itself can be the site of an activist agenda. This multi-site framework helps to explain the apparent contradictions of women's positions and perspectives, associated with endorsement of, and exclusion from, forestry and land use practices and policy debates. It also points to elements of social policy that must attend changes in environmental and land use policy when those changes initiate and/or hasten broader social changes. By this approach, I deliberately account for the variability of social life in the analysis of politics and perspectives of forestry-town women.

Study Area and Research Method

The North Island

My study took place on northern Vancouver Island, described by local residents as "the North Island" and defined here by interviewees as all areas north of Woss (Figure 1.1). The North Island is sparsely populated, with 15,441 residents in the Mount Waddington Regional District (MWRD) in 1996.[11] Women from Port Hardy (population 5,470), Port McNeill (population 3,014), Port Alice (population 1,626), and Alert Bay (population 697) on Cormorant Island were interviewed as well as women from the unincorporated places of Sointula (on Malcolm Island), Holberg, Winter Harbour, Coal Harbour, and Woss, the last logging camp on the island.

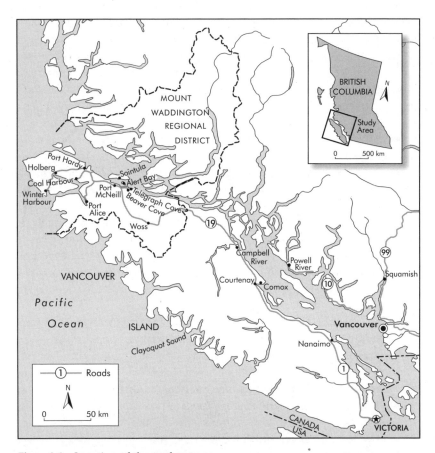

Figure 1.1 Location of the study area

Local women view the communities as isolated from the rest of the island and the province, given that they are approximately 235 kilometres to the nearest movie theatre and full-scale hospital in Campbell River and 500 kilometres to the province's capital city, Victoria. While mining and fishing have also been important for employment and income, forestry remains the largest single employer. Provincial government calculations suggest that 51 percent of after-tax income in 1996 came from forestry in the region (Horne 1999). This number was even higher for particular communities. For example, employment income derived from forestry accounted for 58 percent of all employment income in Port McNeill and 84 percent of all employment income in Port Alice (Horne 1999). The Port McNeill Forest District covers the North Island and a large portion of the Central Coast of the mainland. Six major companies held the largest proportion of the annual allowable cut in the region.

Fishing has also been a major component of the North Island economy and is still important to North Island communities both for commercial fishery and for tourism and sport fishing. In 1995, there were an estimated 240 commercial salmon-fishing vessels registered in the region, employing about 300 people in commercial fishing and creating 300 to 400 seasonal jobs in recreational fishing. Although numerous productive fishing locations exist on both coasts of the North Island, commercial fishing and sport fishing have recently been adversely affected by factors such as reduced fish stocks, changing regulations, and public confusion over which species can be harvested. Aquaculture is a relatively new and growing component in the local economy, contributing to the employment of about forty people at a local fish-processing plant created in 1997.

The North Island has also been a site of local mines. The most important was Island Copper Mine, which closed in 1996 after twenty-four years in operation. Despite the large number of employees laid off, the economic impact was considered small because of the long lead time to closure and the ability of the company to find alternative employment for most of the workers.

Finally, tourism and recreation are small but increasingly important components of the local economy. Whale watching, sport fishing, scuba diving, kayaking, coastal cruising, caving, and other outdoor adventure options shape the tourism "product." As well, many recreationists choose to observe or participate in cultural activities and the arts, which are increasingly offered by many First Nations in the region. The expansion of these activities is limited, however, because of the limited infrastructure, such as accommodation and food services, and the perceived lack of a desirable climate to support year-round visitors.[12]

Like the province as a whole, the North Island has been subject to several important planning and policy initiatives since the early 1990s. In 1994,

CORE recommended establishing several new protected areas for Vancouver Island (see details in Chapter 3). Before the process began, Vancouver Island had 10.3 percent of its land base, or 345,236 hectares, in existing protected areas. In keeping with the emergent Protected Areas Strategy, the plan added a further 2.7 percent, or 90,344 hectares, for a total of 13 percent in protected areas. But the allocation across the island was spatially uneven. Of new lands to be allocated for protection across the island, just over two-thirds (62,000 hectares) were to be located on the North Island (Figure 1.2).

Other planning initiatives were also put in place. The Mount Waddington Community Resources Board (CRB) was formed in the spring of 1995 to act as a subregional group to implement decisions and monitor the effects of the Vancouver Island Land Use Plan. The board is composed of local citizens representing the interests of individual communities, interest groups, and industry sectors. In addition, when I began my research, the region was becoming part of a new planning process along the Central Coast. The planning initiative was part of the province's subregional process of creating land and resource management plans (LRMPs) that was pursued after CORE's dissolution. The LRMPs were designed to interpret government policy for management zones, landscape units, sensitive areas, recreation sites, trails, and interpretive areas and to set rules for individual operators and plans. In 1996, the government initiated its most ambitious and complex process to date. The planning region selected for the LRMP included both land and coastal resources along the mainland West Coast. It involved sixty members – the largest table yet consolidated – representing various stakeholder groups as well as municipalities and provincial, federal, and Aboriginal governments. Once Clayoquot Sound was resolved, this mainland coastal region became a target for international environmental organizations, which renamed it the "Great Bear Rainforest" to galvanize an international campaign for its protection. Thus, there was pressure on the provincial government to put a plan in place for this area. Although the planning region is outside the North Island, many woods workers from the North Island flew out to the mid-coast of the mainland to work. For this reason, residents of northern Vancouver Island were both concerned about, and wanted to participate in, the planning process. While many other similar plans in the province were completed, approved, and implemented within two years of initiation, the Central Coast plan required several adjustments to its time line. In 2002, the government estimated that the plan would be complete in 2003, fully seven years after it began.

When I arrived on the North Island with my research assistants in June 1997, the protests in Clayoquot Sound still resonated.[13] CORE's plan for Vancouver Island still raised hackles; however, the impact of its land use recommendations made in 1994 had not been fully realized. Its recommendations

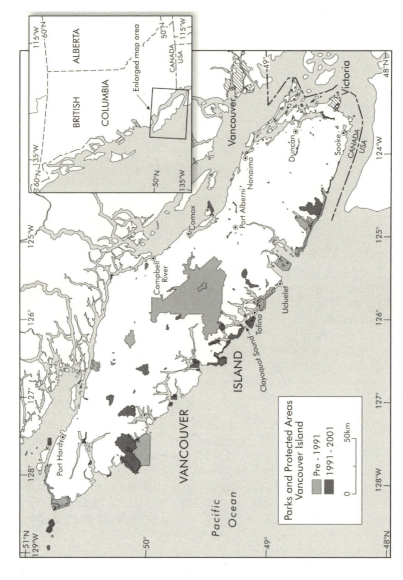

Figure 1.2 Parks and protected areas of Vancouver Island, pre-1991 and 1991-2001. (Adapted from the BC Ministry of Sustainable Resource Management.)

were introduced in rapid succession with changes to forest management and transitional strategies whose potential for success was unknown. The intense international scrutiny of the West Coast, combined with losses in all resource sectors (e.g., fishing and mining), had left local residents weary and wary of government and outside researcher inter- vention. During the summer of 1997, smaller-scale protests occurred in response to the individual actions of environmental organizations. Following these protests, several longer shutdowns by industry took place, and many women expressed concerns that these were structural rather than seasonal in character.[14] The "fighting spirit" that marked the demonstrations in 1994 had been replaced by a more subdued, introspective concern.

A Word about Method

In conducting my research, I followed principles of feminist participatory and case study methodologies outlined by Shulamit Reinharz (1992) and Linda McDowell (1993a, 1993b) and, in particular, the strategies described by Julie-Katherine Gibson-Graham (1994). I call this methodology "interactive applied research," and, for those who are interested, I provide details in the Appendix. As I began the research, I was interested in understanding how women's opposition to environmental regulation was motivated and played out and, in particular, in identifying how the women involved framed these issues. This interest required that I find ways to uncover and illustrate the complexity of women's lives and to allow them ways to represent their own stories. I used data from these interviews in combination with reviews of relevant policy documents, focus groups, and continuous contact with some of the women living and working in the region.

My research assistants and I initially conducted thirty-two in-depth interviews with women who had varying connections to forestry. From this group of local residents, ten women were selected to be community researchers in order to discuss local issues and to be trained to conduct in-depth interviews. In total, fifty interviews were completed for analysis.[15] Upon undertaking the preliminary analysis, I conducted three focus groups with local women who had not been interviewed. The focus groups served a dual function: they gave me an opportunity to provide feedback to the local communities about the nature and status of the research, and they assisted directly in corroborating and refining emerging themes and social categories. After the focus groups were completed, I undertook further analysis and then held a workshop with the community researchers in which I again presented my results. The community researchers offered more suggestions for refining the analysis and for undertaking extension work in their communities.

The sample of women for interview was not selected randomly, nor was it statistically representative of the region at large. Table 1.1 reveals characteristics of women interviewed in 1997 in relation to those living in the census region, the Mount Waddington Regional District (MWRD), in 1996 (see Figure 1.1). Approximately 82 percent of the population of the MWRD is located in the study area, so these census data provide the basis for a general comparison of the study group with the wider population of the region. Table 1.1 illustrates that most of the women interviewed were of employment age. In fact, 98 percent of the interviewees were between 20 and 64 years of age. The women had higher rates of university education and labour force participation and lower rates of unemployment than women in the MWRD. As intended by the sampling strategy, women in this study were almost four times as likely to work in primary industries than women in other parts of the MWRD.

How I Tell the Stories

A major theme of the book is that political concerns about conventional

Table 1.1

Selected characteristics of women in the study group compared to those in the Mount Waddington Regional District (MWRD)

	% in study group (1997)	% in MWRD (1996)
Women aged 20-64	98	59
Women with some university education	35	16
Women living with male partners[1]	84	86
Labour force participation of women	80	71
Unemployed women	7	10
Employed women in "jobs unique to primary industries" (census definition)[2]	15	4
Employed women in "forestry or forestry-dependent occupations" (study definition)[2]	40	n.c.
Women whose employed partners are in "jobs unique to primary industries" (census definition)[3]	39	25
Women whose employed partners are in "forestry or forestry-dependent occupations" (study definition)[3]	74	n.c.
Total Number	N = 50	N = 7220

Notes: Proportions are rounded to the nearest whole number. n.c. = not calculated.
[1] There were no known same-sex couples in the sample.
[2] For this calculation, only 40 women or those participating in the labour force, were included.
[3] For this calculation, only 39 men were included.

forestry and land use practices can be understood if they are considered part of broader rural social changes rather than simply part of anti-environmental rhetoric. Chapter 2 explicitly addresses the broader context of the research by considering how sustainability and transition have inadvertently contributed to the social marginalization of rural communities along the West Coast of North America. In Chapter 3, I introduce the public policies and structural changes affecting rural British Columbia, illustrating how policies and initiatives introduced in the 1990s are part of a broader set of structural changes affecting rural residents more generally and providing a context for suggesting that coastal communities are part of a changing social geography.

In each of Chapters 4 through 6, I examine one aspect of women's perspectives associated with forestry and land use practices. In Chapter 4, I examine how women's lives intersect with paid employment, particularly with forestry-based employment. Chapter 5 takes up the theme of community management by examining how women support forestry through community services that they provide. In Chapter 6, I discuss women's political perspectives in support of forestry practices. I explicitly examine anti-environmental sentiments and illustrate how women forged community consensus through words and actions used to separate their communities from those that they perceived as other, including some women *within* their own communities.

Findings from Chapters 4 to 6 lead me to suggest that policy processes must be created to admit, address, and incorporate geographical and social differences when they are used to plan for environmental and land use change. Thus, I use Chapter 7 to describe in greater detail exclusionary practices that women were subjected to when they participated in planning processes dealing with environment and land use. I address these exclusionary practices by considering how a model of participatory citizenship might allow both environmental and social issues to be addressed. In Chapter 8, I further integrate ideas and themes developed throughout the book. I summarize the location of women in forestry and land use debates and suggest how they might be more effectively included in policy forums, academic theories, and research methods about gender, environmentalism, and political activism.

"Happy 50th Woss," 1997. Woss, which is now incorporated, was the last forestry camp on Vancouver Island.

2
Transition and Social Marginalization of Forestry Communities

> Can we think meaningfully of "sustainable development" in non-metropolitan contexts of the advanced countries?
>
> – Frederick Buttel (1992, 1)

> We are a province dependent on forests for lifestyle and economy, a forested landscape, *a place of changing values.*
>
> – Scientific Panel for Sustainable Forest Practices in Clayoquot Sound (1995, 1; emphasis added)

Ideas about Transition

As cited above, Frederick Buttel posed a provocative question in his 1992 presidential address to the American Rural Sociological Society. His question is particularly pertinent to British Columbia, where the processes of resource extraction, environmental activism, and public policy have combined in overlapping and contradictory ways to establish and reinforce an uneven social, economic, and ecological landscape. In BC, two-thirds of the population live in the Lower Mainland, a highly urbanized region in the southwest corner that is of primary political and economic importance. For the majority of residents who live there, sustainability outside the Lower Mainland has become almost synonymous with the preservation of wilderness. The competing societal demands to protect local society, regional economy, and ecology have prompted some observers to declare that BC's forests, forest industries, and forestry communities are "in trouble" (Barnes and Hayter 1997) and even "intemperate" (Braun 2002). When the state of BC's society and ecology was compared to the objectives of sustainability, some argued that the province must undergo a *transition* in its economic, environmental, and social relations if it is to become a sustainable society (Burda, Gale, and M'Gonigle 1998; Greenpeace Canada 1998).

Since the mid-1970s, several new economic and social challenges have faced forestry communities in British Columbia and Canada. These challenges include the decline in the availability of timber due to the fall-down effect,[1] changes in international market conditions, increased mechanization in both harvesting and processing sectors, corporate restructuring, and more flexible forms of production. Increasing public awareness of, and demands for, environmental protection and wilderness areas, as well as changes in relations with First Nations, have placed demands on policy makers for new land use strategies as well as new ways to incorporate multiple publics in decision-making processes.

For the internationally focused campaigns of environmental nongovernmental organizations (ENGOs), the preservation of wilderness along the West Coast of Canada and the American Pacific Northwest provides one of the last opportunities to protect key species and ecosystems of the temperate rainforests. Furthermore, preservation, it is claimed, will provide a sanctuary from human occupation and satiate the "twin desires of the human heart – wealth and beauty" (Dietrich 1992, 25). Rural communities of the West Coast must now address this imperative (e.g., Schoonmaker, von Hagen, and Wolf 1997). The result has been an increasing chasm between rural and urban ideals of sustainability.

The term "transition" shaped the public policy discourse related to adjustments within forestry communities during the 1990s (e.g., CORE 1994a). Indeed, transition has become the operative word for both practitioners and academics in describing the changes occurring in and necessary for providing a sustainable economy and society for British Columbia. Contemporary issues related to transition refer to large-scale structural changes in technology, the organization of labour, societal attitudes, and government policy. The speed, depth, and geographic extent of changes, as well as the changes in broader societal expectations, are still unknown.[2] In this context, some policy analysts have used the metaphor of "crossroads" to capture the choices that policy makers must adopt if they are to succeed in harnessing changes in the forest industry and economy in order to build a sustainable society (e.g., Binkley 1997; Drushka, Nixon, and Travers 1993; Hammond 1991; Hayter 2000; Hayter and Barnes 1997; Marchak 1991).

I use the notion of transition to describe changes in forestry and land use that are considered permanent and structural, not just temporary and cyclical. These changes, however, do not imply an immediate shift in the priorities of the state, industry, or rural communities. Transition will likely take multiple forms and spur alternative trajectories depending on local conditions and their intersections with nonlocalized changes in technology, market conditions, environmental strategies, and political imperatives – all of which are dynamic and potentially chaotic. Strategies for transition are also embedded within, and constituted by, broad societal, economic, and political relationships and institutions within which forestry communities are situated. I emphasize how rural residents respond to and seek to shape policy and social changes that they experience locally. These relationships and their interpretations are shaped, in part, by the prescriptions and policies formulated to effect a transition in forestry and associated forestry communities.

In this chapter, I tackle various interpretations of transition, beginning by illustrating how the term has been used in contemporary public discourses associated with environmental, economic, and social sustainability. I then show that the discourses on forested landscapes have themselves undergone transition, from "resource landscapes" to "wilderness landscapes," and how forestry communities have become politically and socially marginalized from ensuing public debates.

Policy Perspectives on Sustainability and Transition

It is challenging to conceptualize "sustainability" and "transition" as they relate to forestry communities. These places have been subject to boom-and-bust cycles throughout their history. There is strong evidence that they are already in the midst of transition. Since the late 1970s, rapid technological change and economic restructuring have brought forestry communities in line with the dynamics and imperatives of globalization. The twenty years from 1956 to 1975 saw annual harvests increase fourfold, with corporate concentration and firm size increasing along with vertical concentration by industry players (Pearse 1976). The years that followed saw a levelling off of harvests, retooling of outdated infrastructure, shedding of unprofitable operations, and increased contracting out in remaining firms (Hayter and Barnes 1997). The coastal region of British Columbia was affected most dramatically by industrial restructuring and shifting forestry management practices. According to Roger Hayter and Trevor Barnes, since 1980 "several [BC] West Coast mills have been shut down, wound down, or reconfigured to varying degrees" (1997, 8). These changes have had dramatic effects on rural communities: "While the fortunes of single industry communities in BC have waxed and waned, historically, during the last 15 years they have mostly waned. Twenty-five years ago, the archetypal British Columbia logging town, Port Alberni, was the eighth most prosperous community in Canada; now it is not even in the top 100" (8). Clearly, fortunes are changing! One could argue that, in the dynamic context in which forestry communities are situated, transition is not particularly new. What is new, however, is that the public policy debate itself is also in transition. In particular, the debate about sustainability and land use draws attention to three interconnected policy domains: environment, economy, and society.

By the 1990s, academics had built on the Brundtland report on sustainable development (World Commission on Environment and Development [WCED] 1987) and formulated definitions of sustainability that included environmental, economic, and social components (e.g., Robinson et al. 1990). Drawing from an environmental discourse (International Union for the Conservation of Nature and Natural Resources [IUCN] 1980), proponents of sustainability made an important distinction. They did not condemn economic development; rather, they attempted to promote more socially and environmentally sound economic practices. In British Columbia, public policy makers adopted strategies and plans to advance the aims of sustainability by promoting "balance" among these three elements (e.g., British Columbia Round Table on the Environment and the Economy [BCRTEE] 1993; CORE 1992). When government agencies anticipated that new environmental policy prescriptions would affect the economic and social well-being of local communities, they advocated programs to support workers during transition (see Chapter 3). Even ENGOs began to offer more constructive alternatives to their traditional condemnations of forestry and land use practices. Working individually, collectively, and in supportive networks, ENGOs began to provide specific prescriptions for retaining both jobs and trees on Canada's West Coast, lending greater credibility to the claim that sustainability means more than simply protecting *natural* ecosystems (e.g., David Suzuki Foundation 1999; Ecotrust Canada 1997; Greenpeace Canada 1998; Sierra Club of British Columbia 1997). This rhetoric of maintaining the triad of economy, environment, and society, therefore, became important in shaping public debate.

The *economic* component of sustainability is associated with maintaining a regional economy and ensuring an adequate material standard of living for local people (Robinson et al. 1990). In the context of the BC forestry economy, economic transition would require the ability to anticipate and respond to the changes in the industry.

The *environmental* component of sustainability requires that human activities be carried out in ways that ensure the continued health and productivity of ecological systems (Robinson et al. 1990). This dimension includes maintaining essential life-support systems, protecting biodiversity, and using resources wisely (IUCN 1980). Environmental organizations argued that British Columbia contains some of the last remnants of coastal temperate rainforest on the globe, complete with unique species and ecosystem diversity. They expressed concern about the physical availability of these landscapes for future generations and thus about the ability of the current generation to meet its responsibilities to maintain biodiversity and life-support systems.

The two components come together in prescriptions that the industry make a transition from being volume based to being value intensive. This new form of forestry would require moving from an expanding industry that relies on a large volume of high-quality, high-yield, old-growth timber toward a higher-value, more labour-intensive production system that includes more intensive silviculture with environmentally benign harvesting practices. In addition, it would require a reskilling of forest industry jobs from logging to manufacturing, particularly in specialty products and wood-processing industries (Clapp 1998; M'Gonigle 1997; M'Gonigle and Parfitt 1994). Transition in the economic sphere has also been described in terms of a move from employment in primary resource extraction sectors of forestry, mining, fishing, and agriculture to jobs in nonextractive uses of forests such as ecotourism (Burda, Gale, and M'Gonigle 1998) and/or out of forestry altogether, with job replacement in the service sector (Burda, Gale, and M'Gonigle 1998; Greenpeace Canada 1998; Sierra Club of British Columbia 1997).

According to John Robinson et al. (1990), achieving the *social* component of sustainability requires ensuring that basic needs are met, protecting cultural forms, and ensuring that systems of governance are acceptable and provide a collective sense of social well-being. CORE built on this broad definition by suggesting that its own recommendations for land use planning would have to consider the "distributional equity of land use decisions, support of economic and social measures to address the economic effects of land use decisions, promotion of a good quality of life that included fostering earning a living, obtaining education and training, and access to social, cultural and recreational services, and finally to make decisions in a fair and equitable manner" (1994a, 245). Fulfilling economic and environmental prescriptions such as those above will have dramatic social repercussions for residents of rural communities who have built their lives and their communities along trajectories aligned with resource extraction and production. Thus, these communities need to become more sustainable. During times of environmental and land use change, the social component of sustainability implies the need for changes in the structures, processes, and relationships that characterize community life and that shape relations between rural communities and their urban counterparts.

There are several aspects to these required changes. One aspect can be found in political responses to the changes in broader societal norms and values toward the environment and the economy. Governments at all levels have been called on to bail out local companies and communities in distress; unemployment programs have been reassessed for specific relief for rural regions; "transition programs" have been introduced to provide for early retirement, retraining, and incentives to work elsewhere. These policy initiatives have placed governments in a contradictory position: on the one hand, providing specific regions or places with targeted programs (e.g., job creation or retraining), on the other, reducing access to basic services in rural areas, through decreased expenditures in public health, education, and social benefits such as income assistance.

But beyond these direct policy and program responses, a broader dimension of social transition is relevant. Social transition is also being illustrated by the realignment of political power. Urban regions in Canada have gained significant political clout through changes in population distribution and organizational capacity. By the late twentieth century, more than 75 percent of the population of Canada lived in urban settings within a narrow strip along the southern border. By their population alone, urban residents now have a greater political voice through the electoral system. According to Melody Hessing and Michael Howlett, "The increasing urbanization of Canada precedes and parallels the transition from resource dependency to increased economic reliance on urban-based, tertiary, or service sector, employment. The southern and urban concentration of the population creates a physical and symbolic distance from hinterland areas of resource extraction and economic wealth creation" (1997, 36). Hence, urban residents have greater access to public forums and public figures to ensure that their issues are advanced on political agendas. This aspect of social transition has contributed to the growing sense of political disaffection and marginality present in forestry communities.

In addition, urban-based organizations also have more outlets for their messages that reach into the international sphere. The rise of the Internet is an important element of internationalization. While some would argue that the Internet places rural and urban interests on a more equal footing, geographers and development practitioners have pointed to the real "digital divide" that favours access to the Internet for an urban, male, highly educated elite (Knox and Marston 2001; United Nations Development Program 1999). In Canada, rural communities have lagged behind their urban counterparts in terms of their access to the Internet because they lack the physical connections and the human capital required to build and service the "information highway." This uneven access to information affects the ability of rural communities to participate in societal debates that affect their lives and livelihoods.

In all aspects of transition associated with sustainability – economic, environmental, and social – rural workers and their families will be expected to adapt to changes in the forestry economy and the broader society. Yet there is no reason to believe that transition efforts are uniform, inevitable, or easy to implement (Carroll 1995; Fitchen 1991; Prudham and Reed 2001). The interpretation and effects of transition will differ by gender, ethnicity, class, and geographic and social location. Government policies and programs may be created within and without forestry but have dramatic impacts on how forest workers, families, and communities adjust to changing realities. With these considerations in mind, Matthew Carroll (1995) argued that it is important to re-examine widely held assumptions about the "inevitability" of efforts to engage forest communities in transitional strategies. He suggested that academics and policy makers be able to separate adaptations that might be required by systemic changes from those strategies that might be deliberately induced by one group in another because of differences in community culture.

Transition in the Interpretation of Landscape

> In the end, what South Moresby revealed was a profound clash between world views. The dominant one sees all of nature as a potential resource, of value only for its economic worth. But there is growing support for a different outlook that recognizes that we are biological beings, who, in spite of science and technology, remain embedded in, and dependent on, nature. So we have to fight to keep nature intact and to try to bring ourselves into a balance with the environment. South Moresby could be a watershed that makes a shift toward this emerging world view.
>
> – David Suzuki (1987, D4)

Contemporary debates about the sustainability of forests are embedded within changing values about what constitutes an appropriate environment for current and future generations (Bengston 1994). In BC, this transition of values has had real material effects on people living in forestry communities. Two interpretations of forested landscapes – "resource landscapes" and "wilderness landscapes" – have dominated public debate. No doubt the viewpoint that forests are appropriately resource landscapes to be exploited for economic gain dominated public policy in the twentieth century. However, this viewpoint has been challenged by the interpretation of forests as wilderness, as landscapes to be retained for their noneconomic significance. While this interpretation has not yet come to dominate BC's political economy, it has gained considerable public support, both within the province and on national and international public agendas. The importance of this perspective has also recently shaped government policies and regulations dealing with public lands. As the wilderness interpretation has gained public legitimacy, British Columbia has begun to undergo a transition of values in the societal interpretation of landscape.

Forested Landscapes as Resource Landscapes

Where forested rural landscapes have been considered resource landscapes, they have been deemed "productive" when their natural resources can be assigned economic values. Economic value is ascribed to elements of nature as a result of the application of labour and technology.[3] In public policy debates, this representation has historically been advanced by a triad of industry, state, and resource worker (Roberts and Emel 1992). The primary activity of forested landscapes seen as resource landscapes is timber extraction. Sites that produce easily accessible, high volumes of timber are privileged. Workers and industry ally across class affiliations to protect access to what is known colloquially as "the working forest." This label privileges the work that forests do in contributing to economic enterprise (e.g., in providing fibre for timber harvest), while it omits, in large part, the ecological work of purifying the air, retaining soil nutrients, or providing habitat for nonhuman species. ENGOs and their campaigns have been tolerated as long as they do not pose a substantial threat to economic imperatives. Governments have responded by establishing new parks or reserves where protected areas do not pose a substantial threat to the overall objective of timber production.

The stories that have been told of forests as productive landscapes have reflected the history of white male settlers, while stories of the contributions of other social groups have been slow to emerge. For example, First Nations, as the original settlers of the landscape, have historically been subject to processes of depopulation and marginalization and even erasure (Braun 2002; Willems-Braun 1997a, 1997b).[4] In some forestry communities, there is a significant population of East Indian settlers who undertook jobs in sawmills. Similarly, some early Chinese immigrants who had worked as indentured labourers in the creation of the Canadian Pacific Railway in the late nineteenth century settled in forestry towns. They provided critical services to workers employed in logging and milling; some worked directly in the woods or mills. Yet attention to these workers in academic or popular writings is scant.

The stories of women's contributions within these landscapes are also sparse. Rather, the landscapes of the working forest literally became places of working men's culture (Dunk 1994). There, amid the trees and the technology, male identity was forged, reinforced, despised, and celebrated (e.g., Garner 1999; Trower 1999). Women's contributions to these places were relegated to private spheres of reproduction and consumption. Despite their historical presence in early settlements and camp life (see Garner 1999), women and their contributions as producers have been narrowly interpreted. Consequently, their work has been largely "invisible" to researchers, policy practitioners, and even residents, because it intersects less obviously with predominant patterns of male employment. Contemporary aspects of this issue are taken up in detail in Chapter 4.

In British Columbia, about 95 percent of forest land is publicly owned, and the provincial government has been primarily responsible for the allocation of forest lands and management practices. Until about the mid-1970s,[5] the state's role was that of manager: creating and maintaining top-down institutions to ensure ongoing production. The Ministry of

Forests was considered the sole arbiter of forestry claims. Critics argued that the ministry, as with other resource management agencies, was influenced, and even held captive, by the industries that it sought to regulate (see Williston and Keller 1997). It was not necessary to demonstrate deliberate attempts by industry to influence individual government officials. Rather, government regulatory agents were often trained by the same institutions and shared the resource-centred values of the companies. These values included the widely shared belief that the agency existed to sustain the industry rather than the resource itself (Clapp 1998; Rees 1990).

During the 1970s, increasing pressures on available timber supplies, new public calls for environmental protection, and increasing awareness of nontimber values in forests (e.g., wildlife, water, and fisheries) led policy makers to align themselves with a new ideal of "integrated resource management."[6] In addition, the provincial government responded to calls for greater public involvement and increased public influence in land use decisions by establishing ad hoc commissions and advisory groups to address specific land allocation and management issues (Pearse 1976; Sewell, Dearden, and Dumbrell 1989). Throughout the 1970s and 1980s, other government agencies gained a greater voice in forestry issues.[7] New parks and wilderness areas were established as the government attempted to quell public discontent about particular places.[8] These combined pressures, therefore, led to a new interpretation of landscape – that is, landscape as wilderness.

Forested Landscapes as Wilderness Landscapes
In contrast to resource landscapes, wilderness landscapes are valued for their noneconomic attributes. In some cases, values may be associated with alternative forms of production or consumption that may include transitory, small-scale economic enterprises such as cone picking or beekeeping or, on a grander scale, ecotourism. Alternatively, some groups may seek outright preservation by referring to the scientific, ecological, or intrinsic values of these landscapes. Within these constructions, particular sites (e.g., old-growth forests specifically or the BC central coastal region generally) and species for protection (e.g., spotted owls, bears, or salmon) have been highlighted. For example, in 1997, without consulting local residents, a network of ENGOs renamed the mid-coast of the province "Great Bear Wilderness" (Greenpeace Canada 1998).[9] Web sites, promotional materials, environmental representatives, and even news media now refer to this region as "Great Bear Rainforest." The emotive significance of such a name cannot be underestimated.

As the dominant, industrial interpretation of forests was questioned, so too was the role of the state. Its role shifted from that of manager to that of mediator of public disputes and regulator of industrial practices. Its primary role today is to attempt to "balance" competing objectives through policy instruments and public involvement mechanisms under the rubric of sustainability. The 1990s saw the establishment of new mechanisms of public joint decision making and consensus seeking through strategic land use planning. Within this construct, industry has been viewed as the primary enemy. Often, however, workers have also become the focus of disdain or distrust (White 1995) or, more charitably, been viewed as victims of international capital (Boucher 1994; Burda, Gale, and M'Gonigle 1998).

The promotion of forested landscapes as wilderness areas continues to demonstrate exclusionary practices and exhibit an imperialist bias (Di Chiro 1995; Guha 1989; Neumann and Schroeder 1995; Seager 1993). For example, it is now recognized that First Nations in British Columbia have long laboured in the "wilderness." Canadian superior courts have affirmed that the resolution of Aboriginal "claims" to BC's lands and resources should be addressed by the state and broader society. However, contemporary images of wilderness continue to erase their presence or "permit" Aboriginal people to enter wilderness landscapes only insofar as their activities involve "traditional" and "nonexploitive" patterns of resource use (Willems-Braun 1997b).

Like resource landscapes, wilderness landscapes and their interpretations are also gendered. Ideas about the untouched character and/or maternal qualities of "nature" have given wilderness a feminine character (e.g., Fitzsimmons 1989; Merchant 1980; Rose 1993). Human attempts to "know" nature through adventure, recreation, exploration, aesthetic appreciation, and scientific endeavour have been viewed as acts that assert masculinity (Rose 1993; Seager 1993). This orientation also asserts a particular westernized form of masculinity in which alternative viewpoints about "people in nature" are ignored and effectively erased.[10]

Non-Aboriginal resource workers in the forest industry have also been effectively omitted from conceptions of wilderness. Within this construct, other ethnic groups (e.g., Chinese Canadians, (East) Indian Canadians) who helped to create forestry culture are also excluded from perspectives of wilderness. In a biting critique, Richard White (1995) argued that environmentalists have not come to terms with those who labour in nature, approving of archaic forms of work while condemning modern ones. Leaving aside the challenges of determining what constitutes archaic work and what constitutes modern work, he suggested that wilderness preservation campaigns have contributed to a bitter divide between leisure and labour, the pristine and the sullied.[11] Women, as well as men, who live and work in rural places that rely on forested landscapes are immersed in these debates. Whether they are identified as victims, victors, agents, or opponents of change is a topic discussed in subsequent chapters.

The two representations of forested landscapes have been presented as emerging from alternative and opposing value systems. Yet these representations are reciprocal, if contradictory. For example, the pristine quality attributed to a wilderness landscape requires the alternative vision of a "sullied" or "industrial" landscape against which it gains saliency. These representations are also linked because of their spatial and temporal proximity. Wilderness is viewed as a landscape that is far away in time and place from the hustle and bustle of urban life. It comes into conflict with the values of forests as resource landscapes when wilderness and resources are found in the same place. It is no coincidence that the "best" landscapes for resource extraction (e.g., valley bottoms, old-growth forests) also have the highest values associated with wilderness.

The different values that underlie these representations contribute to the shaping of material practices – that is, the policies and practices deemed acceptable during times of transition. Policy alternatives and individual programs for transition are not initiated in a vacuum. Rather, they are embedded in social relations that have placed residents of forested rural communities in a marginal social and geographic location with respect to prevailing public policy interests.

Interpreting Transition as Social Marginalization

In the American Pacific Northwest, forestry workers are less likely to be unionized, typically work for lower wages, and enjoy fewer benefits than forestry workers in Canada. In British Columbia, male forestry workers and their families are rarely poor.[12] Since the Second World War, Canadian forestry workers have been represented by strong unions[13] and have enjoyed high wages, good benefits, and access to a social safety net that includes employment insurance, universal medicare, and publicly supported old-age pensions. Average incomes have historically outstripped those for the general population. Why, then, should these people be considered marginal? How does transition further contribute to their social marginalization?

Typically, research about environmental destruction in rainforests has focused on tropical zones where destruction is linked to grinding poverty and social marginality that, in turn, drive the practices of degradation (e.g., Friedmann and Rangan 1993; Peet and Watts 1993; Redclift 1987). Working within a broad framework classified as "political ecology," researchers have focused on how capitalist economies promote a structure of unequal relations that, in turn, has resulted in "subaltern" environmental struggles that are rooted in livelihood issues. Political ecologists suggest that livelihood struggles focus on attempts to "gain access to and control over the natural resources upon which their lives and livelihoods depend (Friedmann and Rangan 1993, 4). Thus, they focus on who has power and on which instruments they use in political struggles over environmental and social change.

I am not suggesting that conditions for rural residents living in the coastal forestry communities of the Pacific Northwest have reached the depths of marginality described by scholars of political ecology working in "developing" countries. Nor are rural residents uniform in their marginality. There are major divides within these settings across gender, class, and ethnicity that situate some residents as decidedly more privileged than others. The agendas and "successes" of environmental organizations in gaining more lands or waters for protection from exploitation have been unevenly applied, and their effects have been unevenly distributed across landscapes. However, at least three insights from this literature pertain to the research here.

First, several analysts have argued that international environmental activism has privileged particular landscapes and species. ENGOs based in North America and Europe have made deals with international development and finance agencies and have frequently (intentionally or not) justified the displacement of livelihood strategies of poor and disenfranchised groups in developing countries (Guha 1989; Neumann and Schroeder 1995; Sundberg 1999). Consequently, wilderness preservation movements seeking to protect landscapes in developing countries have been openly criticized for the effective imperialist and colonialist nature of their interventions (Guha 1989). There has also been an uneven application of environmental interest; the bulk of environmental fund-raising by ENGOs has gone to preserve nature in rural settings (Braun 1998; Seager 1993). In contrast, environmental degradation in urban areas has frequently been left to be addressed by marginalized socioeconomic groups whose lives are threatened by household, hazardous, and/or toxic wastes (Bullard 1990; Di Chiro 1995, 1997, 1998, 2000; Pulido 2000).

Second, political ecologists encourage one to consider how the positions of individuals or groups within the dominant economic and social relations will condition how they see environmental problems. For example, Laura Pulido's (1996) notion of "positionality" suggests that, while activists may all be involved in the same environmental issues, different actors hold different positions within the socioeconomic structure. Consequently, they frame their struggles differently.

Third, the protection of livelihood is a powerful motivating force. Many of the criticisms of rural activists in North America are related to their desire to retain a preferred lifestyle. Yet political ecologists and new cultural geographers encourage us to consider whether or not these actions are focused partly on the protection of livelihood – the means to earn a living – and partly on regaining some measure of political voice within a society that appears to have pushed rural issues to the political margins.

This possibility raises the need to understand how these rural communities in North America fit within environmental policy debates. I suggest a multifaceted concept of social marginalization to illustrate their contemporary status.

The Many Facets of Social Marginalization

Perhaps the appeal of the term "marginalization" for me as a geographer is its emphasis on location. According to Linda McDowell and Joanne Sharpe (1999), "marginality" is used metaphorically to define the position of an individual or social group as part inside, part outside the dominant area or region. Virginia Seitz (1995, 6), citing the *New Lexicon Webster's Dictionary of the English Language,* uses the term to mean "to cause to live on the edges of society by excluding from participation in any group effort." Margin (the social or geographic location), marginality (the condition), and marginalization (the process) typically revolve around debates about citizenship, equality, social justice, and economies.

Marginalization has typically been associated with uneven economic relations inherent in capitalism and the global economy, in which access to material benefits for economic security and well-being is unequally distributed. The assumption is that basic material needs must be met before benefits associated with the quality of life can be realized. Marxist notions of marginalization reflect these ideas, linking marginalization to the processes of imperialism and colonial practices that served to incorporate some regions into the global economy while disenfranchizing others (e.g., Frank 1967; Friedmann 1966). Liberal ideas about marginalization are also typically associated with indicators of economic growth and income, defining core and marginal economies or regions on a global map of development. While the two positions differ in their assessments of the desired distribution and the mechanisms for reallocation, both have historically been committed to economic indicators of marginality.

In this context, while residents of post-World War II British Columbia enjoyed high wages and living standards, at least four qualifications must be attached to this observation. First, the economic benefits of the resource economy have not been evenly shared across regional or even local landscapes. There is considerable variation in income for men and women across different job types. As noted in Chapter 4, workers in government forestry jobs do not draw nearly the income that industry workers do. Women in industry are often slotted into jobs that are even more economically marginal than those of men in either industry or government. Second, I suggest that the overall economic well-being of forestry communities is of recent significance. Historically, forestry workers were exposed to many occupational hazards, low or nonexistent pensions, and a lifestyle that often led to retirement in the tenement apartment buildings or on the streets of Vancouver's poorest neighbourhood (Davis and Hutton 1989).[14]

Third, the economic and political strength of forestry workers, tied to the postwar union movement, has waned since the 1970s (Widenore 1995). Within the industry, industrial restructuring, job loss, and renegotiation of contracts have illustrated the waning bargaining power of unions with their employers. In addition, the identity of forestry workers has declined in political saliency within the broader society (see next section).

And fourth, economic well-being does not have an immediate correlation with social well-being (Beckley 1995; Byron 1978; Kusel 1996). Because of the recency of settlement and transience of the population, forestry communities often lack the social infrastructure to coalesce around major social issues in a sustained and unified manner over a long period (Marchak 1983). Residents of forestry communities are unevenly poised to influence the social, environmental, and economic changes that constitute the restructuring of their communities. One can see that individuals within these communities have different prospects for maintaining and/or improving their social well-being during times of transition. In this context, I theorize that a study of the effects of transition for forestry communities will yield very different results within and across these communities.

Furthermore, recent structural changes in the industry and/or in government policy have had and will continue to have differential effects for workers and communities. For example, Clark Binkley (1997) estimated that policies introduced in the early 1990s would result in a twenty-year reduction of about 23.5 percent in provincial total harvest levels, with greater impacts on the coast than in the interior. He further estimated that this reduction would result in the loss of up to 92,000 jobs, $4.9 billion in provincial GDP, substantial losses in government revenues, and increased costs for social services for unemployed workers. While some of these losses will be realized in Vancouver, the impacts will be most strongly felt in thirty-nine of fifty-five rural communities in British Columbia where forestry is the dominant basic industry. Data from previous recessions do not indicate whether professional workers are more likely than waged workers to be affected by job loss or how they will fare upon layoff (see Hayter 2000).

However, if past circumstances are repeated, then it is likely that women in forestry occupations will fare worse than men. While the evidence is sparse, research by Eric Grass and Roger Hayter (1989) suggested that during the recession between 1981 and 1985 female employment dropped faster than male employment, particularly in the coastal forestry region. Hayter later observed that, while the proportion of women in the industry was small, "the recession weakened the already marginal position of females in forest-product manufacturing" (2000, 266). Furthermore, there are indications that upon job layoff labour adjustment is more difficult for women than for men. A report to the Ontario government about the forest industry there revealed that women fared worse than men, not because of family responsibilities but when all other factors are controlled: "women in fact, take a greater cut in pay compared with men when they are displaced ... They experience significantly more long-term unemployment and earn less when they do land a job" (Ontario Ministry of Labour n.d., 75-76). Thus, unequal economic relations within forestry situate workers in a marginal position. And, within this position, some workers are more marginal than others.

Marginality may also be applied to ideas about citizenship, defined as a "contractual relationship between an individual and a territorially-based state-like body which defines a person's eligibility to certain rights that are enforceable through collective entitlements" (McDowell and Sharpe 1999). Citizenship formalizes the conditions for full participation in a community and refers to a range of formal and informal rights and processes that determine people's inclusion in, and exclusion from, a variety of symbolic and material spaces and resources (Smith 2000, 83). These ideas originate in the work of Thomas Marshall (1964), whose writings on civil, social, and political rights of citizenship laid the foundation of the welfare state. Changing entitlements and the associated, shifting patterns of eligibility may result from economic restructuring, cultural transformation, or political realignment. Consequently, social justice, citizenship, and inclusion in civil society encompass concerns for both the material distribution of social and economic benefits and the recognition of identity within mainstream society (Fraser 1997). The importance of this dual set of concerns for this study is that one need not rely on illustrating economic deprivation in order to make a claim about social marginalization. Exclusion of some groups or individuals from the benefits of recognition and legitimacy within a broader culture may also deny them their rights (and attendant responsibilities) to become full participants in society at large.

Theories of marginalization and citizenship have been given practical meaning in recent discussions about the meanings and policies associated with "social exclusion," particularly as they have been debated in Western Europe (e.g., Room 1995; Sibley 1998; Smith 1997). In policy practice, social exclusion has been rather narrowly related to discussions of how social groups have been excluded from the labour market and which mechanisms might be adopted for incorporating them into the workforce (Sibley 1998). Yet, in academic and social activist debates, social exclusion moves beyond simple descriptions of job loss and poverty – defined by levels of income and associated lack of resources – to include relational issues such as inadequate social participation, lack of power, and social integration (Elliott 1999; Room 1995). My use of marginalization is consistent with these multiple dimensions, as illustrated in Table 2.1.

Michael Samers (1998) classifies social exclusions into two categories. Material exclusions relate to one's economic well-being and access to material resources, while discursive exclusions affect how one is represented to the broader society. He points out that both material and discursive exclusions can have real, material effects on one's economic livelihood and well-being. Samers's list reflects a multidimensional definition that focuses on processes as well as outcomes. In this study, I use a similar framework to explore marginalization. My use of social marginalization relates to the inability to exercise both the formal and the substantive rights of citizenship in civil society, as well as exclusion from centres of decision making and popular values. Inequalities between localities and communities can alter the extent to which residents' or members' social, economic, and political entitlements can be mobilized (Marston 1990; Marston and Staeheli 1994). In my research, I found that rural residents in forestry communities have been increasingly marginalized in their claims for

Table 2.1

Social exclusions

Material exclusions
- from a job or "primary sector" jobs (as defined by labour segment theorists and described in Chapter 4)
- from social services (including health and transport services and self-help organizations)
- from adequate housing (in both state and private sectors)
- from political (civic) participation (in local elections and/or regional and/or national elections, local cultural and social organizations)
- from adequate social contacts
- from banking (access to loans)
- from (especially prestigious and/or well-funded secondary) education
- from employment training
- from recreation and leisure (activities and spaces)

Discursive exclusions
- by academics (the question of representation, social invisibility in reports and surveys)
- by government and policy makers (social invisibility in reports and surveys)
- by housing, social service, and immigration authorities (racism, intimidation)
- by schools, universities, and other educational authorities (racism, social categorizing)
- by the media (television, newspapers, et cetera)

Source: Samers 1998, 126.

economic, social, and political entitlements, particularly as environmentalism has emerged as a dominant or core value within forestry and land use debates of the Pacific Northwest. Women living in rural regions in particular are located at the margins of social and political discourse that surround policy makers, activists, and scholars dealing with contemporary environmentalism.

That social exclusion can include both material deprivation and relational concerns over participation and acceptance into the broader society is consistent with Iris Young's (1990) theorization of social justice. Young argued that social inequalities take multiple forms beyond inequalities in the distribution of material goods and resources.[15] According to her theorization, people become disabled through constraints imposed by unfair distributive patterns, decision-making procedures, divisions of labour, and culture. These dimensions create hierarchical divisions between people by defining another group as different from, and inferior to, the "norm," thereby rendering it as "other." Marginalization can take place as a consequence of institutional, structural, and cultural features of well-intentioned liberal democratic society. As Young suggests, "some groups suffer as a consequence of often unconscious assumptions and reactions of well-meaning people in ordinary interactions, media, and cultural stereotypes, and structural features of bureaucratic hierarchies and market mechanisms – in short, the normal processes of everyday life" (41). Consequently, one need not demonstrate the conscious or intentional actions of a group or community toward another to demonstrate social marginalization. Rather, this argument is sustained by explaining the consequences of ordinary daily activities.

I adapt Young's framework to form the foundation of my own theory of social marginalization, which I apply to forestry communities.[16] My adaptation divides social marginalization into four facets: exploitation, social exclusion, powerlessness, and moral exclusion.

Exploitation includes the appropriation of labour by one group to the benefit of another – for example, that of workers by capitalists or women's domestic labour by men. "Gender exploitation includes the systematic and unreciprocated transfer of powers, usually from women to men, including the transfer of fruits of material labour and nurturing and sexual energies" (Young 1990, 50). In this study, I consider exploitation in terms of women's labour in the paid workplace and in unpaid activities in the house and community organizations. I argue that the "work" of forestry communities is much broader than simply the harvesting and processing of timber. Women's contributions – both to the paid work of forestry and to the unpaid work of maintaining forestry communities – are many, yet they remain unacknowledged by partners, policy makers, and even academic outsiders. The issue of "invisibility" is one component of gender exploitation in the context of forestry. The second issue relates to how we conceptualize work outside forestry. This facet of social marginalization is considered in Chapter 4.

Social exclusion is a second facet of social marginalization. According to Young (1990), social exclusion occurs when people are expelled from useful participation in social life and ultimately results in material deprivation. For example, those who become unemployed and seek employment insurance, retraining, or welfare are often forced to give up rights and freedoms that others have. They may be monitored, and professional decisions are often made for them. They may also be required to suspend basic rights to privacy, respect, and individual choice. In addition, people may be rendered marginal in terms of personal efficacy in the form of uselessness, boredom, and lack of self-respect.

This form of social exclusion generated much fear and uncertainty in the communities of my study. Women who participated in this study feared that changes in environmental policy would have significant and marginalizing effects on those whose jobs were rendered "redundant," those who were destined to be "retrained," and/or those who entered the ranks of the unemployed or became dependent on social security. The notion of the family wage was strong; the absence of such an opportunity shook the foundation upon which the forestry communities had been built. In addition, the threats of job loss were more than economic; they also undermined the ideas of self-reliance, hard work, and independence that composed part of the identity of forestry communities, particularly for men who worked in the industry.

The third facet of social marginalization is *powerlessness*, defined as the lack of respect given to some groups according to their apparent professional or relevant qualifications and demeanour. In this study, powerlessness is described in several ways. The powerless have little or no work autonomy, exercise little creativity or judgment in their work, and have no technical expertise or authority. Consequently, they express themselves awkwardly, especially in public or bureaucratic settings. Often, they do not command respect. By contrast, professionals have a progressive development of their personal capacity, greater decision-making authority, and greater respectability in society. While one may consider powerlessness in relation to divisions of labour in workplace settings, it may also apply to the ways in which decisions about environmental policy are made. For women living and working in forestry communities, both were relevant. As members of the paid workforce, most women viewed themselves as disempowered by virtue of their gender and, in some cases, ethnicity (Chapter 4). Women were also disempowered within their own communities since their public service work was devalued or dismissed by dominant male institutions operating locally (Chapter 5).

Powerlessness was also expressed by women in this study who saw themselves as part of a broader rural culture that had become disenfranchised from policy debates about environmental protection and whose grassroots organizations seemed to be out of step with and outmatched by the more professional environmental organizations (Chapter 6). The professionalization of environmental organizations provided them with the ability to speak out clearly on a variety of issues, while at the same time they appealed to the broader middle class. Consequently, environmental organizations were far more successful in gaining the ear of the state as the government negotiated a land use strategy with public interest groups in newly established land use planning processes (Chapter 7).

The last facet is *moral exclusion,* a notion that has been advanced by geographers and sociologists in relation to environmental debates in North America. These authors have explained the timber supply crisis of the Pacific Northwest as a struggle over the legitimation of competing moral communities (e.g., Proctor 1995; Rural Sociological Society of America 1993). Moral exclusion takes place when the views and experiences of some groups become stereotyped and used to construct those groups as "others." This construction then serves to exclude the groups by processes that consider the experiences and culture of the "dominant" group as the norm or standard against which others are judged. This process renders the perspective of one's group invisible at the same time as one is stereotyped and marked as other. These "others" are then placed into a network of dominant meanings by people who are outside their personal experiences, and their placement is usually marked as inferior to those meanings associated with the dominant society. The "others" may then be forced to react to the behaviours of those influenced by these images.

In the battle of woods and words, this facet of social marginalization has been dialectical. According to the Rural Sociological Society of America, "groups for and against contemporary forestry compete for the right to define nature and its socially (morally) appropriate uses with myths or stories about natural objects and their appropriate roles in society. Groups who gain benefit from these myths gain both legitimacy and rights of access and use of the resource" (1993, 159). Both environmental organizations and rural residents have been complicit in stereotyping and marking the other in their battle for the moral high ground. The primary consequence is discursive – that is, it creates myths and icons associated with the dominant society. The secondary consequence is material. It generates social inequality in the attribution of value to nature and in the costs and benefits associated with changes made in that attribution. Those who oppose these tactics are stereotyped and dismissed, ignored and vilified, and seen as undeserving. Furthermore, others may be mythologized through images such as "rapers of the land," "tree murderers," "Paul

Bunyans," et cetera. Rural residents also engage in such tactics, labelling environmentalists as "tree huggers," "hippies," and "social welfare bums." However, in the public policy debates, these images have not budged the dominant public sentiment, which remains unequivocally in favour of protection of wilderness for aesthetic and ecological values. "West Coast" environmentalism, with its focus on protecting old-growth forests along with their ecological structure and integrity, has gained moral ascendancy, replacing both local and global industrial elites who traditionally benefited from access to, and use of, "natural resources."

In sum, the analytical approach to marginalization is multidimensional. The four facets of marginalization are unevenly produced within and across geographic landscapes and societal groups. The facets are linked and are integral to an understanding of the positions taken by residents of rural communities. By examining these four facets, it is possible to illustrate how environmental debates are embedded within their social contexts. I suggest that marginalization of rural peoples and their forestry culture on Canada's West Coast can be understood by considering their relationships to processes of uneven development (including division of labour), environmentalization and anti-environmentalization, and identity politics.

Uneven Development and Forestry Communities
Uneven development is exemplified in current debates about the globalization of local economies. The notion that forest economies are part of a globalized system of exchange implies that international patterns of investment and withdrawal, political events, environmental disasters, and social upheavals may displace people socially and geographically far beyond individual or even national control. The forest industry of British Columbia is part of a global economy. However, its geographic and economic location on the world stage is also an important characteristic. Roger Hayter argues that "the geographic marginality of BC, on the edge of an empire, a continent, and an ocean, is the defining context for understanding the evolution of its forest staple" (2000, 35). According to economic geographers who adhere to political economy, the thesis of uneven development illustrates how decisions and events in distant places can affect local economies and communities (e.g., Barnes and Hayter 1992, 1997; Hayter 2000; Innis 1933).[17]

In Canada, political economists have explained uneven development through the lens of the staple thesis first advanced by Harold Innis (1933). This thesis interprets "staple exploitation within the framework of creative destruction, of instability and crisis, in which the manner of exploitation is itself subject to policy" (Hayter 2000, 24). In this model, the Canadian economy has been built on providing staple or resource (fish, fur, trees) products for metropolitan countries. Institutions, geography, and technology have shaped the development of the staple economy. Core or metropolitan regions (e.g., the United States and the United Kingdom)[18] require and shape the production of staples that occurs in peripheral countries such as Canada.

This core-periphery framework has also been used to interpret Canada's internal economy. Relations between central Canada (including southern Ontario and Quebec) and the maritime and western provinces, as well as relations between southern and northern portions of most provinces, have been characterized by systems of uneven (core-periphery) exchange (e.g., Davis and Hutton 1989; Hayter 2000; McCann 1987).

According to staple theory, Canada's economy has been unusually resource specialized and prone to crisis and booms and busts. In an effort to gain comparative advantage in the international marketplace, firms have exploited the resource base, extracting the best-quality and most-accessible resource first (a process referred to as "highgrading"). Their efforts have been supported by policy makers with short-term political horizons that have evolved in close alliance with the dominant resource industry (Clapp 1998). At the local level, diversification is frequently limited and often related to diversification around the export base. For example, the establishment of a sawmill may be seen as a means to diversify employment prospects that would otherwise rely solely on logging.

This situation makes resource-based communities extraordinarily vulnerable to changes in external circumstances and demand as they become "trapped" in the mode of staples extraction and production (Watkins 1984). For communities that rely on resources for their economic well-being, boom-and-bust cycles are considered inherent features of their economies. Residents become "addicted" to these circumstances, unable to divorce themselves from their expectations of well-being (Freudenberg 1992), and consequently they may pressure the government to subsidize resource extraction to the point of both economic unfeasibility and ecological exhaustion. Because of their marginalized status in directing the economy and their lack of alternative work options, resource workers may in fact contribute to their fate. They frequently ignore the signs of long-term reductions in resource availability and thereby contribute to the inevitable decline of the resource sector and, ultimately, threaten the viability of successor industries (Clapp 1998).

Division of Labour
Within these uneven trajectories, the division of labour affects one's position in relation to issues. Simply stated, division of labour refers to who works for whom, who does not work, how the content of work is defined,

and how it defines one institutional position relative to others. Division of labour commonly intersects with other social divisions such as gender or ethnicity, so that we tend to conceive of particular work roles for particular social groups – such as for women and Chinese Canadians in both the creation and the ongoing maintenance of rural resource towns. One's place in the division of labour translates into particular lifestyle choices based on income, education, status, authority, and power. For example, as described previously, "professionals" are normally accorded more authority than waged workers with respect to advocating or implementing policy changes. One's place in the division of labour may also indicate the relative exposure to job layoff, the likelihood of success in retraining, and the ability to acquire an alternative position after dislocation.

Studies of worker displacement in forestry occupations suggest that the effects of displacement are long-standing and far-reaching (Carroll, Daniels, and Kusel 2000; Hay 1993). While those in managerial positions can draw on a broad range of skills and may be better suited to move to new occupations, those in waged employment appear to have more constrained labour market opportunities and are unwilling or unable to move to larger centres to obtain new employment. Based on experiences of economic transition and diversification in Oregon, Paul Sommers argued that, "for those left out and left behind, the result is not 'an optimistic economic future' but a degraded present. There is a lot of despair and anxiety – people working two part-time jobs with no benefits, and households with all adults working to scrabble out a living" (1996, 2). This observation illustrates how quickly rural workers can become marginalized when jobs are lost in the forestry sector.

Division of labour may also influence the way in which people become situated within particular class positions and social relations. Historically, the term "class" has referred to a specific relationship between workers and owners. That is, class has emerged as a particular social grouping, a social category, or a structural feature of capitalist production and society. This conception has been extended in two ways that are useful for this study. The first extension is presented by Karen Sacks (1989), who suggested that class membership need not be based on individual status but can emerge as a relation between a group and the means of production. Her definition includes struggles that are community based rather than individually constituted and may (by extension) encompass the activities of women who are not employed in waged labour. However, her conception is limited in that it is still firmly related to issues tied to the means of production.

In a second extension, economists and geographers have explored the potential of examining class as a process of change (e.g., Gibson 1992; Gibson-Graham 1996; Resnick and Wolff 1987).[19] For example, Katherine

Gibson defined class as "the *social process* of producing and appropriating surplus labour ... and the associated *process* of surplus labour distribution" (1992, 113; emphasis added). By focusing on how surplus labour is produced, appropriated, and distributed, they include labour processes within both capitalist and noncapitalist systems and include numerous other economic relationships that actively shape people's lives and the landscape. Both efforts to extend and revise the notion of class provide opportunities to consider how "workers," broadly defined, may be situated within multiple class processes. An individual, for example, can simultaneously occupy a number of class positions, including worker, self-employed individual, and exploited homemaker (Gibson 1992). By emphasizing class as a process, rather than a social grouping, Julie-Katherine Gibson-Graham (1996) expands the spheres where appropriation and distribution occur to encompass not only the shop floor, the forests, and the fields but also the household and the community.

These conceptual developments are relevant to the study of forestry communities of northern Vancouver Island because rural individuals and households are involved in diverse economic pursuits that defy easy classification. For example, within a single family, individuals may simultaneously be small-scale commodity producers, property owners and landlords, and engaged otherwise in subsistence activities such as hunting or fishing. How, then, would they be classified? These extensions to the concept of class illustrate the multiple positions in which rural people might be situated. They also suggest that their activism can occur across a range of sites – ranging from the household, paid work site, and forestry community to the front lines of protest events. In short, broad-based economic and social relations such as uneven development, division of labour, and class are considered societal processes that shape the lives of rural residents and situate their positions in environmental debates. Attention to "environmentalization" and "identity politics" also illustrates the themes of multiple positioning and multiple sites of activism.

Environmentalization and Anti-Environmentalization
Much of this book focuses on the divide between "environmentalism" and "anti-environmentalism." Neither movement represents a singular philosophy, ideology, or practice. By describing each separately, I risk reinforcing this divide against the current wisdom of postmodern theory and practices of organizations that sustain the movements. Yet environmentalism, as it has been practised in the Pacific Northwest, has led to a marked division between rural and urban places with respect to the protection of wilderness. I argue that the polarization of sustainability in environmental debates and the associated standoff between pro- and anti- factions have played crucial roles in constructing "rural identity" and in reducing the

voices of rural residents to a singular, oppositional, and negative status with respect to environmental regulation and land use.

An introductory text on environmental issues in Canada characterizes environmentalism as a movement that supports the protection of ecological integrity and sustainability by advocating a set of transformations of society and economy (Draper 1998). Environmentalists demonstrate a concern for policies and values that affect the long-term viability of non-human systems and place value on aspects of the environment that require knowledge of how the uses and aesthetics of the environment are judged as well as moral commitments to other living things and future generations.

Environmentalism has had a long history of theoretical and empirical study to trace its origins, philosophies, and impacts (e.g., Doherty and deGeus 1996; O'Riordan 1976; Snow 1992). In contrast, the anti-environmentalism philosophy and movement have been given far less attention (e.g., Beder 1997; Rowell 1996; Switzer 1996, 1997). Consequently, anti-environmentalism is not as easy to define. Both Robert Paehlke (1992) and Duncan Taylor (1992) suggest that an expansionist economic worldview is contrary to the perspective of environmentalism. Related to this worldview is a preoccupation with the monetary costs of environmental cleanup or a consideration of jobs and employment as paramount over environmental controls (Draper 1998). Anti-environmentalism has sometimes been linked to ideas about citizenship, particularly in the United States, where groups who seek to protect property rights and personal wealth argue that these are necessary conditions for participation in society. In more popular writing, anti-environmentalism has become synonymous with terms such as "green backlash" (Rowell 1996; Switzer 1997), and is depicted as a movement determined to roll back gains made by environmental activists since about 1970 and ultimately to destroy environmentalism (Beder 1997). According to these depictions, its followers are envisioned as right-wing and pro-industry, bent on a campaign of information distortion, personal harassment, collective name-calling and intimidation, and suspected of using threats or acts of violence to further their aims (Rowell 1996).

Concerns to protect the natural environment are brought forward in social and political life by processes of environmentalization defined by Frederick Buttel as "the concrete processes by which green concerns and environmental considerations are brought to bear in political and economic decisions in educational and scientific research institutions, in geopolitics, and so on. Environmentalization is thus the concrete expression of the broad force of greening in institutional practices" (1992, 2). He argued that greening is largely an ideological or symbolic phenomenon and a response to environmental destruction. He suggested that researchers "must take into account the reciprocal interactions between this ideological force and the social structures within which it is located" (2). If environmentalism embraces both philosophy and practice, then environmentalization refers to the means of mobilization. Strategies of mobilization, however, are not just the purview of environmental groups but are also used by those in "anti"-environmental movements. Thus, one might also be able to conceive of processes of anti-environmentalization. As with environmental activists and campaigns, the identities and strategies of anti-environmentalists may be adopted in opposition to other groups.

Part of the mobilization efforts on both sides of the debate has been to classify the tactics of the "other" group. Anti-environmentalists have been associated with the "wise use" movement of the United States (classified as the "SHARE" movement in Canada). The labels are derived from rural communities that promote the wise use of natural resources defined as providing for multiple uses of the environment and including extraction and production of resource commodities. They also maintain that urban and rural residents must share equitably in both the costs and the benefits of resource management. Of course, while the wise use adherents may borrow the wording of environmental activists, their positions are decidedly more in line with industrial forestry. The depiction by Andrew Rowell (1996) that the wise use movement is a vicious attack against environmentalists and environmental imperatives describes only its most extreme elements. For example, in the United States, a handful of leaders have focused on radical and extreme positions and proponents of the environmental movement (e.g., Earth First!) and on elements to which rural people will be most hostile – animal rights, anti-hunting, and (in the Pacific Northwest) the spotted owl campaigns. Adherents of wise use have engaged in their own acts of stereotyping by denigrating environmentalists as welfare dependants and/or white, overeducated preservationists who serve elite interests (Beder 1997). In the United States, those in the wise use movement tend to share a dislike of environmental regulation, and the aims of their movement are often conflated with American ideals to uphold the rights of private property (Beder 1997; White 1995).

In Canada, there are important connections and significant differences between the aims and the tactics of SHARE (a.k.a. wise use) organizations. SHARE organizations entered Canada from the United States via Ontario and British Columbia in the late 1980s and early 1990s, at the height of increased uncertainty about the viability of Canadian resource economies. American activists were invited to speak in Canada about the potential dangers of allowing an environmental agenda to take over the livelihoods and social fabrics of rural communities. For example, in June 1993, the SHARE organization in Squamish invited a compatriot from Washington state who warned listeners of the social dislocations that would result if environmentalists were successful in reducing access to timber resources in their region. In a community of about 12,000, over 1,000 people attended the talk. Other connections were also made with more high-profile organizers of the wise use movement in the United States. These citizen groups flourished with financial backing from large industry-supported organizations. In British Columbia, the Forest Alliance, a worker-industry dyad, spoke on behalf of SHARE. By the mid-1990s, at the height of SHARE's local influence, thirty-three SHARE organizations were active (CORE 1994a). The mayor of Port McNeill, at the centre of the controversy and located in the study area of my research project, was an important spokesperson for SHARE in British Columbia.

Part of the appeal of SHARE was that it linked forestry workers with the broader dimensions of forestry communities. In this context, women became important spokespeople and activists within the movement, engaging in emotional speeches about the potential devastating impacts that would be unleashed in their communities and spreading fears of family distress and social unrest arising from environmentalism. Women in the SHARE organizations wrote letters to policy leaders and coalesced in women-only groups such as Canadian Women in Timber (CWIT) (modelled after its American counterpart Women in Timber). These strategies and perspectives, as well as some of the contradictions of these organizations, are addressed in some detail in Chapters 5 and 6.

However, while the Canadian movement gained momentum from activities south of the border, it also had distinctive interests. In the United States, the link between wise use and the protection of private property rights is strong. This link has not been developed in the Canadian movement since most forestry lands are publicly owned. While SHARE organizations may have blamed the provincial government for its mismanagement of forest resources and conflicts, they have made no concerted effort to alter the configuration of property rights.[20] In addition, while there is evidence of financial support for SHARE groups early on from large corporate interests through organizations such as the Forest Alliance, this support was not long-standing.

At the time of my research in 1997-98, most SHARE organizations were present in name only. Their membership and activities were dormant. They did not have the longer-term history or the appeal of the American movement, nor did they draw on constitutional or customary institutions (e.g., property rights) to gain public legitimacy. In addition, SHARE organizations were linked by a common agenda but had a loose affiliation across organizations. Membership and activities were voluntary; Canadian activists were not professional organizers. As a result of these circumstances, the interests, perspectives, and positions of people in SHARE organizations were likely more diverse than those depicted by the popular media of the day. Notwithstanding their own attempts to pursue a common front "against" positions of environmentalism, my research revealed a range of expertise and opinion among various elements of this movement. As I discuss in Chapters 5 and 6, some women who held official positions in SHARE groups also lobbied for significant policy changes to the forest industry and within forestry communities.

At one time, environmentalists argued that they represented disadvantaged people and interests whose efforts were outside the mainstream of political power. With reference to environmental activism, this claim is increasingly difficult to sustain. Recognizing the variety of philosophies and tactics of environmental organizations, I consider "mainstream" environmental organizations as large groups who have become recognized by policy makers at provincial and national levels, are solicited by media outlets, and have gained international media attention (after Fitzsimmons and Gottlieb 1988). Throughout the 1970s and 1980s, these groups became increasingly professionalized. They were transformed from a loosely knit coalition of groups into highly organized institutions complete with lawyers, scientists (including social scientists), and professional lobbyists ready to study, advise, advocate, and in some cases in Canada even sue.

With this definition, ENGOs seeking to protect wilderness along the West Coast of Canada can indeed be considered mainstream. By and large, most organizations in British Columbia are headquartered in Vancouver. They sustain large budgets and staff levels, make links to other organizations both regional and international, and have media savvy developed from years of organizing and garnishing public attention.[21] Consequently, organizations such as Greenpeace have become shapers of public agendas, not merely respondents. Membership in these organizations is largely drawn from the ranks of the middle class – especially those employed in professional services – rather than from primary or manufacturing sectors. These groups have attracted the sentiments of the most privileged and economically secure individuals in these debates (Schrecker 1994). Accordingly, these groups help to frame the public policy agenda with respect to land use.

By emphasizing that the protection of industrial forestry is solely anti-environmental, they misrepresent the complexity of the struggles of rural communities and overlook the economic and social contexts in which complexity is embedded. Laura Pulido points out that, while "environmental ideas and activism may be marginal at times, the voices carrying them are not. Moreover, if they are, it is, perhaps, because they choose to be" (1996, 192). In contrast, residents of forestry communities have fewer resources with which to "choose" their social status. That is, they are less likely to determine for themselves if they are to be included or excluded in mainstream society. More commonly, such status is inscribed by economic structures and forces, social and political institutions, ideologies, and customs. Women living in forestry communities, many of whom lack levers of social, economic, and political power both within and without their communities, have fewer opportunities still.

In North America particularly, the temperate rainforests of the Pacific Northwest have been a focal point for environmental activism. This region has been subject to long-standing, politically astute, and increasingly international campaigns to protect it from logging, while other ecosystems across the country have received relatively minor attention.[22] Environmental organizations have formed strategic coalitions to increase their overall influence in the international arena of public opinion. British Columbia's rainforest, for example, has been assigned global value; public sentiment to protect it has drawn from an international audience. For example, the protests in Clayoquot Sound noted at the beginning of Chapter 1 brought people from all over the world, including several international celebrities, such as Robert Kennedy Jr. In 1998, environmental organizations initiated an advertising campaign in British Columbia and the United States that highlighted firms that still used products from old-growth forests (see Dearden and Mitchell 1997). This "international markets" campaign has more recently been pursued over the Internet, where environmental organizations list, lobby, and pass judgment on companies according to their purchasing policies. While they promote the noneconomic values of wilderness, their methods and strategies are clearly associated with global economics.

In British Columbia at least, coastal forestry communities are vulnerable to the international strategies of environmental organizations because these strategies go to the heart of their livelihood. These communities are more likely than urban ones to bear the costs of social dislocation from the pursuit of environmentalist agendas (Schrecker 1994). While these communities also have access to the Internet, their ability to reach out beyond their borders is constrained by their class position, their lack of political savvy, and their increased social distance from the centres of moral authority. In short, urban-based environmentalism has taken over labour as a "progressive" social movement and a site of "progressive" politics (Buttel 1992), leaving residents of forestry communities without a base of political support from which to develop their positions. The political consequence is an attempt to regain moral authority through activities designed to reaffirm rural identity and its place in the economy and the culture of the province.

Identity Politics: Reinforcing Rural Identity and Forestry Culture

It is important that people in this study identify themselves as rural residents and members of forestry communities. These self-references are the materials with which a shared forestry culture can be described. According to scholars of new social movements, the formation of a collective identity is a necessary first step in building a movement (Eyerman and Jamison 1991; Jamison, Eyerman, and Cramer 1990). Furthermore, identity and culture can be sharpened and hardened when they are shaped by oppositional politics. As Pulido points out, "a shared identity must be cultivated and refined through interaction and struggle with other groups ... The development of a collective identity allows people to forge an emotional attachment to each other, but it is also an opportunity to generate an affirmative identity, particularly if they believe their identities have been maligned, distorted, or subject to attempted erasure by the dominant society" (1996, 46). This study considers culture very broadly, including economic forms of organization, power relations, gender dynamics, material artifacts, religion, and language (Pulido 1996).

Following Pulido's lead, this study also adopts Zygmunt Bauman's conception of culture. According to Bauman (1973), culture incorporates particular values and beliefs as well as material icons. Rural identity is grafted onto particular cultural forms considered endemic to local culture and different from those outside it. These forms may include accepted patterns of gender relations and family formations, work habits, and local celebrations. For example, in rural communities, the average age of childbearing tends to be lower than in their urban counterparts. In virtually every forestry community (if not every forestry town), annual celebrations of "logger sports" offer local residents opportunities to showcase local skills and practices particular to forestry (e.g., using heavy equipment, climbing, and even target practice).

Bauman also considers praxis as an element of culture. Praxis is action, usually referring to practices of which people are not overtly conscious but that appear to be the natural way of doing things. For example, how people organize their family obligations and mobilization efforts is an important element of praxis in the protests held by rural residents. The yellow ribbon campaigns mobilized up and down the West Coast of North America were modelled after other ribbon campaigns of different colours (e.g., Mothers against Drunk Drivers, AIDS awareness, the white ribbon campaign of men working to end men's violence against women). By choosing a ribbon campaign, forestry communities signified their association with other important social issues of the time (see endnote 2, Chapter 1).

The celebration of culture marks both solidarity with, and separation from, other groups. It may celebrate these groups as different and place them along a hierarchy in which some cultures are viewed as better than others. For example, many people interviewed for this study argued that their rural culture not only differed from, but was also maligned by, mainstream urban residents and environmentalists. They attempted to invert this perception by discussing how their culture was superior to that of environmentalists. In doing so, they drew on notions of "real work," "hard and physical work," comparing the "honest jobs" of loggers to the "holidaying," "free-wheeling" environmentalists. It is in this sense that celebration and reification of culture may be engaged in by both "sides" of environmental debates. To the extent that symbols, praxis, and hierarchical conceptions are valued by all players in the debate, they may be sources of empowerment. Campaigns to win over public sentiment and policy makers are undertaken by manipulating cultural symbols through popular media. However, if admiration for these traditions is not mutually sustained, then tactics that seek to amplify rural identity and forestry culture only serve to exemplify and reinforce processes of marginalization. This issue has already been taken up in the discussion of moral exclusion, and specific tactics and implications are discussed in Chapter 6.

Worker culture also embraces common-sense knowledge and the ability to learn by doing (Dunk 1991; Satterfield 2002; White 1995). These elements of knowledge acquisition are set against those of formal education, which is more likely to be found among people from urban places. Common sense and bodily knowledge are viewed as worthwhile and usable as opposed to that which is intellectually and physically distant from the necessities of everyday life. Usable knowledge may be applied to one's understanding of nature and ecosystem processes, where daily exposure to the "great outdoors" engenders understanding of and respect for those processes that cannot be fully understood through book learning. These elements of culture and identity imbue the perspectives of women who are quoted throughout Chapters 4 to 7.

These dynamics are difficult to classify. The three societal processes – uneven development, environmentalism/anti-environmentalism, and identity politics – are all mixed up within forestry debates. As Pulido pointed out, "In previous times, we might have tried to make these struggles conform to our narrow definition of class struggle, ignoring the critical roles of identity formation and quality-of-life issues that social agents care enough to mobilise around and that are, in fact, critical to any form of collective action. By the same token, however, we must strive to connect identity politics to a larger materialist analysis instead of focusing on the actions of what appear to be autonomous individuals" (1996, 30). While difficult to classify, these dynamics will be important in understanding the positions that people from forestry communities take with respect to environmental and land use change. It is in this sense, then, that pro- and anti-environmental organizations have tended to render essential and fixed their environmental positions and differences. By maintaining that wilderness must have a pristine quality, pro-environmental positions have excluded a frank debate about livelihood and ultimately have contributed to the growing schism between rural society and urban society over wilderness protection. Indeed, one might speculate, as Pulido does, whether or not "this tendency to disaggregate environmental concerns is a reflection of mainstream environmentalism's propensity to deny that its own environmental interactions are couched within a context of political economic privilege" (193). The concrete processes associated with environmentalization, combined with the increasing polarization of social and economic status between urban and rural areas, have ripened conditions for the marginalization of rural people and their claims for social justice. These forces and relations reinforce an apparent show of solidarity by "forestry communities" and, unintentionally perhaps, serve to fan the flames of an appositive rural identity.

To clarify, I do not seek to blame the environmental movement for all the challenges that currently face rural resource communities. Yet, as it is expressed in coastal British Columbia, the environmental movement has significantly shaped rural issues. In doing so, however, it has largely omitted the social, economic, and even political needs of rural communities in its critiques of government policies or in its blueprints for social change.[23] By this I mean that, while some environmental organizations have identified prescriptions for forestry communities and workers, few have worked directly with rural communities to seek alternatives of mutual interest (see Pinkerton 1993; Schoonmaker, von Hagen, and Wolf 1997). By framing environmental debates in the context of transition and marginalization, I have argued that rural resource communities have been both materially and discursively affected by social trends that favour environmental protection, yet in large part they have been excluded from influencing their trajectories. I take up this theme in the next chapter, in which I provide some of the public policy context that has shaped the economic and social dimensions of rural change in British Columbia.

A bird's-eye view of Port McNeill, 1997.

3
Policy and Structural Change in Rural British Columbia

> Over the last decade and a half British Columbia's forests have become an increasingly troubled landscape.
>
> – Roger Hayter and Trevor Barnes (1997, 1)

Changing Policy Landscapes

The landscape of changing social values described in Chapter 2 had profound impacts on rural communities and policy makers in British Columbia in the 1990s. In 1991, social democrats represented by the New Democratic Party (NDP) were elected and held power for almost ten years. When first elected, the party was given an overwhelming mandate to "make good" on a number of environmental promises. Yet its power base was historically built on its support by labour or, in its words, "the working people." Thus, it faced two historically opposing constituencies. In this chapter, I explore how the government addressed this challenge by documenting its public policy agenda in the early 1990s and by linking its contemporary efforts to longer-term and broader social changes affecting rural places across Canada. This chapter, then, sets the practical context in which women's perspectives and activism can be interpreted.

Sustaining Forestry Communities in British Columbia: The Public Policy Agenda

From Sustained Yield to Sustainability

The need to sustain rural communities has been an explicit, if ill-effected, policy objective since the Second World War. In the years immediately following the war, forested landscapes were viewed as timber reserves, to be harvested for maximum sustained yield. Sustained yield was primarily concerned with the physical characteristics of supply; it did not focus on other economic or social objectives. Instead, other forest values were incorporated into sustained yield policies as constraints on this objective (Haley and Luckert 1995), while it was assumed that sustained yield would lead to socially desirable objectives such as community stability (Byron 1978). New ideas about the sustainable development of forests arose in the 1970s (Pearse 1976), but they were not advanced until the 1980s and

1990s.[1] These new ideas were less concerned with maintaining the yield of fibre over time and more concerned with the broader contribution of forests to human welfare. Consequently, investments in reforestation were intended not simply to replace harvested stands but also to create forest ecosystems that would maintain multiple values and goals – including ecological integrity, biological diversity, as well as productivity of sites and ecosystems (Haley and Luckert 1995). Sustainability also came to mean concern for the well-being of future generations, although this general objective was interpreted differently for different interests. For ENGOs, this objective meant protecting forested ecosystems, while for resource workers it meant sustaining rural communities (CORE 1994a).

The distinction between sustained yield and sustainability, and the contest about their contemporary meanings and effects on forested landscapes and peoples, have continued to plague contemporary disputes on the West Coast. Unlike in most other industrialized countries, most of Canada's forest lands are held under public ownership (and referred to as "Crown land"). With some exceptions (e.g., lands for First Nations and lands of federal jurisdiction – national parks, ports), the provinces are responsible for the allocation and management of lands and resources contained within their borders. Under these arrangements, British Columbia owns 91 percent of the 94.5 million hectares that make up the province's land base and about 95 percent of the forested land base. According to conservative estimates, in 1991 "productive" forest land (land suitable for timber harvesting) accounted for 51.2 million hectares, 24.4 million of which were designated for commercial forestry and about 3.9 million of which were located on the West Coast (Price Waterhouse 1995).

The history of public policy related to forestry and land use in British Columbia has been marked by a basic assumption that localities can be maintained by sustained yield policies. As with other rural communities whose fortunes were tied to resource commodities such as fish and foodstuffs, policy makers assumed that a steady supply of resources would, more or less automatically, provide the necessary and sufficient conditions for building stable resource-producing communities. This was a logical fallacy because it did not account for changes in market demand for the products, nor did it account for changing public values over time. Yet this position was advanced in British Columbia through two royal commissions in 1945 and 1956, respectively, in which Commissioner Sloan argued for sustained yield forestry.

In 1976, after undertaking a comprehensive review of forest tenure, Peter Pearse noted that provincial forest policies had failed to accomplish their original goals and to respond to the changing needs of the population. He recommended several measures, including more intensive regulation of the forest, increased forest inventory information, and the use of technology to improve the utilization of timber. He also noted that increasing public pressure for environmental protection included the desire to protect nontimber values and the dwindling timber supply. Consequently, he questioned the capacity of the existing forest tenure policy to meet changing forestry objectives, and he warned the forest industry to expect an increasing government and public interest in its development. Yet it would be many years before government and industry were willing to acknowledge these observations and warnings.

Policy Initiatives in British Columbia in the 1990s
By the late 1980s, the protection of wilderness had become a driving goal of large, well-organized environmental interests. Valley-by-valley conflicts to protect particular ecosystems marked the landscape. The widespread protest in Clayoquot Sound was part of an ongoing saga of conflict that plagued both policy makers and industry in their drive to maintain conventional forestry. In addition, environmental organizations began to take their protests to the international arena, encouraging boycotts of BC forest products that were obtained from old-growth forests. On the other side of the issue, workers and families united in their own protests. Worker and community groups, union locals, and community leaders became vocal about the potential economic and social dislocations that would result in their communities if more lands became wilderness preserves. For environmental organizations, protection of the temperate rainforest ecosystems was the linchpin for the long-term sustainability of human communities. For forestry workers and their families, the long-term economic and social well-being of their communities was a major concern. If environmental and worker organizations did not share a common definition of sustainability, they did share a growing uncertainty about the sustainability of timber harvest levels in the province and a distrust of government attempts to reconcile and integrate disparate values in resource management initiatives.

During the 1990s, sustainability became an official public policy goal of the BC government (CORE 1992). With respect to forestry, several new acts or major policy initiatives affected Crown land allocation and management practices, and new policies were introduced to assist in economic transition (see Table 3.1). I consider each in turn.

Land Allocation Initiatives
CORE was created in July 1992 by the provincial government. It had a mandate to develop a Provincial Land Use Strategy that included regional and community-based land use planning and management processes. CORE undertook four regional planning initiatives across the province. Each plan allocated land for different purposes, ranging from resource

extraction to wilderness protection. In June 1993, CORE established a land use charter, which described eighteen principles of sustainability that would guide its planning efforts. The principles included a commitment to maintain natural ecosystems for present and future generations, to foster a strong and sustainable economy that would provide the means for increased environmental protection and conservation, and to respect the concerns of individuals and communities in seeking a balance between environmental and economic needs. Its land use strategy was designed to incorporate economic, environmental, and social values into its overall approach and design (CORE 1992). Although the commission lasted only four years, its efforts generated influential documentation about sustainability and created a framework for land use planning that continues in the form of local or subregional interagency public planning initiatives throughout the province.

Vancouver Island was chosen as the first region to receive attention from CORE in the hope of resolving some of the land use conflict and uncertainty plaguing the region. CORE was charged with developing a plan for the island, excluding Clayoquot Sound.[2] The Vancouver Island CORE process began in November 1992. A planning table composed of fourteen sectors representing both government and nongovernment interests

Table 3.1

Selected changes in forestry and land use policy in British Columbia and Vancouver Island, 1991-97

Policy/initiative	Year introduced
Land allocation	
Provincial Land Use Strategy	1992
BC Treaty Commission	1993
Protected Areas Strategy	1993
Clayoquot Sound Land Use Decision	1994
Forest Land Reserve Act	1994
Vancouver Island Land Use Plan	1994
Forest management	
Forest Resources Commission (final report)	1992
Provincial Timber Supply Review (ongoing)	1993-
Clayoquot Sound Scientific Panel	1995
Forest Practices Code (proclaimed)	1995
Transition/mitigation strategies	
Forest Jobs Commission	1994
Forest Renewal Plan	1994
Jobs and Timber Accord	1997

Source: Adapted from Price Waterhouse 1995, 18.

negotiated recommendations for a land use plan. After fourteen months, the table could not reach a consensus. CORE collapsed the table and submitted its report to the government in February 1994. Shortly thereafter, the government gave its support to the plan and its formal approval in June 1994. The report and the approval were both general documents. The final plan, documented with specific borders, was completed in February 2000.

The Vancouver Island CORE regional plan was highly contentious, and large, organized protests were made to the provincial government by forestry communities of Vancouver Island and beyond. The central issues were the loss of timber-harvesting areas to protected areas and the consequent economic effects on communities. The CORE plan proposed a zoning system that involved allocating 13 percent of the land base to protected areas, where resource extraction would not be allowed. A further 8 percent was allocated as "Regionally Significant Lands," where environmental priorities would take precedence over resource extraction. Multiresource use areas were to comprise 73 percent of the plan area. In these areas, intensive logging activity was allowed.

One implication of this land zoning for forestry communities was an estimated 4.5 percent reduction in the total harvest from Crown land or about 580,000 cubic metres per year for three years. Recommendations for an economic transition strategy to address adverse impacts were also included in the CORE plan. A major impact identified in the strategy was the short-term loss of between 900 and 1,500 direct and indirect jobs in the forest industry due to the reallocation of land to different uses. By the mid-1990s, when this research was undertaken, the large job losses predicted by the plan had not yet occurred. Since then, job losses have occurred as a result of a mix of factors, including soft international markets, a tariff dispute with the United States, company restructuring, industry mechanization, and stricter harvesting standards. In addition, the final boundaries associated with CORE's plan became legal only in 2000, deferring the impact of the land use plan for almost another decade. These factors have complicated any effort to attribute the cause of job losses to any individual intervention.

CORE was not the only environmental policy initiative of the 1990s. However, its efforts were swift and far-reaching. The commission broke new ground in attempting to practise the themes articulated in the three-part framework of sustainability. CORE made an effort to consolidate disparate government policies and practices and to develop a coherent normative and strategic approach to addressing them. CORE proposed and worked through a model for public decision making and even proposed a new sustainability act for the province. It was also the focus of direct attacks both by environmental organizations and by community-based groups who sought, with varying degrees of success, to influence planning processes, politicians, and the general public toward their ultimate ends. Despite its relatively short tenure (1992-95), CORE's legacy remained long after in the institutions and language of public land planning that succeeded the commission.

Beyond CORE, the government took other initiatives. In June 1993, the provincial government announced a new policy called the Protected Areas Strategy (PAS). The PAS was a set of policies and procedures for selecting and managing areas to be protected from resource extraction activities such as logging, mining, hydro dams, or oil and gas development. Protected areas (including land and water) were set aside for a variety of uses, including nature preserves, nature appreciation and recreation, scientific research, education, and cultural heritage. The goal of the PAS was to allocate 12 percent of the province's land base by the year 2000 in order to protect representative ecosystems, ecologically significant areas, and special natural, cultural, and recreational environments and features.[3]

In July 1994, the provincial government established the Forest Land Reserve Act to protect the commercial forest land base of British Columbia. This act was designed to protect lands designated for forestry production from conversion to nonforestry uses. A proportion of Crown land was to be allocated to forest land reserves upon completion of local and regional planning and consultation processes. Privately managed forest lands were automatically included in the reserve. Legislation was passed under logic similar to that of British Columbia's Agricultural Land Reserve, an institution of more than thirty years in which lands for agriculture were to be protected from conversion to other uses, particularly urban development. In 1995, 15 million hectares of provincial Crown forest land were added to the Forest Land Reserve provincewide, after land use plans were completed for Vancouver Island and the Cariboo and Kootenay regions. This total represents 17 percent of the area of provincial Crown land in British Columbia. On Vancouver Island, approximately 72 percent of Forest Land Reserve is private forest land, while 18 percent is Crown land (Government of British Columbia, Land Reserve Commission 2000-01).

Beyond these specific acts and policies, ongoing debates emerged around the system of forest land tenures. Under several kinds of leasing and licensing arrangements, the provincial government provided licences in return for harvest. Tenure is a key and contentious institution of public forestry policy. Problems associated with the tenure system have been an ongoing feature of royal commissions and public debates (e.g., Pearse 1976; Sloan Commission 1945, 1956; Williston and Keller 1997). Public debates have revolved around the ways in which tenures have contributed to a lack of investment in silviculture, low levels of stumpage, and royalties paid to government for use of the forest resource. Furthermore, when forest tenures were codified along the coast, the government granted allocations to larger firms. The coastal forest industry is now characterized by a small number of large, integrated, multinational firms. Some have argued, persuasively, that at least since the Second World War this system has given larger operators significant political influence (Williston and Keller 1997) and ultimately increased workers' and forestry communities' dependency on and vulnerability to globalizing forces (Burda, Gale, and M'Gonigle 1998; Marchak, Aycock, and Herbert 1999; M'Gonigle 1997). For some, a strengthening of private property rights (probably for current operators) should increase the pool of capital to invest in forest productivity and provide greater flexibility in responding to rapidly changing circumstances now found in British Columbia and abroad (e.g., Binkley 1997). For others, policy makers should dismantle the current tenure system, dominated by large companies, and move toward a network of individual woodlots, community forests, and First Nations territories (e.g., Burda, Gale, and M'Gonigle 1998; M'Gonigle 1997). In the 1990s, the government undertook a small-scale experimental project to allocate a handful of community forest tenures; however, it never demonstrated the political will to dismantle the current system of property rights regimes.

Compounding the complexity of tenure is the role of First Nations in land and resource issues. In the latter part of the twentieth century, First Nations became a powerful voice in the politics of land allocation and use in British Columbia. With some minor exceptions on southern Vancouver Island and in the northeast portion of the province, the governments of British Columbia and Canada did not sign treaties with Aboriginal peoples living in "British Columbia" at the time of European settlement in the nineteenth century. While Aboriginal protests occurred throughout the twentieth century, by the mid-1980s many Aboriginal peoples had mounted effective protests against resource users, submitting land claims and seeking to protect lands and resources until their claims were resolved (Tennant 1990). Increasingly, legal decisions by the federal and supreme courts began to favour the rights of First Nations and compelled the federal government to negotiate the basis of these claims. While the federal government is empowered to sign treaties, the provinces have jurisdiction over lands and resources. In short, Aboriginal protest, litigation, and confrontation throughout British Columbia generated economic and social uncertainty and threatened to damage the province's economy and credibility (BC Treaty Commission 1998).

As a consequence of successful legal challenges by First Nations, provincial decisions about land use must now be made "without prejudice" to potential future property rights. This means that, while Aboriginal peoples may be involved in planning, their agreement to plans does not override any future claims to lands and resources. Ongoing negotiations with

Aboriginal peoples may alter the configuration of property regimes in the future. In 1999, the first contemporary treaty in British Columbia, the Nisga'a Agreement, was ratified after almost thirty years of negotiations. This landmark agreement, however, has created much debate for both Aboriginal and settler British Columbians and serves as a reminder of the growing importance of Aboriginal rights and interests and the uncertainties associated with their recognition and resolution.

Forest Management Initiatives
But land allocation initiatives were not the only elements of changing forest policy. Forest management practices were also being altered. In the early 1990s, British Columbia developed a timber supply review process designed to adjust allowable annual cuts for the province. Both physical and socioeconomic analyses for each supply area were completed by the chief forester of the province, and new overall priorities were set. In many cases, this review resulted in reductions in the allowable annual cut.[4] Beyond these reviews, other management initiatives were in the works.

Clayoquot Sound, a spectacular watershed located on the west coast of Vancouver Island, has been the subject of intense concern by environmentalists, logging companies, and First Nations for at least thirty years. The massive protests in Clayoquot Sound noted at the beginning of Chapter 1 were sparked by an April 1993 BC government land use plan for the region. After years of public advisory committees and negotiations, the government decided that one-third of the 260,000 hectares of land in the sound would be permanently protected from logging and other forms of resource exploitation, while 45 percent of the land area would be available for resource use, including logging. This decision was a compromise between long-standing adversarial interests, and the compromise failed to achieve its objectives. After the announcement, during the summer and fall of 1993, thousands of people protested, and over 800 were charged with criminal contempt of court because they physically blockaded loggers, who had the legal right to enter the region, from going to work.

Subsequently, the province established a scientific panel composed of fifteen scientists and four people designated by the Nuu-Cha-Nulth Tribal Council, the First Nation whose territorial lands incorporated Clayoquot Sound. In May 1995, the panel recommended that a holistic ecosystem approach to forestry be adopted. Among its recommendations was the idea of a "variable retention silvicultural system" under which clearcut openings would be reduced to four hectares or less. Openings larger than four hectares would require that a minimum of 15 percent trees be retained, either singly or in patches. Other recommendations required that logging plans for the area be based on the area in question rather than the volume of trees to be removed; specific plans be defined by natural topographical boundaries rather than administrative ones; the number and type of logging roads be restricted to 5 percent of any watershed's harvestable area; and traditional ecological knowledge of the First Nations be incorporated into planning and harvesting processes. In July 1995, the ministers of forests and of the environment announced that the province was accepting all of the 127 recommendations in the final report of the scientific panel and that new rules would be put into effect immediately, with measures initiated to maintain existing employment levels in the region.

The impacts of this decision went far beyond Clayoquot Sound. For First Nations, it represented joint ownership in both the decision-making process and the economic development brought by the decision. Subsequent to the panel's report, the Nuu-Chah-Nulth Tribal Council joined with MacMillan Bloedel (now Weyerhaeuser) to form a joint venture to log according to the standards set out in the panel's report. Industry was able to declare that its role in Clayoquot Sound was a victory for environmental protection and partnership with Aboriginal peoples. For Weyerhaeuser, Clayoquot Sound became a positive public relations icon. For ENGOs, the decision was also a success. Having refused to compromise, the organizations declared a victory for sustainable forestry and set their sights on the next domain of temperate rainforests, the Central Coast of British Columbia's mainland (or so-called Great Bear Rainforest). For residents of forestry communities, however, Clayoquot brought fear and protest. They viewed the decision as an attack on forestry culture generally and feared that the protests and tactics used in the Clayoquot region would soon be seen elsewhere.

But perhaps the most widespread and contentious management initiative was the introduction of the Forest Practices Code ("the Code"). It was introduced by the provincial government in 1994 and brought into effect in April 1995. It provided new standards for forest harvesting across the province in order to protect forest resources, including fisheries, wildlife, biodiversity, cultural heritage, soils, and community watersheds. The Code required enforcement of strict new practices with the aim of ensuring sustainable use of forested lands and watersheds. The Code replaced hundreds of overlapping and often contradictory federal and provincial regulations that had previously regulated timber-harvesting operations.

Under the Code, several important changes occurred. Clearcut size was reduced to a maximum of forty hectares in southern British Columbia. Clear-cutting was banned where alternative harvesting systems were deemed more appropriate. Stricter controls were brought in for the protection of nontimber values such as fisheries, wildlife habitat, cultural heritage, biological diversity, soils, recreation, and old-growth forests. New visual quality objectives required foresters to consider the aesthetic impacts of logging, especially in areas likely to be used for recreation or tourism. Fines and penalties for noncompliance were increased substantially. Some fines were initially set as high as $1 million for first offences and $2 million for repeat offences, and irresponsible operators faced the potential loss of their licences. Higher-level plans such as regional or strategic plans and subregional land and resource management plans (LRMPs) were to be designed to comply with the Code, with the implication that lower-level operational plans prepared under the Code would also meet the objectives, strategies, and targets outlined in the higher-level plans.

Importantly, the Code enshrined new practices in regulation and legal requirements that had been established only in policy and procedure. Accompanying the regulations were dozens of guidebooks, which stipulated standards of practice to be achieved by all who worked in the woods. The Code provided for legal sanctions for noncompliance, where previously compliance had been left to the discretion of local government officers and subject to tailoring of local conditions and/or bargaining between public and private agencies. Loggers, professional foresters, and government agencies were made legally responsible for demonstrating "due diligence" in regard to these standards. Individual forest workers – both waged and professional workers – feared that they were to be held individually accountable.

Transition and Mitigation Measures
New land allocation and forest management measures would have direct impacts on workers in the forest industry. The government of the day, with social democratic roots, was obliged to consider the social impacts associated with the inevitable decline in access to timber and new management requirements. Thus, the provincial government introduced "transition measures" aimed at re-creating new employment prospects for displaced workers and ultimately retaining the social sustainability of forestry-dependent communities. But the provincial government was slower at developing these social measures than it was at implementing its environmental agenda.

Several initiatives formed the foundation of the government's plans in the early stages of changes in land use planning and regulation. However, these initiatives were introduced after CORE was well under way with its land use allocation activities. In July 1994, the Forest Jobs Commission was established to address economic transition and mitigation issues, particularly job loss and retraining, resulting from land use decisions. Vancouver Island was one of the first regions where a commissioner was appointed. However, this commission was created without a budget, thereby limiting its functions to advice and assistance to communities that sought funding through other provincial or federal agencies that delivered job-related programs. In 1997, the British Columbia government announced the Jobs and Timber Accord. The accord subsidized firms that chose to hire new workers by cutting current employees' work hours or overtime. This accord was supposed to provide openings to retain employment in the industry and effectively distribute current work and income to a greater number of people. An advocate was hired in 1999 to ensure that commitments made by industry and government under the Jobs and Timber Accord were implemented. This position was closed in 2001, with duties of the advocate going to other people and government ministries. During the tenure of this position, several review processes were introduced, but the impact on job provision was not measurable.

The Forest Renewal Plan (FRP) was introduced as law in the BC legislature in April 1994. This was two months after the Vancouver Island Land Use Plan was submitted by CORE to the government. The goal of the FRP was to ensure that more of the wealth generated by the forest was reinvested back into the forest and communities to protect the resource and forest-dependent jobs. The plan was to raise about $400 million per year through increased stumpage and royalty payments, to be reinvested by the government back into silviculture, environmental restoration, worker retraining, value-added initiatives, research, and economic development. Forest Renewal BC (FRBC) was created as a Crown corporation, with representation from the forest industry, the province, ENGOs, First Nations, and communities, to manage the plan's investments.

Initially, the government intended to prevent a serious decline in employment in those localities by creating new jobs in environmental restoration, habitat protection, and value-added industries. Its intentions were to provide new skills for workers within a new definition of forestry that included new harvesting methods and more intensive environmental management measures. It also intended to increase the participation of First Nations in forestry, establish a coordinated approach to government economic development initiatives, and thereby stabilize local economies. New funds were made available for companies to invest in silviculture, value-added initiatives, and site rehabilitation. However, within a short time, FRBC became the focus of constant criticism for mismanagement of funds, uncoordinated program delivery, waste, bureaucracy, and overall failure to meet the needs of either forestry communities or "the environment." Seeing a large purse and a shrinking government budget, the provincial government raided the fund for general revenues in 1999 and cut into the FRBC watershed and Ministry of Forests land-based programs.[5] By doing so, the government called into question its commitment to communities and placed significant limits on the benefits delivered by the program. Notwithstanding both of these initiatives, from 1995 to 1998 jobs in timber harvesting and processing declined from 87,600 to 75,000 (Auditor General of BC 1999-2000).

While these transitional measures were specific to forestry, broader labour initiatives were also introduced. During the 1990s, the NDP government established measures that linked the labour market and infrastructure development. The NDP's major labour market policy initiative, Skills Now, was announced in May 1994. It was a $200 million training plan over 1994-96 to boost the skill levels and employability of people in British Columbia. Touted as a new partnership between industry and labour, Skills Now included a twenty-six-member labour development board with co-chairs from the BC Business Council and the BC Federation of Labour. The board's role was to provide advice to the government on the job market and training measures. This skills strategy had four themes: linking high school to the workplace, opening more doors and the right doors to college and university, retraining workers closer to home, and moving from welfare to the workforce. Retraining programs for forestry workers obtained some of their funding through this initiative.

On the social front, forestry workers and communities were receiving mixed messages. While these measures were intended to support forestry workers through the transitional phase, there were nevertheless dramatic and contradictory changes to social welfare programs in the 1990s. During that decade, welfare provisions – the purview of the provincial government – changed. New rules required low-income people to become involved in skills training and work searches, and reforms were implemented to combat welfare fraud. Attention was also paid to upgrading social infrastructure in the form of school and community facilities. In the early 1990s, the provincial government engaged in the regionalization of health and social services. For many small communities, this initiative resulted in a loss of local services and the transfer of decisions about individual cases to larger centres. For example, on Vancouver Island, restructuring of the Ministry of Social Services resulted in the transfer of some programs from Port Hardy to Nanaimo, located a five-hour drive to the south. These limitations were exacerbated due to reduced federal transfer payments for health care and education. At the federal level, provisions for employment insurance had changed dramatically, requiring longer work periods before workers could collect benefits. The result was a dramatic reduction in the number who qualified for benefits and in the amount that each claimant received.

While many of these restrictions were also placed on people living in larger urban centres, the effects on resource communities were significant. For example, due to the cyclical nature of resource-based employment, a larger proportion of forestry workers came to rely on employment insurance as a means of supplementing their incomes. Throughout this period of changing rules and government restructuring, it was often difficult to determine which agencies and individuals were responsible for various social services – be they related to health care, housing, education and training, financial aid, employment assistance, supports for children and youth, seniors' housing, or other needs. Consequently, the social well-being of rural communities began to decline on many counts. These changes in land allocation, forest management, and social well-being were greeted with massive protests by people living in forested rural communities across the province. Community residents argued that people who laboured in the woods were now the endangered species and that their communities were now in need of protection.

These protests and policy changes were not simply the outgrowth of an emergent policy agenda introduced by a newly elected and enthusiastic political party. Rather, they were embedded within broader structural changes affecting rural areas that went to the roots of their economic base, environmental regulation, and social well-being.

Structural Dimensions of Rural Change

Economic Structure and Restructuring

As noted in Chapter 2, rural areas have long been subject to cycles of economic growth, stagnation, and decline (Clapp 1998; Freudenberg 1992). Some of the reasons relate to the physical supply of resources. In this regard, rural areas reliant on renewable resources (e.g., forestry, agriculture) have not fared any better than those reliant on nonrenewables (e.g., mineral and fossil fuels). Other reasons relate to the social effects that these economic boom-and-bust cycles associated with natural resource industries have on local communities. These economic cycles generate and perpetuate patterns of transience, placing pressure on the provision of social services and infrastructure during both boom and bust periods (Freudenberg 1992).

Forestry workers have also suffered from the uncoupling of production from employment. This means that automated and less labour-intensive technologies have been substituted for labour nearly across the board in the manufacturing sector (Carroll and Daniels 1992). In logging occupations in British Columbia, the number of employees per 1,000 cubic metres of timber harvested dropped from 0.42 to 0.25 between 1963 and 1995. During the same period, the number of all employees in production jobs (harvesting and processing) declined from 1.32 to 0.85 per 1,000 cubic metres (Marchak, Aycock, and Herbert 1999). In addition, the complexity of economic links increased and became more widely dispersed geographically. Capital and information flows became instantaneous across the globe, and producers were able to transcend national boundaries that they considered potential markets and competitors (Carroll and Daniels 1992). In British Columbia, the forest industry has always been geared to exporting raw logs to an international market. This global orientation made the industry vulnerable in the international marketplace during the 1970s, when much of the easily accessible old-growth timber was gone and rival regions began to establish viable industries based on new growth (Marchak 1991). The resulting economic restructuring of the industry brought an overall downward cycle in employment. The combination of automation and economic restructuring has meant that, since the late 1970s, employment in logging, wood industries, and paper and allied industries has experienced rounds of *permanent* downsizing (Hayter 2000).

It is possible that labour savings accruing from advances in technology might be offset, at least in part, by more expensive harvesting practices. These practices include harvesting smaller logs in steeper, less accessible locations, executing the more complicated harvest patterns required by environmentally sensitive forest management prescriptions, and taking greater care to leave the harvest sites in better condition (Carroll and Daniels 1992). New methods of harvesting, such as variable retention cutting, selective logging, and helicopter logging, are now being tried and are even required in some cases. However, these methods are very expensive and limited in their applications by the province's physical geography. Furthermore, many commentators have concluded that the industry has simply expanded its reach well beyond the capacity of the resource base to sustain it (e.g., Burda, Gale, and M'Gonigle 1998; Clapp 1998; Marchak, Aycock, and Herbert 1999). Thus, it is unlikely that the industry will ever support the number of workers that it employed in the 1960s.

These economic conditions suggest that many of the problems faced by workers in the forest industry are occurring irrespective of contemporary policies associated with land use and societal value changes. They are exacerbated by the fact that the economic fate of many such communities is often in the hands of corporate entities whose headquarters are located at great distances from where the consequences of their decisions will be felt (Hessing and Howlett 1997; Marchak 1991). Yet, as discussed throughout the book, practices associated with environmental and land use policy making also exemplify this pattern. In public policy arenas, "extralocal" interests are not just private corporate interests or insensitive government bureaucrats but also, increasingly, ENGOs whose targets are international (i.e., consumers of wood products) but whose successes are marred by local economic and social dislocation. Consequently, in addition to dramatic and fundamental restructuring of the industry, social issues related to environmental regulation and provisions for social well-being have heightened the plight of forestry communities.

Restructuring of Environmental Regulation

Environmentalism has become a cogent political force within public policy in North America in general and British Columbia in particular. The importance of environmentalism has been matched by a restructuring of the ways in which environment and land uses are allocated and regulated. During the 1990s, "ecosystem management" became a catchphrase for environmentalists, scientists, and policy makers. This approach addressed concerns about ecological integrity by integrating scientific knowledge with local knowledge and with socioeconomic concerns about environmental resource use (Grumbine 1994). This ideal was matched by demands for stronger rules and regulations to direct the industry as well as a more effective enforcement regime.

In Canada, regulation has been the most popular means for governments to control the activities of individuals and companies involved in various forms of resource extraction, processing, and sales (Hessing and Howlett 1997). Policies have generally guided industry, while regulations have rarely been unequivocally articulated. Enforcement of policy has been characterized as a process of cooperative bargaining between government and industry in which noncompliance has usually led to renewed negotiations of regulatory goals and industrial practices rather than punishment (Harrison 1996). However, during the 1980s and 1990s, increasing public concern about the extent and ongoing character of noncompliance placed pressure on governments to get tougher with enforcement and to move increasingly to judicial remedies.

The availability of new technology has also effected changes in policy implementation in at least two ways. First, improvements in technology have driven changes in harvesting and processing practices, providing opportunities to impose new standards. Second, a "tougher approach to regulatory enforcement reflects an increase in administrative capabilities in monitoring and enforcement" (Hessing and Howlett 1997, 183). New computer-based capabilities for data collection, administration, and regulation, as well as the emergence of the laptop computer and the World Wide Web, have provided new tools for government regulators. Improvements have literally taken place in the field in varied tasks such as cataloguing baseline conditions, monitoring changes, and surveying and mapping. The ability to document and distribute information on forestry practices quickly and accurately has also given rise to a public demand to enforce regulations immediately and publicly.

The World Wide Web has also increased the availability to the public of data from government agencies, public interest groups, and private corporations that can now be used to debate openly the merits and shortfalls of contemporary management practices. In addition, the Web creates a public forum for monitoring and relaying information about industry and government practices, allowing a broad public audience to be informed and make choices accordingly. This Web publicity brings an added dimension to the internationalization of environmental regulation, making companies and governments accountable to shareholders and consumers on an international stage rather than to local populations. One may argue that this level of scrutiny heightens accountability, but to which audience should the government be accountable – local, regional, or international? Each audience has different issues and concerns with respect to the interpretation of these data, and each can mount different campaigns to address outstanding issues. If the government responds to international pressure, it may neglect its responsibility to maintain the social well-being of its citizens. Once an issue enters the international domain, it is exceedingly difficult to return it to the local citizenry to resolve outstanding details.

Changing Provisions for Social Well-Being
Social and economic well-being is shaped not only by changes in the structures of economies and environmental regulations that specifically target the forest industry. Fundamental changes have been made to welfare states in "westernized" countries since the early 1980s. Like residents of other welfare states in the post-Second World War era, Canadians believed in a significant social role for modern governments within the community and economy. Here I consider the welfare state in a broad sense, covering a large area of public policy activity and employing several instruments, including cash transfers between levels of government, tax measures, service provisions, laws and regulations, symbolic gestures, public ownership, and even privatization (after Prince 1996). Since the 1930s, the Canadian welfare state has provided social services and income support programs designed for those "in need" as well as policies, programs, and legislation to redistribute status, rights, and life opportunities (Evans and Wekerle 1997).

Social policy is a political activity used by the state to articulate public values. The state uses legal and policy initiatives to allocate public resources and opportunities. According to Michael Prince, "social policy is more than providing relief for those in trouble"; it also "entails providing essential services and benefits to the general public, building social infrastructure such as schools and parks, and investing in people through learning and training as a way of both promoting human development and managing the economy" (1996, 240). While health, education, and social services have been the main activities associated with social policy, other matters – such as Aboriginal affairs, human rights and justice, corrections and policing, recreation and tourism, the arts, multiculturalism, income maintenance, immigration, women's equality, employment and the labour market, and housing – may also fall under this rubric. In Canada at least, economic policies, such as regional development initiatives to help create or maintain employment in rural areas, have also had a strong social dimension.

At the national level, during the 1980s and early 1990s, the federal government, like governments in western Europe, turned to the political right. The consequences included reduction in public services, devolution of powers to the provinces, and privatization of functions previously provided by the state. In April 1996, the federal government introduced changes affecting federal-provincial fiscal arrangements for health and social transfers.[6] These changes both reduced the total amount of money transferred from the federal government to the provinces for social programs and altered the structure of funding arrangements. This restructuring of social programs marked a retreat by the federal government from its involvement in the public sector and a renewed emphasis on market and family as providers of social assistance. Provisions for employment insurance were curtailed, social assistance benefits were reduced, and income testing for old age security (an allowance previously considered a universal right) was introduced.

In British Columbia, a major economic recession beginning in 1983, coupled with the installation of a neoconservative Social Credit government, led to major cuts in the civil service and reductions in provisions of social welfare and services. Although some of these services had been reinstated by the next decade, they were never provided at the same levels as previously. During the 1990s, with the election of the NDP government, some modest changes were made in the provision of health care, education, and some social services, but the die had been cast. Funds were placed into the creation of regional health authorities, the upgrading of educational facilities, and job development programs; however, for people living in poverty, prospects became bleaker. Priorities were placed on training programs for welfare recipients and on reforming the welfare/income assistance program to combat fraud. The result was that the proportion of the provincial population living in (pre-tax) low-income poverty rose from 14.4 percent in 1989 to 18.4 percent in 1996, with poverty among families accounting for a large proportion of this increase (Ministry of Industry 2000).

These alterations at the federal and provincial levels had particular effects on women, who are typically the major recipients of services and workers in the fields of health care, social services, and education (Evans and Wekerle 1997; Jennissen 1997). This is especially the case for single women with children, elderly women, women with disabilities, and Aboriginal women. Many women are dependent, at some points in their lives, on the welfare state for financial support and/or services such as subsidized child care, counselling and referral services, homemaker services, maternity leave, and legal aid. Women, especially those of childbearing age and older women, are more frequent users of the health care system than men (Jennissen 1997). But gender is not the only divide in the distribution of social welfare.

The effects of social restructuring and access to state institutions and benefits also vary by region, social class, and ethnicity. The effects of restructuring of labour markets and reorganization of relations between individuals and families and the state occur within specific places and to specific people (e.g., Halseth 1999). Furthermore, as Marjorie Griffin Cohen points out, "social welfare relies as significantly on *economic* policy (e.g., budgets, taxation, trading relationships, development policy) as it does on those state programs more normally associated with ... redistributive policies [e.g., income assistance]" (1997, 29). This connection was exemplified during the 1990s, when layoffs of BC forestry workers occurred because of ongoing trade disputes with the United States, which claimed that BC lumber was unfairly subsidized by the provincial government. These layoffs increased the reliance of forestry workers on employment insurance and other social services while governments wrangled in legal battles to resolve these issues. The "exposure" of and the choices for residents of rural communities under these uncertain circumstances are markedly different than for those living in urban centres. Thus, when growing public sentiments across the province began to favour withdrawal of lands for environmental protection at the same time as the public purse reduced provisions for social well-being, perhaps it is not surprising that rural resource communities began to feel beleaguered and marginalized.

Social Effects on Rural Communities

While social activists and academics have illustrated how race, class, and gender intersect in the analysis of changes to the welfare state (Evans and Wekerle 1997; Griffin Cohen 1997), in Canada there have been few efforts to determine the uneven effects of social restructuring across regional economies (Hessing and Howlett 1997). Consequently, I turn to findings related to deindustrialization generally and to forestry regions in the United States as well as Canada to document potential social effects. Findings from the United States suggest that economic shocks such as those brought on by a plant closing begin a pattern of intergenerational poverty and diminished life chances that is enormously difficult to break (Conger and Elder 1994; Fitchen 1981, 1991). Where the socioeconomic structure of communities breaks down, loss of opportunities contributes to selective out-migration, in which more prosperous and upwardly mobile residents migrate, leaving behind a less skilled population in which poverty and social marginalization become more concentrated (Conger and Elder

1994). Local communities become less attractive to potential employers searching for new locations because they have inadequate support services and infrastructure. This dynamic illustrates one of the difficulties with proposals made by environmental organizations to diversify local economies. Ironically, during the 1980s and 1990s, in much of rural Canada, these losses were realized at the same time as governments relied on private and voluntary sectors to patch up the pieces of the social safety net that policy makers tore up in the first place (Roseland 1999).

Deterioration of social relationships becomes evident in diminished social satisfaction with community life, feelings of isolation within communities, tensions between groups, and feelings of isolation from decision making (Beckley 1995). The erosion of social relationships in the community may socially isolate economically stressed families, leading to chronic depression *within* family groups, higher rates of spouse and child abuse, substance abuse, and suicide. Individuals and families also suffer from the social stigma associated with job loss, economic stress, and social marginalization (Young 1990; see Chapter 2). For those in the forest industry, this stigma may involve being labelled as "bad managers" or "high rollers" who have outlived the benefits to which they are no longer entitled (Carroll 1995). For those individuals who are unemployed or displaced, the stigma may define them as lazy or "taking advantage" of the welfare system. This may place them at odds with others still working in forestry who take pride in their rugged individualism, their work ethic, and their ability to carve out a living in harsh physical and social circumstances. These losses may be felt across generations as parents realize that the way of life they have known cannot be passed down to their children.

The choices facing these people are often not positive. The lack of employment locally may result in a difficult choice between being able to provide for the family elsewhere and staying in the community to accept a reduced standard of living. In the latter case, family members may have to work at low-wage jobs that offer few or no benefits and/or accept employment with little chance of long-term advancement (Fitchen 1991). Even for those who have not suffered direct personal financial loss, there may be a social loss associated with these changes as rural residents reflect on the lives of their friends and neighbours. Politically, local communities also become disenfranchized from the economic and political system that seems to have so little regard for their plight.

While many of these effects have been attributed to the rural ghettos of the Ozarks and Appalachia (e.g., Caudill 1962; Hall 1986; Seitz 1995, 1998), West Coast forestry communities may also exhibit some of them. For example, the 1980s and 1990s brought structural changes to the economy of Oregon, along with dislocation and uncertainty for many of the residents of forestry communities there (Brown 1995; Carroll, Daniels, and

Kusel 2000). A report by American regional economists cited widely by environmental organizations on British Columbia's West Coast stated that the environmental qualities and the West Coast lifestyle were major attractions for many high-technology companies thinking of moving to Oregon (Power 1996).[7] For example, the report indicated that between 1988 and 1994, despite declines in forestry and aerospace industries, economic well-being in Oregon, Washington, Idaho, and Montana had increased by 18 percent, or two and a half times the national average (see Durbin 1996, 287). Yet studies undertaken at a local level have told a different story. Paul Sommers (1996) observed that, while the state succeeded in diversifying into new sectors, *resource workers* were unable to make the transition into high-technology and other sectors because they lacked the necessary preparation, job skills, or personal mobility to enter the emerging job situation. Beverly Brown (1995) documented how people arriving for new jobs bid up land prices, closed off public access to rural areas, and were associated with concerns about personal safety, squeezing out the rural working class, and changing the social character of rural communities.

These kinds of concerns led the biannual report of the Oregon Economic Development Commission to suggest that "prosperity still eludes many of our distressed rural communities ... Too many Oregonians don't qualify for all the new, well-paying jobs created because they lack sufficient education and work skills" (1997, 2). Furthermore, the report identified that, while total jobs had increased, many communities still experienced high levels of unemployment and poverty. There was a serious need to raise Oregon's educational standards to meet workforce skill demands. In the words of the commission, "Oregon should do more to help its depressed rural communities ... [to] help those left out of Oregon's success by geography" (3). This is more than an economic or environmental geography. I suggest that this is also a social geography reinforced by the specific public policies that deal with land use, economic development, and social well-being. By examining policy change and political protest as *social* phenomena, we can read the stories that follow – their consistencies and contradictions – with coherence and compassion.

"Caulk boots built this country!" A sign of affirmation placed on the lawn of forestry supporters.

4
Women and Woods Work: The Gender of Forestry Jobs

> Let me tell you about loggers. I married one 18 years ago. I couldn't resist the smell of utter maleness in damp, sweaty black wool underwear sweetened by the heavy scent of fresh sawdust and chainsaw exhaust ... I still love the romance of big men, big machines and big trees ... Loggers are the last of a dying breed of men who "work" for a living. Their work is dangerous and back breaking. I hope ... [names an environmentalist] doesn't live in a woodframe and plywood house, because if she does she owes an apology to the logger who fell[ed] a few trees so she could have a home. (I always wondered what kind of houses environmentalists live in.) She should try hugging a logger – she'll never go back to trees!
>
> – Maureen Henderson (1993, 9)

> Women are not viewed as equals. It's a man's community.
>
> – Interviewee, 1997

The Paradox of Paid Work

Caulk boots[1] are the steel-toed, spike-soled work boots designed to assist the wearer to walk on logs both in and out of water and/or to move up and down steep slopes without slipping. As the photograph on page 78 illustrates, caulk boots represent the hard physical labour, danger, and drama associated with logging. Planted on the front lawn of a forestry family, this sign illustrates the unstinting solidarity that forestry families share with the dominant occupation. Forestry-town women, who share common personal histories, economic dependencies, and material desires, bind to their partners in uncritical support of the masculine imagery used to characterize the paid and productive work of forestry. Or do they?

This singular depiction of forestry-town women dominated research in labour studies during the 1970s and 1980s. Scholars of that time established an image of women's unwavering devotion to explain perspectives and activism of workers' wives in resource towns during times of economic strife (e.g., Ali 1986; Maggard 1990; West and Blumberg 1990). This explanation has also been used by environmentalists who attempt to criticize forestry without criticizing forestry workers (for discussion, see

Satterfield 2002). The result is one of "social pathology" whereby forestry workers and those allied with them are considered to be bound together in an unhealthy addiction to a dying industry. By explicit reference and logical extension, those who support forestry are portrayed as myopic, conservative, and dependent (as described in Chapter 1) or, in Terre Satterfield's words, as "passive pawns," "psychologically impaired," "addicted to timber dollars," and ultimately "disposable" (2002, 91, 94). In short, they become dupes of the larger corporate interests that shape their lives and their desires.

This chapter adds a deep wrinkle to this apparently smooth and seamless scenario. Consistent with this scenario, I acknowledge that women retain a strong attachment to forestry as an occupation and a way of life. These attachments are made, in part, by their association with, and support of, their partners and other family members in forestry. They are also made from their own rich working experiences within the industry and within the broader forestry community. In contrast to academics and policy makers who point to the relative insignificance of women in the paid work of forestry, I use this chapter to illustrate that women do have a significant role to play in the paid work of forestry. As women have entered nontraditional occupations in forestry, they have become part of the transformation and restructuring of the industry. From this experience, they have gained an inside vantage point from which to observe the problems and issues of the industry. Many women, like the one quoted in the epigraph above, reported feelings of exclusion from predominant employment opportunities in forestry, as well as sexism and alienation for those who did work within forestry. Thus, the dominant perspective of women's blind and unstinting support of forestry and/or forestry workers falls far short of women's own experiences. The women of this study posed a paradox. They acknowledged their experiences of social marginalization within forestry. In particular, they documented forms of exploitation and social exclusion occurring within forestry communities. Notwithstanding these experiences, many women in this study retained strong support for their partners in forestry and/or the forest industry or forestry work more broadly.

The purpose of this chapter is to explore and explain this paradox. I suggest that women's forestry communities are constructed, in part, by a network of shared understandings and obligations associated with forestry. This network moves beyond material attachments associated with income. It also provides meaning to the lives of women who live within these communities. Thus, to understand women's perspectives and activist choices, it is important to locate women within the dominant employment structure. But it is also important to interpret the meanings granted to paid employment – both for the women themselves and for how women perceive changing opportunities for their partners and other family members. Therefore, in this chapter, I explore women's direct involvement in the paid work of forestry and examine the meanings that women give to forestry occupations. Attention to their positions within the paid work of forestry communities illustrates that women have multiple locations within forestry culture and exhibit contradictions and conflicts in their support for the forest industry. I make visible the contradictions and continuities that mark the lives of women who support industrial forestry.

Looking for Women in the Woods

Feminist scholars (including geographers and sociologists) who have explained employment choices and circumstances within their broader social and geographical contexts are well suited to an understanding of women's contributions to the paid work of forestry (e.g., Carroll 1995; Carroll, Daniels, and Kusel 2000; De Bruin and Dupuis 1999; England 1993; Hanson and Pratt 1995; Massey 1994; Parr 1990; Smith 1997; Tigges, Ziebarth, and Farnham 1998). Like other elements of social life, paid employment illustrates how women's experiences are embedded in multiple layerings of "community." According to Leann Tigges, Ann Ziebarth, and Jennifer Farnham, consideration of social embeddedness "means being alert to the influence of structural constraints on the range of choices available and to the costs and benefits of pursuing certain strategies given available resources" (1998, 204). Social embeddedness emphasizes the ways in which social relationships affect choices and actions. In Mark Granovetter's words, "actors do not behave or decide as atoms outside a social context, nor do they adhere slavishly to a script written for them by the particular intersection of social categories they happen to occupy" (1985, 487). Their attempts at purposive action are instead embedded in concrete, ongoing systems of social relations that link economic and noneconomic goals (Granovetter 1985).

Within a framework of social embeddedness, the workplace, family, and community dynamics are important elements in an analysis of paid work in forestry communities. By making these links, we can bring women more centrally into forestry debates. First, a focus on embeddedness gives women greater visibility in work sites that are directly and indirectly related to forestry. This position derives from the perspective that women's employment even outside forestry work sites continues to form part of the context for forestry. Second, such a focus helps to explain both the paradox of paid work described above and women's perspectives and actions described in this and subsequent chapters.

The historical disparity in opportunities for men and women in paid employment is reproduced across Canada and within the study region. Job segregation – the association of women or men with particular kinds of employment – remained strong even in the 1990s. According to Statistics Canada, in 1996 just under 4 percent of women in the paid workforce in the Mount Waddington Regional District (MWRD) were employed in occupations unique to primary industries, representing less than 2 percent of the total workforce of the region. This figure compared with 25 percent of men in the paid workforce, representing 14 percent of the total workforce of the region. However, this is an incomplete and inaccurate assessment of the importance of forestry as an employer in the region and as an employer of women and men, respectively. Societal norms about what to expect in these places have shaped our research programs, emphasizing men's employment and marginalizing women's. These norms are deep-rooted.

Societal Norms and Working Assumptions

The distinction between men's and women's work that developed historically in the Western economies throughout the nineteenth century promoted women's rightful place in the home (Leach 1993; Marston 2000). The notion that work and home were separate spheres became crucial in shaping a gendered division of labour that is often considered "traditional" (Leach 1993).[2] Sallie Marston points out that "the separation of work and home that accompanied capitalist industrialization and the cultural ideals and practices that emerged as part of this separation have been enacted along class and gender, as well as sexuality, race, ethnicity, *and locational axes*" (2000, 234; emphasis added).

The idea that geography is important in constructing ideals, ideologies, and practices of work and home, even within similar economic structures (i.e., within westernized capitalist economies), is an important insight of feminist geographers for this work (e.g., England 1994; Hanson and Pratt 1995). Forestry towns (like mining towns) were first created by recruiting large numbers of single men and some families in isolated locations. As these towns matured, single men married, married men settled, and the "surplus of women who might wish waged employment often became acute ... The social implications of the prevailing twentieth-century pattern that privileged men in the work force are familiar: the struggle for a male breadwinner wage, the predominant view of women as consumers rather than as producers in the market economy, and the persistent poverty of female-headed households" (Parr 1990, 235). This historical context has set the stage for both the marginalized status of women within forestry communities and their relative invisibility to labour theorists.

There is a paucity of theory that explains labour practices particular to rural places and resource sectors (Halseth 1999). In labour segmentation theory advanced by Peter Doeringer and Michael Piore, the primary segment is characterized by "high wages, good working conditions, employment stability, chances of advancement, equity, and due process in the administration of work rules" (1971, 165). In contrast, jobs in the secondary segment tend to have "low wages and fringe benefits, poor conditions, high labour turnover, little chance of advancement, and often arbitrary and capricious supervision" (165). A long-standing scholar of forest policy in British Columbia, Roger Hayter (2000) suggests that this model is an effective representation of labour market conditions in British Columbia's forest economy in the post-Second World War era.

While Hayter (2000) identified small and medium-sized enterprises at a regional or provincial level as forming the secondary segment, one might also view segmentation in terms of a local labour force. In this context, the secondary segment is composed of nonunion peripheral workers whose wage levels and employment stability are typically less structured than in the primary sector. Workers in the secondary segment are more likely to be nonunion and female and to belong to a visible minority. According to feminist geographers Susan Hanson and Geraldine Pratt, women's exclusions from the primary segment "build on the sexist practices of male employers and employees. Male employers may be reluctant to hire women for the most prized jobs because of gender stereotypes, worries about complaints from male employees, and their more general fears about losing male advantage ... White, male employees also have organized through unions and professional organizations to shelter jobs for themselves" (1995, 6).

Indeed, the male-dominated nature of occupations within resource-based communities has created and elevated the importance of a working*man*'s culture (Dunk 1991). Institutional factors, local practices, and sexist attitudes shape the culture of forestry towns, rendering less important and in some cases invisible the nature and extent of women's employment within forestry communities. In this light, the classification of "primary" denotes not only occupations based on the extraction of raw materials but also those that hold primary importance in the local culture and economy. In short, jobs in "primary" (extraction) industries have "primary" importance to local communities and policy makers. Women's employment within these communities is viewed as secondary or tertiary, not only because women are more likely to be in manufacturing and service sectors, but also because they are seen as being of second- and third-order importance to the overall workings of the forestry community.

Yet even two decades ago, Patricia Marchak (1983) argued that, although women's paid jobs were mainly located in the secondary and tertiary sectors, they were of *primary importance* to the maintenance of forestry towns. In her words, "though women are not employed in the forest industry in these towns, their presence is an important part of the context for these industrial processes. Women do the maintenance tasks in the homes and the service tasks in the offices, stores, shops, schools, and hospitals. In their absence, the forest company employers could not maintain company towns, and the overall cost of obtaining a male labour force would sharply increase" (213). Indeed, company recruitment policies during the 1970s (when labour was in short supply) tacitly acknowledged this observation. During the 1970s, companies actively recruited married men because they were considered a more stable and reliable workforce (Hayter 2000). Women interviewed for my study confirmed this observation.

This rendering of women's paid work in forestry towns as "secondary" does not simply include women in secondary and tertiary sectors. Even women who figure in conventional counts of forestry-related occupations are subject to limitation and erasure. Women employed in forestry jobs discussed restrictions in hiring and promotion and the lack of recognition of their direct contributions to the industry. These observations will be discussed later in the chapter. The bias that focuses all attention on male wage earners is also evident in potential databases and academic work that might otherwise provide accurate empirical descriptions of employment. These sources, in turn, shape policy debates and strategies advanced during times of economic and social transition (see Chapter 7).

Counting Women "in" Forestry
Reliable, valid, current, complete, and commensurable data on gender and employment in forestry are not readily available from government agencies or private companies. Company records typically do not distinguish between women in nontraditional jobs (e.g., planers) and those employed in traditional jobs (e.g., secretaries) within the firm. Employment counts by resource sector, location, and gender in combination are not routinely made available by Statistics Canada, other government agencies, researchers, or industrial employers. Special tabulations cost extra money, but they reveal slightly different results. For example, in a special tabulation of the 1991 census, it was revealed that approximately 10 percent of the provincial workforce in logging industries was composed of women and that 28 percent of jobs related to forest services was held by women (CS/RESORS Consulting Limited 1997). These numbers are higher than those of academic studies, but they are still derived from an unnecessarily narrow definition of forestry employment, thereby underestimating the number of women who work in forestry occupations. For example, the workers in forest services counted by the census do not include workers in management, information, or administrative services.

These "other" kinds of positions are likely significant in both the number of women they employ and the quality of jobs they provide. For example, in 1997 the Ministry of Forests District Office located in Port McNeill had a workforce of eighty-nine, thirty of whom were women. Sixteen of eighteen administrative jobs were held by women, while eleven of fifty-three people with occupations as technicians, foresters, and planners were women (Ministry of Forests, Port McNeill District, 1998). None of these jobs was classified as a forestry job by the census.

Academic work reinforces and is shaped by biases in the availability of data. Empirical studies that use standard census categories continue to report the very limited participation of women in forestry occupations (e.g., Halseth 1999; Randall and Ironside 1996). Other studies about work in forestry towns focus on worker mobility (Halseth 1999) and displacement (e.g., Carroll, Daniels, and Kusel 2000; Daniels, Gobeli, and Findley 2000; Kusel et al. 2000). Like other studies in the forest industry, these research efforts tend to favour consideration of men's employment. Some researchers have attempted to address this bias by undertaking employment counts within specific firms (e.g., Grass and Hayter 1989; Hayter and Barnes 1992), but these data, collected for other purposes, are incomplete from a regional perspective.

In one study, Eric Grass and Roger Hayter (1989) collected data from a random sample of sixty-three plants from 1981 to 1985 to determine the employment characteristics of workers who experienced layoffs during the time of widespread recession in the industry. They noted that, with the exception of female middle managers (who were few in number), female job losses were greater than men's. This was particularly evident in clerical and production jobs. They noted that the region of Prince George, which had experienced some growth, involved solely male employment. Their data also revealed that women occupied more than 50 percent of the clerical positions but only 3 to 4 percent of the industry jobs, including administration, trades, and production work. These figures later led Hayter to conclude that, "given that female employment is a relatively small proportion of total employment in this industry, this trend should not be overstated. Nevertheless, the recession weakened the already marginal position of females in forest-product manufacturing" (2000, 266).

While this analysis revealed a higher vulnerability of female workers to job loss, the data do not provide a complete picture of women's paid work in forestry for the purposes of this study for at least two reasons. First, the data are now quite dated. Second, by the authors' own admission, the study omitted employment in other sectors of the industry, notably in head offices of firms, in woods work (e.g., loggers, camp cooks), in research and development, as well as in regulatory and planning positions of the Ministry of Forests. All of these sites are important components of the industry and increasingly important places of paid employment for women.

Perhaps the most complete regional study that discusses women's employment remains *Green Gold* by Patricia Marchak (1983), a sociologist who undertook research in the late 1970s. She estimated that in the late 1970s between 63 and 87 percent of the men in these communities worked in the forest sector, compared with 3 to 7 percent of women. She noted that women and men formed two virtually distinct labour pools, in which men were largely employed in production, trades, and professional or managerial positions in the forest sector, while women worked as housewives or in nonindustrial occupations (mainly clerical and service work or lower-level management outside forestry). Her findings led her to state that gender was a primary division of labour in these towns.

In more recent work in the forestry town of Port Alberni, Brian Egan and Suzanne Klausen (1998) confirmed that gender remains a fundamental determining factor in the distribution of jobs, status, and income in single-industry towns. They surveyed research dealing with gender and the restructuring of British Columbia's forest industry, noting that, while some investigations used a gender-sensitive approach (e.g., Grass 1987; Grass and Hayter 1989; Hay 1993; Hayter and Barnes 1992; Mackenzie 1987; Stanton 1989), "the bulk of recent research ... neglects gender as a central category of analysis (e.g., Drushka 1985; Ettlinger 1990; Hayter et al. 1993; Drushka et al. 1993; Barnes and Hayter 1994; Hayter and Barnes 1997) ... and overlooks the marginalized position of women in the paid labour force and forest-sector unions and, moreover, ignores the broader issue of the sexual division of paid and unpaid labour in forest-dependent communities" (9).

Women whom I interviewed openly challenged census definitions, arguing that many jobs conventionally classified in other ways directly rely on forestry. To "test" the potential discrepancy, I used the census definition of "jobs unique to primary industries" to classify the number of women whom I interviewed as forestry workers. In this tally, 15 percent of the employed women whom I interviewed would be classified in forestry jobs. However, I also tallied women in forestry according to the definitions provided by the women themselves. This classification revealed that 37 percent of employed women whom I interviewed[3] might be counted as forestry workers. Using a similar strategy, I classified and reclassified the jobs of the partners of interviewees and found that the proportion of their jobs classified as forestry or forestry related rose from 39 percent to 66 percent. This exercise revealed that outside researchers may practise exclusion in determining what counts as forestry activity. However these numbers are tallied, these kinds of calculations have important policy implications since they determine whether employment, retraining, or other social programs are necessary and who can qualify to receive them. The more limited the numbers, the less likely workers will obtain assistance during times of economic and social change. Given the ways that academics and the census delimit the definitions of workers in the industry, it is not surprising that policy debates reflect and reinforce the same biases.

Policy Debates

In policy debates, forestry is considered a primary industry in terms of its reliance on the extraction of "natural resources"[4] and its economic importance to local communities and to the provincial economy. For example, while forestry employs only 5 percent of the total workforce of the province (Marchak, Aycock, and Herbert 1999), the forest sector accounted for more than half the value of all manufacturing shipments in the province in 1993 (Forgacs 1997). Individual rural communities across the province still rely heavily on forestry to anchor their economic bases (Horne 1999). Clearly, forestry remains a large element of rural British Columbia.

During times of economic transition, there is a distinct policy preference for protecting only those jobs that are directly dependent on forestry. Government programs have focused on retaining, retraining, or retirement packages aimed at the male wage earner in forestry occupations – specifically, woods workers and those who work in sawmills and pulp and paper mills. When CORE recommended changes in land allocations to protect more land from extractive uses (logging, mining), it also estimated job losses (see Chapters 3 and 7). Although CORE predicted that at least as many jobs in secondary and tertiary sectors would be lost as in the primary sector, no recommendations were made to support these workers. Instead, new government programs were put in place for those who qualified under arrangements with (un)employment insurance.[5] Most of these programs targeted male workers. In contrast, CORE provided a brief catalogue of employment prospects and social impacts affecting women, suggesting that the information it presented about women might be useful in designing "social services support to better respond to the needs and roles of women in communities affected during economic change" (1994a, 205). The information provided to CORE did not form part of its recommended transition strategy, nor did it signal the need for specific policies or programs to address the impacts of job loss. Indeed, as described in Chapter 3, social service provisions were reduced, restructured, and regionalized at the same time as forestry was experiencing employment losses. The consequences of this bias for women of the region are discussed in greater detail in Chapter 7.

In sum, women's work has been largely invisible to researchers, policy practitioners, and residents themselves because it intersects less obviously with male employment. Women's employment (whether on the "main stage" of forestry jobs or in "supporting roles") is viewed as secondary, both in terms of its relation to the primary industry and in terms of its importance to the overall workings of the community. In the following section, I turn to women's overall employment status on northern Vancouver Island before examining their employment within forestry more specifically.

Gender at Work on the North Island

Employment is key to living on northern Vancouver Island. In 1996, 85 percent of all income was derived from employment, as opposed to 70 percent for the province as a whole. These levels rise to 92 percent for Port Alice, where the pulp mill is the major employer, and 88 percent for Port McNeill, where private forest companies and the Ministry of Forests have regional offices. Less than 3 percent of all income in the region came from pensions, as opposed to almost 25 percent for the province as a whole. These data indicate that, as people attain retirement age, they leave the region possibly for better medical and social services or to escape the isolation. The demographic structure is truncated; only 8 percent of the population is sixty-five or older, compared with 23 percent of the population of the province.

Labour force participation, occupational status, and wages provide an initial indication of the gendered dimensions of paid work in the study region. Given that employment is a primary factor in men migrating to the region, perhaps it is not surprising that men living there participate in the workforce at higher rates than men across the province. In 1996, 84 percent of men in the region were participants in the workforce, compared with 73 percent provincewide (Table 4.1). Census data also revealed that women from the region participated in the workforce at a significantly higher rate (71 percent) than women across the province (60 percent). In two-spouse families, 72 percent had both spouses in the labour force. These data were surprising since the conventional interpretation suggests that women living in resource communities come in larger numbers to support men's employment opportunities and are less likely to take up paid employment themselves (Marchak 1983; Parr 1990). Consequently, the stereotype that women in forestry towns are less likely to be employed in the paid workforce is not substantiated by census data. However, these data support another important dimension of women's paid work in forestry towns. It is hard to get a well-paid, full-time job, and the impact of this reality on women's income is severe.

As shown in Table 4.1, women dominate in sales and services as well as business and financial occupations, while men are overwhelmingly slotted into trades and occupations unique to primary industries. Women are more than three times more likely than men to enter service occupations, while men are more than six times more likely than women to be found in primary industries. One result of this job segregation is a large differential in wages. In 1996, women in the region earned 87 percent of women's average incomes in the province or 54 percent of male income in the province. Table 4.2 reveals that men in the region earn 23 percent more than their provincial counterparts; by contrast, women's share of men's incomes in the region drops to 48 percent. Part-time income is important both for women generally and for men in forestry occupations. Women on the North Island are more likely than women elsewhere or men generally to work part time, with the wage differential most marked in this classification. Women's part-time incomes for both British Columbia and the region are virtually the same and represent 66 percent of men's part-time incomes for the province as a whole. However, in the MWRD, women's part-time income is only 46 percent of men's part-time income. These "factual" data illustrate a strong divide between women and men. So, too, do the women themselves.

Women's Experiences of Paid Work

> The [forest] industry is why we're here. Like you've seen, you've gone to one-horse towns, and when the company leaves it people are upset, but eventually the town dies unless something else comes in to replace it. Now this is not entirely a one-horse town, but it comes pretty close.
>
> – Interviewee, 1997

> This community, this area, [is] male oriented – forestry, fisheries – it's really hard to get in, even if you are smart. I think it's even harder if you're Native.
>
> – Interviewee, 1997

The quotations above were taken from different women employed at the time of the research. Despite holding paid jobs, women were virtually unanimous in describing the limitations placed on women in both finding and retaining work. Only two of the fifty women interviewed (one employed, one a homemaker) refused to acknowledge specific barriers for women in seeking and retaining employment. For all the others, the towns were not simply one-horse towns; they were also uniform in terms of gendered opportunities for paid employment. Women's attempts to attain paid work and to be valued within paid occupations were constrained by practical limitations of opportunity, such as infrastructure and services that might support their employment. Importantly, however, the culture

Table 4.1

Provincial and Mount Waddington Regional District: Male/female participation in industries, 1996

Industry type	Provincial total (#)	MWRD total (#)	Provincial %	MWRD %	Provincial male %	MWRD male %	Provincial female %	MWRD female %
Management occupations	60,200	565	1.9	6.9	2.1	7.5	1.9	6.0
Business, finance, administration	230,600	985	7.4	12.0	7.0	1.9	1.5	25.6
Natural and applied sciences	106,200	470	3.4	5.7	4.0	8.4	3.0	2.1
Health occupations	183,400	195	5.9	2.4	2.3	1.0	10.2	4.3
Social science, education, government, service, and religion	117,600	505	3.8	6.1	2.8	2.9	5.1	10.6
Art, culture, recreation, and sport	84,800	125	2.7	1.5	2.9	1.1	2.8	2.1

Sales and services	1,645,800		52.9	22.4	49.7	11.5	59.9	37.0
Trades, transport, and equipment operators	393,400		12.6	19.7	14.8	31.4	11.8	3.9
Occupations unique to primary industries	84,800		2.7	15.9	4.2	25.0	1.3	3.7
Processing, manufacturing, and utilities	205,800		6.6	7.4	10.2	9.5	3.2	4.4
Experienced labour force (in numbers)	3,112,600 1,557,900 (male) 1,454,800 (female)	8,220 4,725 (male) 3,500 (female)						
%	N/A	N/A	100.0	100.0	100.0	100.0	100.0	100.0

Note: Proportions may not add up to 100 due to rounding.
Source: Statistics Canada 1999, 24 and 474-5.

Table 4.2

Mount Waddington Regional District: Income levels for males and females fifteen years and older, 1996

Type of employment	Mount Waddington Regional District			British Columbia		
	Income, all persons	Income, male	Income, female	Income, all persons	Income, male	Income, female
Full year, full time: Average income[1]	41,589	48,439	28,758	39,414	44,784	31,218
Part year or part time: Average income[2]	22,370	30,207	13,912	17,379	21,071	14,034
Average income[3]	29,161	37,702	18,077	27,480	33,366	20,722

[1] Full-time work of thirty hours or more per week in 1995, as reported in 1996.
[2] A part-time job for part of the year or a full-time job for another part of the year.
[3] Total income during the 1995 calendar year from wages and salaries (before deductions), net income from unincorporated business, professional fees, and net farm self-employment income as reported in 1996.

Source: Statistics Canada 1999, 28 and 478-79.

of forestry reinforced women's employment as secondary to the primary goal of timber production. This culture had multiple effects on women who lived there.

Women believed that employment opportunities for them were in extremely short supply or simply did not exist. In the smaller communities, such as Holberg, Woss, Port Alice, and Winter Harbour, women stated again and again that they simply wanted jobs, any jobs at all. They perceived that their options were severely restricted compared with those in "larger" centres such as Port Hardy and Port McNeill. Yet even there jobs for women were scarce, and most paid only the provincial minimum wage of $7.50 per hour. "There is a lot of challenge here because, number one, there's not the jobs ... Women in Port McNeill do not have the opportunity to get a job ... It's really a battle for a woman to get a job. And it doesn't matter, any kind of job. I mean, like, in Vancouver they might think waitressing is a low-paid, bottom-of-the-line job, where in Port McNeill you're darn happy to get it." Women in this study argued that forestry directly affected the wage prospects for them. One woman, holding down four part-time jobs, was asked why. In her words, "Why do I have that many jobs? Because a woman in this area cannot get a one full-time, forty-hour-a-week job that pays properly to support a family ... Women are still making seven-fifty an hour. I can't get full-time work in town *because it's a logging industry town* and a fishing industry town. There's not that many jobs to go round for women. If you're not self-employed, it's very likely you'll just continue to make seven-fifty an hour" (emphasis added).

While one can argue that these low-paying jobs were available to both men and women, interviewees suggested that there was a pervasive perception among employers that women, particularly married women, do not require the same salaries or benefits that men enjoy. One woman who was self-employed at the time of the interview had previously worked for many years in a position within the local public service. She had been part of several hiring procedures. She explained sexual job-typing this way: "The minute a man applies for a job, the ... [employer] thinks, oh, this is a person who has to look after a family. They don't consider that a woman looks after a family until she's a single mother; then they'll look after that, and consider that that's different, and they'll pay her more money than they would a married woman." Women who participated in focus groups confirmed that women who held positions not protected by union contracts frequently got paid "as little as possible." Consequently, for women living in dual-adult households, labour market participation may depend on a process of social negotiation about their home and outside work obligations, not solely with their partners and families, but also with their prospective employers (Smith 1997).

The spatial entrapment of women who try to juggle domestic and paid work responsibilities is also evident in forestry communities. The spatial entrapment thesis was first promoted almost two decades ago with reference to urban labour markets. It linked the empirical observation that white middle-class women had smaller labour market areas than men because they preferred shorter journeys to work in order to fulfill their domestic responsibilities. Their employment opportunities were accordingly more limited (Hanson and Johnston 1985). Rural and urban women who seek paid employment share similar problems, including lack of affordable, convenient, and safe child care, adequate public transportation infrastructure, and training opportunities. Women in the paid workforce require supportive partners and/or other family or social networks to assist in meeting multiple demands of home and paid work.

In small forestry towns, these problems are often more challenging than in urban localities. For example, there was no institutional group day care located on northern Vancouver Island. There were only a few "family day care" operations and many informal arrangements made between family and friends. For those who worked shift-work schedules outside nine to five, day care was a major and ongoing source of frustration and anxiety. One woman described her experiences in this way: "for me, who works shift work, there's been times I've had to have a baby-sitter until midnight, and I'm at work from four-thirty, or four o'clock on, sometimes from twelve o'clock [noon] ... It's hard for single parents ... but, for the most part, child care, for me, is a big concern."

This problem was made more acute by the lack of extended family to provide informal child care services. Provincial legislation passed during the study period required that child care providers over the age of sixteen be paid minimum wage. This new law meant that, for women in low-paid employment without additional family members to assist them, paid child care was impractical financially. For many women, particularly those with children, the lack of basic infrastructure and family networks limited their possibilities for work and discouraged them from seeking paid employment, especially since the monetary rewards were minimal.

Transportation to and from work sites was also a significant barrier for some women. From an urban perspective, several communities in the study area appear to be located within commuting range. For example, Port Alice, Sointula, Port McNeill, Port Hardy, and Coal Harbour are all within fifty-five kilometres of each other. However, the roads that connect these places are not urban highways and they are not linked by regular public transit. Some roads are active logging roads; some are paved, while others are not. Many of the roads were considered treacherous by women, particularly in winter, when days are short, roads may be covered in snow or ice, and logging trucks may continue to roam. Many women refused to drive regularly under such conditions, and those who did described their commute like this: "It's a long drive over here. I drive it every day. It's forty-five minutes, and in the winter it takes often twice as long. And it's not fun to drive a twisty mountain road at thirty kilometres an hour when you're afraid of sliding into a 400-foot chasm."

Lack of education was another hurdle to employment prospects for women. Both women in the workforce and those wanting paid employment saw themselves as undereducated. Local institutions for further education provided uneven availability of educational programs for women living in the scattered communities of the North Island. However, in the vicious circle of limited infrastructure, simply acquiring "more skills" does not necessarily lead to more opportunities:

> In order to get a higher-paid job in this town, of course, you have to further educate yourself, and that wasn't possible here, until the last few years ... Since then I have further educated myself to the point where, now that I'm educated, and I have five years into my accounting, I can't get a job because the town doesn't service that. It doesn't have the population mass that you need for these jobs that are going around, that you want to be able to survive on. There's one accounting office, ... and it employs two people, ... and every year ... [North Island College] puts on this course for office training ... Do you know how many people, how many women, take that course every year? At least twelve. So every three years twelve people are coming out of there with these qualifications, with no jobs, because there's none here for that ... So they're being educated for jobs that aren't here. It's stupid. It's a waste of money.

One woman, dissatisfied with her current occupation in forestry, considered how several of these issues constrained her mobility in searching for alternative employment. She identified the barriers in these words: "The fact that I'm female. The fact that I'm undereducated. The fact that I have four children. I'm not free to move around ... I'm the only, sole support of my children too. So it's not just a matter of taking a few months off ... I can't afford that luxury. Economically, I can't afford to indulge myself. I have to be very careful in what I decide to do. I don't have a lot of skills. I have marketing skills, sales skills, but I don't have the background that companies would want."

Family considerations are rooted in geographical communities, and they constrain choices about acceptable training options. Even (or perhaps especially) for families that have separated, women's "choices" about training and employment may be confined to opportunities that support family unity:

Let's put it this way. Families have split up. The women go on welfare, and then they're encouraged to retrain, and then they basically leave the community because the only place they can get retraining is to attend North Island College full time in Port Hardy or Port McNeill or down island or somewhere, and then they don't have the family support, and then the fathers lose contact with their children, and it puts tremendous pressure on the families to have the women leave. I've seen that happen over and over. Also, in small communities, especially one-industry towns, they only employ males in the jobs that can support a family ... There's very few jobs for women; then that means that women leave to find jobs ... And it's hard. It's hard on the families. And it's not fair to the kids.

These challenges are ideological as well as practical. Power relations within the household influence decisions concerning employment (Morris 1990). These relations are particularly significant when considering the effect of financial control within the household on the employment participation of women. In a reversal of the "traditional stereotype" that places women in the home, one woman described how she felt compelled to contribute to her partner's desire to lead the high life, despite her own wish to scale down their consumption and allow herself more time to pursue personal interests:

My husband decided he wanted to build this great big beautiful forty-six-hundred-square-foot home. And I said, I don't want a home that big, you know. We [family of four] were living in 900 square feet, that was just adequate, you know, I could do anything. I didn't have to work anymore. And I started going back to school then. Now all of a sudden we had this great big home that I have to maintain because he has chosen to build this big home. He has chosen to own a big boat. He has chosen to own a big truck. He has chosen this lifestyle, and I have kind of fit into it, and I'm part of his way of paying for it. And I'm quite angry about it ... But in order to do that, I think he had this concept in the back of his mind, well, he has one job. He makes thirty bucks an hour. I can go out and find the same thing. But it doesn't happen that way, sweetie. I have to have five jobs to accommodate the lifestyle that he has chosen for us. But I've allowed him to do that ... I was angry. I'm still angry about it. But I allowed him to do it. I just allowed him to do it to me. I did. It's just pissed me right off ... I can't even be working five jobs, working four jobs, and trying to maintain that house. The girls don't do dick-all in the house, they don't do anything. They've always got commitments and lots of studying to do and lots of sports. And I want them to have a good life. You know, things that I never had. So. It's my own fault. I have created this mess. And I have to be held accountable to it. And now ... I'm trying slowly to change it and fix it. It's going to take a long time.

In this case, a much larger contribution to the household income allowed the husband to make decisions about the lifestyle that his family would lead. However, his income was not quite sufficient to provide all of the components. Thus, the interviewee felt compelled to "go to work" against her wishes, working several low-paying, part-time jobs to meet the demands of her partner and, increasingly, her children. In the end, she blamed her own inability to assert herself for the predicament.

For women in forestry communities, logistical and ideological factors often combine to create conflict about paid employment and domestic duties. Limited availability of child care, for example, reinforces the attitude that women "should be in the home." However, some women in this study chose not to risk affecting the "manliness" of their partners by taking jobs. In the smallest and/or least diversified localities (e.g., Port Alice, Holberg), where a forestry company may account for more than 80 percent of paid jobs, company policies sometimes preclude the employment of more than one member of a family. Men, therefore, whose jobs almost invariably account for the larger economic benefit, are more likely to come first. This bias was sometimes reflected by female residents themselves. As a woman from one of these places explained, "I understand why the logging companies aren't hiring women over the men, for the simple fact that they don't have enough jobs for the men, let alone the women."

Finally, for some women, disengagement from paid employment was a deliberate and desirable choice. For example, some women valued the opportunity to stay at home and engage in the full-time "reproductive" work of maintaining the household and raising children. This perspective was adopted by a small group of the women interviewed. Perhaps surprisingly, this decision did not always correlate with women's educational or previous employment status. For example, one woman, who was university educated and had several years of work experience as a professional forester, decided not to return to her job once her second child was born. She explained her decision in this way: "I'm lucky. I have an option in a small community. I think you'll find most of the women in the Lower Mainland [in which Vancouver is located] don't have the option I have to stay [at home] ... I'm lucky that ... my husband is in the forest industry. And I think you'll find that there's a lot more women that stay home in the smaller communities."

Here we see how elements of forestry culture not only *constrain* women in the home but also, in some cases, *contain* women by *allowing* them, both practically and ideologically, to remain in the home. Where families are supported by the higher wages of forestry, women may find opportunities for well-paid employment limited and limiting; however, they may also find that the decision to stay at home to raise a family is a choice that is validated and affirmed. These choices form part of the very definition of forestry communities located on Vancouver Island.

These perspectives are important to an understanding of women's activism because they illustrate that women who support forestry often do so with a keen appreciation of the employment structure and the community culture that place women at a distinct disadvantage from men. The employment structure and culture shape women's perspectives and participation on the "front lines" of political protest. For example, the woman holding down several part-time jobs raised issues about the materialistic lifestyle with which she was increasingly uncomfortable. Yet she continued to engage in actions to support forestry families publicly as she delivered food hampers to families in need during times of economic dislocation (Chapter 5). No doubt, her household was a site of disquiet, although it was not yet a place of placards and protest marches. This disquiet was not unique to women formally outside forestry occupations. Women within forestry occupations also illustrated their ambiguous relationship to the industry and the culture that it has engendered.

Working at the Margins of Forestry
It is still rare to find a female logger on northern Vancouver Island. Women in this study worked as forestry technicians, scalers, front-end loaders, enforcement officers, stream restoration workers, and camp cooks. In addition, they worked in the industry as administrative officers in the Ministry of Forests or for companies. For some women, transition meant new job opportunities, particularly in forestry. For example, while jobs in logging have declined, opportunities have opened up in silviculture, planning, engineering, enforcement, and administration. Women also worked as private consultants, accountants, public educators, and administrators – all related to the forest industry.

In this study, I classified women into three categories according to their occupational connection to forestry. First, I identified "forestry employees" who held a range of jobs, including truck driver, scaler, loader, forester, personnel officer, or accountant. Second, "women in forestry families" did not work in the forest industry but had partners employed in it ("loggers' wives"). And third, "women in forestry communities" had no member of their families working in the forest industry. In selecting interviewees, I sought out women who supported conventional forestry, and thus the interview sample as well as the focus groups reflected this bias. At the time of my research, forty-three of the fifty interviewees were in the paid workforce, sixteen of whom worked in forestry occupations. Thirty-three of the fifty women (including eight of the sixteen forestry employees) were in relationships with men in forestry.[6] Of thirteen women who participated in focus groups, eight were employed, and four were employed in forestry occupations. In addition, within the cohort of fifty women, many had been employed in the forest industry. These women had held jobs as log scalers and graders, camp cooks, and professional foresters. Although they were classified outside "direct" dependence on forestry, they did provide a rich resource in terms of understanding the structure of the industry and perceiving contemporary challenges as the industry goes through restructuring.

Obviously, I took a broad view when I classified women as employed by, or dependent on, forestry. This tactic revealed a much higher level of dependency than official statistics might indicate. For example, one woman, a certified general accountant, had obtained all of her practical experience in the forest industry. Her knowledge of life in a logging camp had helped her to relate to the industry, and she had become specialized in dealing with problems particular to the industry. While presumably she could switch to another industry, I classified her as a forestry employee. As one woman stated, "As a teacher in the logging community, my job is dependent on the survival of the community. If the logging industry folds in this area, then my job goes as well." Nonetheless, I classified her outside the category of "direct dependence." With this classification, I can now examine women's experiences of employment in forestry.

Women's marginality in jobs within the forest industry was a dominant theme for most women in this study. For those working in union jobs, salaries were standardized along the scale for training, work experience, and seniority. Women reported being able to earn additional income through overtime. However, sexist practices within the union and the jobs were subtle. They related to women being (in)visible for new training and promotional opportunities, having to prove over and over that they were capable of undertaking new tasks, and simply being heard in union meetings. For those working in nonunion positions, women believed that hiring, wage-setting, and promotional practices were extremely irregular. Women from all job classifications experienced sexism in their daily work lives.

Table 4.3 illustrates five forms of sexism identified by women working in forestry. This situation was pervasive, in part, because of the strong attachments of forestry occupations to masculine identities. Such identities have been built, in part, on the notion that forestry jobs, from logging to manufacturing, require hard, dangerous, physical work, with long hours and in rough-and-tumble logging camps. Women who attempt to enter nontraditional occupations in forestry challenge this gender ideology directly. Some whom I interviewed did so without success. One woman was told during a job interview that she wouldn't be hired as a logger because she couldn't handle the language. She viewed this excuse as a metaphor for other activities that might be expected during work in the woods and the logging camps. Another woman, a professional forester seeking an engineering position to match her training, said, the company "wouldn't hire me, and I'm pretty sure it's because I was female. And they've hired people with less experience than I had, that couldn't even read a compass. You know, so it was kind of upsetting to find that they'd do that and not hire me."

Women's paid work within the forest industry was varied. It ranged from the short-term work of cone picking to full-time, permanent employment as professional foresters. Women who "worked in the woods" were limited in number, but opportunities for their skills are growing. One of

Table 4.3

Forms of sexism expressed by women in forestry occupations

Form of sexism	Quotation	Job classification
Stereotyping	There's a tendency for a lot of the guys that may not really know you, especially if they're new, to call you the secretary. You know, if you're a woman, and you work, then you must be the secretary.	Accountant in a private company
	There was a lot of camp work, a lot of guys. They wouldn't allow me to go into that situation. They had problems with a female sleeping out there, so they figured all females are the same. So I was sort of stuck in silviculture.	Registered professional forester
Limited promotion	I haven't heard of anyone from up here [scaling] ever being promoted to any position like [quality control].	Scaler
Not being taken seriously	Basically, you don't get anything unless you bang on your hands and feet. They won't give you a promotion or a raise because you're doing such a great job or you've exceeded their expectations. The only way you'll get a raise is by begging or threatening to leave.	Registered professional forester
	I swear, if I was six-foot four, had a big hairy chest, I probably could be a lot more persuasive, but as a	Scaler

	woman it's really hard because they look at you as not serious.	
Underestimating	Even when I first applied for the job, even though I'd worked with the guys for twenty years ... They still have this closed mentality that they don't really want a woman in that position, you know? And I really had to prove myself, that I could do the job. And that I could learn. And that I could take the risks, and that I could do it.	Front-end loader
Lack of networks	Men are perceived as being more competent, in a lot of cases. And there's a lot of mentorship that goes along with men. Like men will promote men under the buddy system, but they won't do the same for women, necessarily. Like men have an edge. I'm not saying that women can't get where they want to go to, but it's usually they have to work harder, be smarter, and they have to be lucky.	Scaler

the traditional woods jobs for women is the picking of seed cones. One woman described it as well-paid, backbreaking work in which "you sit under a roof in an open shed, on chairs, open chairs that they throw there. They come in and dump the branches, and it's kind of a race to see who can pick the fastest and fill the white buckets. Then you run with the buckets and dump some more. The trick for the logging company is to get as many clean buckets of cones that they can ... Some women get very good at it. They look forward to doing it, because they become proud because they can pick so many cones faster than anybody." But she also described the treatment of women as demeaning; women were subjected to verbal abuse as they worked to pick cones for different species: "the ... [boss] walked around and shamed anyone who accidentally threw green in with the cones, because they have to be cleaned, and they are going to be inspected, ranted and raved at all the women, because it is only women that do that, or it used to be ... He said it's not acceptable, not acceptable – it was a terrible thing. I only did it once."

The other types of woods work in which women were hired on the North Island were log scaling and grading. Under a short-lived government policy during the 1980s, the provincial government subsidized the salaries of women who entered nontraditional occupations. Companies were required to provide training and opportunities. Once in the jobs, women clung to them and moved through the ranks. Consequently, a significant number of women worked as scalers in Beaver Cove.[7] Scalers are responsible for assessing the volume of timber and the quality of wood derived from each tree brought to the sorting area. Although women did not have to climb the slopes, some found that their bodies became worn out over time:

> When I worked in that industry, after nine, ten years, you know, I got really bored because it's a treadmill job. You're doing the same thing hour after hour. The hours are long. You know, here I work seven and a half hours a day. In that industry, I was working ten hours a day. And that's sort of a regular shift. And it's physical work. So you're walking eight miles a day. You're up on the logs jumping all the time. It's a, you know, by the time I hit forty-five, I kept thinking, "Is this all there is?" You know, and there's no room, there's no opportunity, to go anywhere else with this. I'm just going to be doing this until I'm sixty-five, another twenty years of treadmill ... It was good money, but I was just very bored. So when my physical body started to break down, that was my excuse to get out.

As documented earlier in this chapter, the number of women in professional forestry is increasing across the province. When the Forest Practices Code was first introduced, the demand for registered professional foresters in both government and private industry increased. Unable to meet demand locally, companies and the government sought qualified students at forestry programs across the province. One woman noted that in Ontario "I competed in woodsmen's and lumberjack competition all through university, and I came second out of fifty. I came out here, and it's Oh, my God, don't touch that, oh, you might hurt yourself, so that is quite different. So it's harder for me, like even though when I graduated I wanted to be an engineer, [in] logging, I couldn't get a job ... I had interviews where they wouldn't [hire me]; basically, it's because there was a lot of camp work, a lot of guys. They wouldn't allow me to go into that situation."

In the manufacturing jobs, the challenges were similar. Another woman described them in this way:

> The pulp mill doesn't hire women into the general population. The pulp mill hires women for clerical positions or cleaning positions, but the wider progression through the pulp mill is through the finishing room, where

you have these great bales of, rolls of, pulp that you're heaving around, and you have to be of a certain physical build to handle the job, and that excludes women ... There's lots of jobs in there women could do, but they don't hire them. So, ah, I understand that somebody's brought a suit before the Labour Relations Board or something, they've taken it to the next level, but in the past it's been you don't fight it because if you scream about not getting your job in there then that jeopardizes your husband's position.[8]

Women applying to work for the provincial government in the Ministry of Forests reported the least incidence of overt sexism. Union contracts, clear job classifications, regular work hours (including flexible time) and a local administration that provided logistical and moral support for women employees had established conditions that were favourable to women's employment. For women in office jobs, the salaries paid by the Ministry were comparable or better to administrative positions in private companies. Ministry jobs also provided favourable benefits (e.g., extended maternity leave, flexible hours, etc.). However, the Ministry did not match the salary possibilities provided in job categories dominated by male workers by private companies for union or professional workers. Thus, the occupational division of labour, coupled with public sector union representation and benefits,[9] likely contributed to women being over-represented in government-related forestry occupations.

New administrative positions created openings for women. Ministry positions increased jobs in compliance and enforcement. Existing jobs became more complex, and women moved from clerical positions to more administrative and regulatory ones requiring advanced computing skills, regulatory knowledge, and "customer" service. The ministry itself provided training for its employees. This training was provided in part to women as part of general provisions to keep staff abreast of new regulations and to ensure that the local workforce met changing regulatory needs. Partly, the promotion of women through the administrative ranks was due to the forward thinking of the manager of corporate services at the district office. She worked hard to ensure that women were able to improve their job skills as changes took place in the regulation of forestry and, subsequently, as new demands were made on ministry personnel. One woman, who began doing data entry and secretarial work, explained her experience: "So ... [my job has] expanded and just grown, and now I'm being trained again. We're getting a lot into the Forest Practices Code for contravention with the companies whoever they are. And that has opened a whole new area where I have to sit in on the hearings, do the minutes, prepare the packages. I'm now going down to learn this tracking system so that I can come back as a trainer to the district and train all the technical staff." Consequently, for some women, changes in government regulations opened opportunities for employment, in terms of both the number of positions and the opportunities for enrichment and advancement.

But the most pervasive and formidable challenges were ideological. It appears that old attitudes about women's (in)abilities die hard. Women from all occupational groups expressed frustration with the constant and consistent theme that they were inadequately suited to work in forestry. This view affected men's perceptions of women's duties while on the job (e.g., only female professional foresters were required to make coffee and clean up after meetings), the opportunities for promotion (women were passed over), and, ultimately, the size of the paycheque taken home each month. Once in jobs, women believed that the need to prove themselves was constant. Those employed for more than twenty years still believed that they had to prove their worth; women employed for only two years believed that they never would be able to do so. Instead, many women stated that recognition of their abilities on the job would require a new generation of managers to replace the "dinosaurs" currently in positions of prestige and power. Prospects for improvement appear bleak in the near future at least. Women believed that sexism was endemic, pervasive, and enduring.

Yet to leave the impression that women experienced sexism in the same way would be misleading. Two women reflected generally about their work experiences:

Beaver Cove dry land sort, where many women worked as scalers.

I'm one of these people that the last thing I ever wanted to do is get somewhere because I'm a woman ... I don't know. We work in a typically male area, and we're in camp lots of times ... I don't mind. I go out there by myself. *They treat you like gold.*

There's sort of a different mentality from when I worked in Ontario, say, and where I worked up here ... I actually worked part time when I was going to school for raising money doing a cut and skidder operation. So I was using chain saws, driving skidders, and everything else. If I even mentioned that I did that to somebody out here, they would probably freak because women, you know, you might hurt yourself. There's a different kind of philosophy, I guess; *you're still handled like gold.* (emphases added)

These two quotations express directly the contradictions of women's experiences. Almost a generation apart, these two women used the same expression to illustrate the absence of sexism and the prevalence of sexism at their respective work sites. This difference of opinion, however, was uncommon among women in the study group. Only two of forty-three interviewees in the paid workforce stated that they did not experience some form of sexism in the workplace. Women's differential positioning across age, job category, and socialization, however, may have shaped their interpretations of their situations. As the quotations indicate, this sexism took different forms. Notwithstanding their differences about sexism, though, both women were strong advocates of the continuation of industrial forestry in the region. Participation in the paid workforce gave women direct experiences from which to interpret the past and present conditions of forestry and upon which to draw motivations for political actions.

Women's Interpretations of Past and Present Conditions

The "past" of commercial forestry on the North Island is a recent past. Most of the logging has taken place in the past century, particularly the past fifty years. The work of the past was hard work, but young men could begin employment as teenagers, setting chokers and then moving up through the system as machine operators or other tradespeople. They did not have to complete high school to complete their education. Rather, boys became men in the woods.

Forestry occupations, particularly logging, were dangerous. One woman, who had lived all her life in a logging camp, said, "It's terrible to say about your own kids, that you don't want them to be a logger, because there's nothing wrong with being a logger ... But I've lost too many friends in logging accidents." This sense of danger, however, was an important component of forestry culture – it created pride in skills necessary to avert ever-present dangers and bonding among those who shared those dangers. The bonds linked all members of forestry communities – men, women, and children.

The forestry culture created in these places was built on hard work and hard play (Dunk 1994; Satterfield 2002). Workers were well paid for their labours. In the words of one woman, "they had huge wages. They would go on a WOBBLY strike if there was no cherry pie in the cook house.[10] The companies gave them exactly everything that they wanted. They had steak night every Friday night. They had two dollars a day that was completely for living expenses in the bunk houses ... And when you went to town it was time to party." In good times, there was no shortage of work. Workers could move to other companies or locations and pick up work if local conditions changed or there was a falling-out with other workers. One woman stated that her father did "everything. He ran every piece of equipment in the woods. He was never out of work. He used to quit jobs left and right. And the phone would be ringing off the hook as soon as he quit because jobs were that plentiful and you had someone as talented as my dad."

The pride, skill, and ability to find work both constituted and secured a manly identity that continues to prevail today. The physical build required, the dangers associated with logging, and the hard work in pulp and paper mills were thus viewed as barriers for women seeking employment in the industry. Men started in the workforce as teenagers and retired by age fifty-five, their bodies spent, their retirement incomes secure. Yet, while these characteristics remain important elements of male identity and forestry culture, new circumstances have created cracks in the foundation of solidarity.

Contemporary conditions, described in relation to changes during the 1990s, have been marked by great uncertainty and stress. Part of the stress relates to planning initiatives such as CORE, while part deals with the uncertainty of market conditions and the restructuring of the industry as a whole. People working in the industry have recognized that these changes are not merely seasonal downturns but also structural adjustments with long-term repercussions. As one of the women stated,

> It's looming on the horizon that there are going to be job losses. We've been very lucky up until now because we have lived in an area of the province that has been the most prolific producer of wood. And, up until recently, we've had and enjoyed a tremendous resource that seemed unending, but of course we see the writing on the wall ... We will not be in the position that we've enjoyed in the past ... We are going through, outside of the CORE period (1992-94), the most stressful time I've ever experienced in the industry up here.

Logging (and associated occupations) remain dangerous. Many women described the death of one or more friends or family members in logging. But most of their concerns dealt with daily health and safety issues. For example, repetitive-use injuries affected the necks, backs, and hands of their partners and friends, and injuries to body parts (e.g., knees) led to job losses for others. The sense of danger was not alleviated by contemporary work standards or technological capacity. Women described new hazards resulting from new methods of logging, such as helicopter logging, or new company policies. There was concern that, with the downturn in industry, companies attempted to cut corners by recycling old machines, running shorthanded, and demanding flexibility in job tasks for workers. These dimensions of men's work added to family stress and heightened worries about partners' health and safety. One woman described the pressures in this way: "they got ... [him] at the age of forty with a bad ankle, he's had a fused ankle for a few years now, and he limps. They had him out running a hydraulic logger loader in the middle of nowhere. All winter long, all alone, in the middle of the night, he would have to walk out to the machine, which was sometimes hundreds of feet off the road in the dark, with a flashlight, and they could never have done that years ago."

Work in forestry manufacturing was also considered dangerous. Women described physical work in the pulp and paper mill in Port Alice in which men had to haul large loads and were susceptible to back injuries. Hearing loss remained a problem for those running big equipment, particularly in the mills. Women also described the hazards from exposure to chemicals used in the milling process. One woman pointed out that "people with allergies to gases that get emitted at different times ... can't breathe that muck in day after day and have it not do anything to your body."

As with other sectors of the economy, real wages had begun to level off. Nonetheless, it was recognized that forestry workers continued to receive above-average wages and salaries. One woman remarked that "They have fallen behind so much in wages compared to what they had before. Which was really inflated before. So maybe this is a good thing."

Women recognized that environmental regulations were not the only source of restructuring in the industry. Economic or technological changes were viewed not as targets but as inevitable and necessary components of a "modern" economy. Consequently, women's apportioning of liability was clearly skewed toward changes in environmental and land use policy and government regulation of the industry. For example, one pro-industry activist argued that the media and government were responsible for 92 percent of forestry reductions, the remainder being attributable to cost-effective logging. In her words, "if you can get a machine to do it, you're going to get a machine to do it because, after all, a machine is very reliable, whereas staff has, you know, marital problems, sicknesses." Some women pointed out that the technological changes that had reduced jobs in the woods had taken place over twenty years earlier. Experimental technologies, such as helicopter logging, were extremely expensive and restricted in use. Thus, contemporary job losses were directly attributed to reductions in the land base available for logging under new government policies. As women in one of the focus groups pointed out, planning and regulatory efforts by the government provided a focus for the expression of fear and frustration, whereas other processes associated with restructuring appeared extremely diffuse and difficult to target and mobilize around.

While women expressed fears and concerns for all workers in the industry, they pointed out that the different groups of workers would be affected differently. Through seniority arrangements, most senior-level wage earners with twenty or more years of experience would make it to retirement. This meant that, for workers in their mid-forties and beyond, current jobs were likely safe, or early retirement packages would shield the blow of job loss. Perhaps at greatest risk were workers under forty-five. Shutdowns are a regular feature of forestry work. They take place in winter and summer because of the weather (snow and heat, respectively) and occasionally because of market conditions. Workers return to their jobs on the basis of seniority. Women noted that workers with seven years of seniority or less had long waits before being called back, sometimes remaining unemployed for five to seven months at a time, only to be called back for a few months. Unlike in the old days, men did not move to take up work during shutdowns. With limited job skills, workers did not have incentives to go elsewhere.

For professional foresters, changes in forestry practices and land use regulations had brought greater job opportunities and more responsibility on the job. The Forest Practices Code and a more general sensitivity in the industry to environmental issues were cited as reasons that foresters were finally "being recognized for the training that they have." For people employed as foresters, jobs seemed to be more secure because managers were generally moved by the company rather than let go. Also, they had skills that are arguably more transferable to other work places.

However, changes in practices and regulations also brought stresses home. One woman expressed concern that foresters had to engage in more paperwork and less outside work – the latter a characteristic of the profession that may have first attracted them. She said, "He comes home certainly more depressed than what he used to be after a day's work. He says that some days he feels that he's accomplished nothing. The sad thing is he's spending so much time doing paperwork and probably not getting out in the field as much as he should to supervise the junior foresters who are actually on the ground making decisions." The Code provided much less room for discretion, instead dictating requirements through its regulations. Many women referred to this as a "cookbook approach rather than a scientific approach." The underlying critique, however, was that the Code downgraded some of the interpretive or professional skills of foresters.

There is no doubt that the Forest Practices Code added a layer of stress and uncertainty to the lives of forestry families. Women argued that more established and more reputable companies were likely in compliance with the Code prior to its introduction. However, smaller, less reputable companies were more vulnerable to prosecution. And yet, in both cases, there had been many violations. Loggers were involved in new training programs to inform them of their responsibilities in the woods. Work had to be completed according to code, and any variations required formal application, extending waiting periods during operations. The requirement that individuals and companies demonstrate due diligence meant a daily record of intentions and activities. These tracking devices increased stress loads for management personnel, who worked late nights to complete them; for workers, who feared that their jobs were under increasing surveillance; and for families, who shared concerns that due diligence would leave them vulnerable to prosecution. Fearing the legal implications of due diligence, one woman suggested to her partner, "Maybe we should put everything [household assets] in my name ... in case you are fined. Because they don't just attack the company if something goes wrong. It could go to the individual" (see also Chapter 6).

For officials in the Ministry of Forests (MOF), changes were also apparent. Expansion of regulatory functions increased the number of jobs and created demands for people with new skills. Jobs as forest technicians, planners, and enforcement officers grew, and opportunities for advancement through the ministry were enhanced. During the 1980s and 1990s, a cultural shift occurred in the ministry that was derived from at least three sources. First, the introduction of the personal computer, with a local area network, a wide area network, and the Internet, resulted in significant changes in operation. All staff, whether forestry staff, operational staff, or even field staff, were now dealing with mobile communications and with computers. This change in technology required changes in hiring and training practices. Second, initiatives taken as matters of policy, discretionary procedure, and indeterminate scientific or "professional" judgment were now required to meet legally enforceable standards of the Code that left much less room for error or personal judgment. And third, the ministry was required to become much more open about its operations and decisions and to be more effective in its communications with the public. One employee within the ministry suggested that recent changes in the Forest Practices Code and other regulations had altered the culture of the ministry from "Smokey the Bear," the warm and fuzzy steward of the forest, to a litigious character focused on compliance and enforcement. Some of the implications of this shift are described in greater detail in Chapter 6. In sum, these concerns contributed to the sense of uncertainty for the future of forestry.

Uncertain Futures

The future of forestry is uncertain for people caught within contemporary changes. The most stressful accounts came from women concerned about the future of employment. Among the hopes for the future were "prideful jobs." In the words of one woman, this meant that "A real job has to pay reasonably well; I don't mean large amounts of money ... A reasonable wage that you could keep a family on. Plus, a prideful job, not a make-work project." The notion of the family wage is strong; absence of such an opportunity shakes the foundation upon which the forestry community is built. However, the most vulnerable group, middle-aged men with low levels of formal education, has few opportunities and many barriers. One interviewee, a former social services worker, talked about the challenges that she faced when she tried to create long-term and fulfilling jobs for the workers: "I'm looking at people in the thirty-five- to fifty-year-old range. They're skilled, you know, they are. They're skilled in what they do ... I was really stumped on how to work with these guys, and I just didn't think there was anything up here that could fulfill their needs ... A lot of these guys have grade ten education ... It's a huge problem, it's Mickey Mouse, what they're doing. You don't want to take these guys and give two months' work on a trail. What's that going to do?"

Barriers to the placement of forestry workers in new jobs are formidable. For some men, these barriers are physical and logistical. The government placed money in special projects dealing with trail development, watershed renewal, and silvicultural work. However, some men requiring retraining had sustained physical injuries that precluded such work. Others, such as machine operators, no longer had the physical conditioning to meet the demands of pruning, planting, and spacing. In other cases, the problems were structural; trail-building and silvicultural jobs were not necessarily new jobs but ones that had formerly been given to other contractors. Displaced forest workers, therefore, only displaced other workers when they took up these positions. Many of the jobs created by the government were short-term ones. As one social services worker pointed out, placement in these positions was not a long-term solution.

Proposals for new jobs created outside forestry met with considerable resistance. Investment in recreation-based tourism, especially ecotourism, is often touted as a potential replacement for job losses in industrial sectors. To be a successful option, tourism requires specialized skills, investments in local infrastructure, good weather, high levels of hospitality, and enticements to spend money within the local community. Even successful tourism operations rarely match the incomes of union wages in the forest sector. Part of the challenge is to overcome the shock of the wage differential:

> They're used to having it all. They're used to drinking in the pubs. They're used to eating out. They're used to buying whatever toys they want, and they're going to have one helluva comeuppance coming. I know some of these people were raised in logging families, so they've been used to this all their lives. You want it, you see it, you have it ...
>
> You live to the lifestyle, and I think the younger generation hasn't ever had to work hard for anything ... They started washing buses and working weekends making ten, fifteen dollars an hour. When they got out of school, they followed their families into the logging industry.

Another woman gave a similar description of a situation faced by her partner. He, along with a number of other men, took ten months of leave to learn an alternative trade. After obtaining their certificates, however, they returned to logging jobs because, even with alternating paid work and layoff, they could sustain higher incomes and retain social connections.

Women also noted that the forest worker has particular demographic and sociological characteristics that make him (gender intentional) an unlikely candidate to seek retraining. Two interviewees described the situation:

> You know, I've seen in the logging industry ... [men] with injuries or [older] men ... coming in to see me. They've gone through their UI (unemployment insurance). They're down to collecting welfare, and they're in shock; they don't have the training to do anything else. They have low education, they've raised their families, and now they're unemployed – it's really frightening.
>
> You know what? We've got an unemployed logger here. Do you think he's going to walk into a skills centre? No. He's already intimidated. And he's already feeling bad because he doesn't have a job, and he probably doesn't have an education. And now you want him to walk into your office and take computers. No ... You're not dealing with somebody who's just out of high school and is still gung ho for learning. You're dealing with a man, probably in his mid-forties, late thirties, never mind the older generation like us [fifty-five plus], who's done nothing but log all his life at eighty thousand, a hundred and twenty thousand, dollars a year, you've taken away his job, he's bitter. He feels useless. He knows he doesn't have

an education, so he's already intimidated. And you tell him, come on in, we've got all these computers for you ... You're still thinking like an academic. Like think like the man you're trying to deal with.

To classify these statements as "attitudinal," however, suggests that these people and their prospects are pliant and easily modified. This logic, which often guides the dictates of environmental organizations (e.g., see Reed 1999b) and public retraining programs, suggests that transition strategies that combine job skills with suitable behaviour modification will improve the job prospects for displaced forest workers. This logic, however, discounts the aspects of culture discussed in Chapter 2. Concern for elements of local culture places emphasis on particular values and beliefs as well as on material icons and opportunities. Forestry-town women revealed that the attitudes are embedded within long-standing notions of forestry culture and masculine identity that have been handed down from the previous generation(s). They are embedded within a political and ideological framework that gives "logging" and "loggers" (or forestry practices and workers) social as well as economic status. In addition, the identity of the (male) forestry worker is given value by (his) beliefs in (his) hard work and the importance of (his) work as measured by (his) income, the contribution of (his) labour to the provincial economy, and (his) understanding of (his) contribution to the social well-being of (his) geographic, occupational, and social communities. These values and beliefs are not easily altered. The interviews supported this interpretation. One woman explained the situation like this:

> One of the hardest things I see around here is that the fathers who got jobs when they were seventeen or eighteen ... setting chokers now ... have worked their way up and are now the machine operators with the beer bellies [and with] the attitude that their sons should be able to do what they did, you know, get out there, get a job, get off your ass. They treat their sons very roughly about this, a lot of them ... A lot of them take the hard line like their fathers did. Get out there and work like a man, be a man.

She described attitudes being handed down from one generation to another, attitudes that serve to shape masculine culture and identity within these places. This description suggests that alteration of the social fabric is not simply a matter of providing retraining opportunities. Instead, because of generational social networks, long-standing gender practices, and expectations, the social reorganization of forestry communities will be a long-term enterprise. While government policies attempt to "soften the blow" through job training and transition measures that may provide short-term relief, the alteration of the foundation and culture of forestry will be profound and long-standing, requiring a shift that may take generations to be absorbed.

For example, a turn to tourism shakes the foundations of worker identity. Women pointed out that men who have worked "in the woods" are unlikely to go from such work to changing beds for visitors who have come to appreciate the natural surroundings. In the words of one interviewee, "I don't see tourism increasing to fill the town's needs ... I mean it would take a couple of generations to get that bitter taste out of their mouths, I think."

These cultural changes will take years to infiltrate forestry communities. Women are well aware of the negative aspects of forestry culture as well as the immediate and substantial economic benefits that it has provided for forestry workers and their families. While economic aspects of forestry work can be addressed in the short term, the social and cultural dimensions of changes in the paid work of forestry will take much longer to overcome.

Conclusion

Women's relationship to paid work is contradictory. For forestry communities on northern Vancouver Island, the pay packets of women and men illustrate greater polarization than those of the "national average" across Canada. Women and men have played different roles in the economic relations of forestry communities, so waged work has taken on different meanings for men and women. Women documented how paid work for men reinforced their contributions to forestry communities, particularly occupational communities, as well as to their masculine identity. In their paid work, men learned the value of hard work and hard play, the rewards of physical work in the bush, and how to deal with occupational hazards. They were rewarded with high incomes and a promise of "the good life." Women, in large part, also became part of these community ideals. In their support of forestry jobs, they were part of the struggle to maintain the family wage. They had a clear understanding of the culture of forestry work as described by characteristics such as danger and physical strength. However, in their own paid employment, women became marginalized both within the industry and within the community at large.

Women's employment choices cannot be explained by singular expressions of material desire or maternal practice. Rather, they represent part of a more complex network that embeds their understanding of the paid work of women in local sociopolitical, environmental, and economic practices and meanings. These practices and meanings in forestry communities place women's paid work in a marginal economic and social position in relation to the paid work of men. Two observations in this regard shape our understanding of women's activism. First, as a result of gendered divisions of labour within forestry communities, women's direct attachment to the industry is contradictory: women want in, but they are simultaneously repelled by structural and patriarchal norms within both the industry and communities. Consequently, despite their public displays of solidarity (Chapter 6), their support of the labour process is not wholehearted. Most of the women interviewed were quite open about the sexism in their places of work. This was as true for women who were active supporters of the industry as it was for those who were critical of it. Second, women's support of the labour process extends beyond material attachments. Women's identification with "logging" and forestry more broadly is key to how women present themselves to others, regardless of whether they are directly employed or whether they feel included in or excluded from the workplace. Their shared interest in, and support for, forestry embed them within the culture of forestry communities. The notion of embeddedness is examined further in Chapter 5 as I explore women's other community work relating to the management of forestry communities.

"Logging – Renewable Resource." Support for logging can be found in gift shops on Vancouver Island.

5
Women's Lives, Husbands' Wives: "Managing" Forestry Communities

> What we do is not glorious. Planting a tree is not glorious ... Standing in a boycott is glorious.
>
> – Interviewee, 1997
>
> You can't eat your boat.
>
> – Focus group participant, 1998

The epigraphs above illustrate the contradictions and complexities of the roles of women who support local culture in forestry communities. In the first quotation, the interviewee uses tree planting to describe the silent acts of community building that support the forest industry. Tree planting exemplifies a commitment to hard work, renewal, and ongoing stewardship (dare I say "wifery"), the hallmarks of "women's community management."[1] This comment is in keeping with the observation of Maria Garcia-Guadilla (1995), who suggested that gendered identities lead women to mobilize around domestic or community issues that are endemic, commonplace, and hardly newsworthy (Chapter 1). In the second quotation, the interviewee speaks openly to the high levels of consumption afforded to some forestry workers and their families.[2] Women within and outside forestry described the high incomes and expectations associated with forestry. During times of economic dislocation, workers have had to obtain food hampers to support their families. In some cases, workers have still displayed the possessions of their previous lifestyles; a boat may have rested in the driveway, while the worker has been unable to eat it or sell it. In both forest restoration and consumption, women have been active in "managing their communities." They can be found behind the front lines of political protest; they can be found planting trees, cleaning local streams, providing food, and lobbying for improved access to social services, training, and infrastructure in the wake of economic and social transition. Many of their activities are not glorious or newsworthy. These attachments are material, maternal, and more, and they carry values that are sometimes viewed as contradictory – values of hard physical work, production, exploitation, consumption, renewal, contemplation, and nature appreciation. In this chapter, I illustrate a range of community-based activities by women who support conventional forestry. I begin by tracing academic interpretations of women's community work and activism, and then I illustrate consistencies in and limitations of these explanations based on the experiences of women on northern Vancouver Island.

Interpreting Women's Community Work

Several strands of feminist scholarship shed light on how we might interpret women's perspectives and activism. A major divide in this diverse literature concerns the distinction between women's politics and feminist politics. Sara Ruddick (1989) distinguishes between women's politics of resistance and feminist politics of peace. Women's politics is identified by three characteristics: "its participants are women, they explicitly invoke their culture's symbols of femininity and their purpose is to resist certain practices or policies of their governors" (222). Through these actions, women affirm the obligations that have traditionally been assigned to them, without disrupting the dominant gender norms, practices, and relations within their local communities. In this context, women resist when they are confronted with policies or actions that interfere with their right or capacity to do their (traditional) work. Women's politics is not predictable, nor is it necessarily progressive. Women may resist racial integration, conscription, or, in my case, environmental regulation. This politics is different from a feminist politics that is "dedicated to transforming those social and domestic arrangements that (minimally) deliberately or unwittingly penalize women because of their sex" (234).

Women's politics – sometimes referred to as maternal politics or social mothering – builds on historical relations between men and women. From at least the early twentieth century, women have reinforced cultural norms of appropriate work for men and women by extending their roles as wives, mothers, and managers of the household to their activities in the broader community. According to Sallie Marston, "a notion of citizenship ... revolved around women's right to negotiate the deployment of a particularly female construction of home and community and their responsibility to be active in shaping both" (2000, 237). For Marston, the linking of home to the broader issues affecting community became part of women's experience of becoming worthy citizens. Women's identity and consciousness of particular issues are seen to coalesce with particular community ideologies that shape their community-based activities.

In a contemporary context, women "use their own image as 'good women' who are clean, hardworking, maternal and the caretakers of the family, the home and even the community" and transfer their "traditional maternal, nurturing and caretaking role to the public sphere" (Murray 1995, 165, 166). They use skills learned in their domestic roles to participate in the public arena and use domestic spaces (e.g., the kitchen) as arenas to organize socioeconomic and political change.

Scholars of women's work in rural and resource towns picked up this historical theme, attributing women's activist roles in community-based organizations to their roots in a conservative ideology related to social mothering. They suggested that women become involved to a far greater extent than men in self-help, voluntary, community-based caring activities as an extension of traditional family values and priorities (Cloke and Little 1990; Marchak 1983). Women's volunteer labour was used to support self-help initiatives and/or to compensate for limited access to social welfare and public services (e.g., Little 1987; Seitz 1995). The roles of women within these communities, therefore, were viewed as part of the informal or voluntary sector that is both shaped by and reinforces traditional notions of femininity and gender roles (Cloke and Little 1990; Marchak 1983).

As described by those studying rural and resource towns, social mothering is politically conservative. Women are seen as taking supportive (not primary) roles in working-class struggles to retain male employment, family incomes, and ways of life (Ali 1986; Maggard 1990). Their activities rarely challenge either the decision-making responsibilities within rural communities or the structure of gender relations and the division of labour (Little 1987). The dominant local demographic structure and lack of social infrastructure (e.g., lack of child care options, lack of employment prospects for women) continue to contain women in the home. These empirical findings have reinforced a theoretical ideal that suggests that "traditional" conceptions of masculinity and femininity are strong in rural resource communities, where women are seen as rightfully the primary caregivers and nurturers and men are seen as the providers and decision makers (Gibson 1992). This theoretical conceptualization has opened up opportunities for understanding women's community work in new ways, but it has also established new sets of blinders. One of the central contradictions in both feminist scholarship and activist communities relates to the ways in which notions of family and community care have been used to mobilize or describe particular actions. Western (white) feminists have tended to view actions tied to supporting the "family home" as conservative ones aimed at retaining the status quo.[3] Yet there have been challenges to this interpretation.

For example, Kathleen Murray (1995) argued that in conservative culture a community may legitimate women's political participation if it is considered an extension of the patriarchal views of women as wives and mothers, particularly in places where the primary role of men has been difficult or impossible to fulfill. Thus, women do not passively accept the boundaries of social behaviour; rather, they actively manoeuvre within the boundaries of patriarchal structures to use their roles as caretakers and nurturers within a political context. Murray's research in a logging community on the East Coast of Canada is particularly instructive since it overcomes earlier work related to the victimized and passive status granted to women in resource towns (e.g., National Film Board 1979) and the rendering of all actions "conservative."

Because of its long-standing attempt to link ideas about women's structural place in society with their organizations and local political debates and policy practices, scholarship in gender/development planning[4] is relevant here despite its application to other geographic settings. In this literature, women's participation in community/local affairs has been linked to their domesticity, while men's participation in local life has been seen as political in terms of their class interests and paid positions. For example, in Latin America, Caroline Moser (1993) described women's community management roles as extensions of their reproductive roles, while men's roles associated with local politics "comprise activities undertaken by men at the community level organizing at the formal political level. It is usually paid work, either directly or indirectly, through wages or increases in status and power" (34). Thus, women are seen to mobilize politically not as members of the working class but as wives and mothers, in recognition of what Maxine Molyneux (1985) calls "practical gender interests."

The theoretical premises of gender/development planning have also been extended and applied to studies of women's activism in North America. For example, Virginia Seitz (1995) used gender/development analyses to explain women's activism in Appalachia, arguing that in both Latin America and the United States women's community management work is important within the context of economic restructuring. She described how, despite the marginalized status of women in these communities, their labour was used to compensate for the decline of government commitment to the provision of social services. Community protest events were organized by women because such events required skills perceived as extensions of their domestic roles. For some women, the emotional satisfaction of volunteer work was as important as money. Volunteer work had nonmaterial rewards, contributing to participants' self-esteem and possibly to their capacity to change their material realities.

An important distinction, however, is that researchers of gender/development challenge the assumption that community management work is conservative. Seitz (1995) suggests that participation in new social movements formed for others bound to one as "family" does not preclude the development of revolutionary consciousness. She sides with Helen Safa, who argues that "Latin American women think that their roles as wives and mothers legitimize their sense of injustice and outrage, since they are protesting their inability to effectively carry out these roles ... In short, they are redefining and transforming their domestic role from one of private nurturance to one of collective, public protest, and in this way challenging the traditional exclusion of women into the private sphere of the family" (1990, 355). Similarly, African American women may develop an oppositional consciousness and strategies of resistance within the familial and community context of the social role of "other mother" and the traditional roles of black women within the church (Collins 1990; hooks 1990). These insights are relevant to a fresh interpretation of the activities of forestry-town women.

Finally, a new emphasis in geography attempts to illustrate how *multiple* experiences and processes shape social relations within particular places (e.g., Fincher and Jacobs 1998). I consider two types of work in this category. First, the environmental justice movement has arisen from activism and scholarship in the United States. This work focuses on the effects of power imbalances on decisions about the location of environmental hazards and noxious facilities or the spatial distribution of environmental quality. The literature emphasizes how racial and ethnic identities and the institutions of racism help to explain spatial differences for environmental quality, particularly in urban environments (Bowen et al. 1995; Bullard 1990, 1994; Pulido 2000), and it examines strategies of political activists against taken-for-granted assumptions about gender, environmental activism, and new social movements (Di Chiro 1995, 1998, 2000).

This literature has challenged contemporary ideas about environmental activism in at least two ways. First, it deliberately adopts as progressive a human-centred notion of the environment, defining it as "the place you work, the place you live, the place you play" and assuming that "people are an integral part of what should be understood as the environment" (Di Chiro 1995, 301). This definition is a deliberate challenge to environmental activists who seek the preservation of wilderness by demanding that concern for people, their communities, and their environments be considered equally and simultaneously in any action to protect environmental quality.[5] Second, female activists in the movement have challenged the way in which their own actions have been classified. While many women in the movement are mothers and may seek to protect their children, others are not. Giovanna Di Chiro (1998) points out that motherhood may be mobilizing, but not all women in the movement are motivated by motherhood. Nonetheless, many activists simultaneously resist the derogatory uses of terms such as "irrational mother" and "hysterical housewife" and use them strategically (regardless of their empirical accuracy) to achieve their political aims (Di Chiro 1998).

In a rural context, Elizabeth Teather (1996, 1997) examined the community work of women from the perspective of how the associated activities give meaning to women's lives and how women express their attachments to place. She argued, following Dorren Massey (1994) and

Allan Pred (1991), that voluntary organizations offer various strategies for an individual to express his or her attachment to place in practical ways, providing opportunities for personal growth. Her studies spanned the experiences of women in agricultural settings in Canada, New Zealand, and Australia. She illustrated that women have used voluntary, structured organizations not only for vital social interaction but also as vehicles for community development from which attempts are made to influence government policy.

Teather identified several kinds of space for members of rural women's organizations. These organizations may act as emotional refuges for like-minded women who share values and "feel comfortable" together. Alternatively, they may provide a focus for the limited time and energy of particular women. These organizations may be a means to reach beyond local geography and connect with rural women elsewhere through newsletters, meetings, and other means. Such organizations may also be used to affirm rural geographical space. The names of particular organizations may affirm the dominant occupation. They attempt to keep rural issues on their own as well as on broader political agendas, "despite the changing nature of 'rural' to which their daily experience bears witness. In fact this implies a particular significance to voluntary organizations in the rural sector: through membership, participants may be defending the very existence of particular places within their distinctive community life" (Teather 1997, 228). Therefore, these organizations may be a mix of self-help within the community and political force beyond it. As part of their agenda, women may become involved in lobbying or other activities to draw attention to the needs within their communities.

The strength of Teather's work is that it provides a means to discuss motivations and meanings that women attach to their efforts without predetermining gender identities. It also serves to illustrate how ideology and identity particular to individual communities shape choices for activism, paying attention to how social norms are locally constituted. This strategy is consistent with the notions of social embeddedness advanced in previous chapters and allows me to consider women's multiple subject positions, contrary motivations, and actions without dichotomizing women and their activist choices into "progressive" and "conservative" camps.

The Home Work of Forestry

The context for women's work in community management is established by the lived conditions for women in forestry communities. Gender identities are bound up within physical and social environments. Women in this study told stories of geographic and social isolation that shaped their agendas and abilities to act. In many cases, these stories were consistent with research undertaken during the 1970s that highlighted the social isolation experienced by women living in resource towns (Marchak 1983; National Film Board 1979). During this study, women discussed their geographic and social isolation from one another within communities, from extended family and friends beyond their communities, and from the social values of the rest of the province. Even women who had lived in the community for up to twenty years and were extremely active in community affairs spoke of being isolated. While I do not share the conclusion of previous research that these women were victims of these environments, I recognize that isolation has remained an important element shaping women's lives and their interpretations of community. Ultimately, their isolation has contained and constrained their choices about activism. Isolation and community issues were raised together during interviews, illustrating how these aspects motivated some women to take public actions and restricted the public activities of others.

Isolation within the home was particularly keen for women with children. Women living in forestry households discussed long hours and frequent separations from their partners. Both waged and salaried employees in forestry may commute up to three hours a day or choose to live in camps some or all of the week, returning home for weekends. The pattern of shift work and long hours created complications for families. The result was increased household and parenting demands, usually for the female partner.

Elements of everyday life that may be taken for granted in urban areas are simply unavailable on northern Vancouver Island. As discussed in Chapter 4, reliable, year-round transportation is not guaranteed. Primary transportation is by private vehicle since there is no public transport within these places and intermittent transportation between them. To move between these places, private vehicles must compete with large trucks on active logging roads, on which conditions are poor even during dry months. However, mobility is particularly limited during winter months, when extended hours of darkness and poor conditions make driving precarious.

Women also pointed out the lack of a collective history and opportunities for networking, particularly for women at home. In the words of one woman, "We're a community that's very raw and very new and has just stabilized in the last seven years." As these women described, there were few jobs for them, few opportunities for them to use their skills, and few places for them to share opinions, ideas, skills, and help. Some women discussed contemporary or historical attempts to create a women's drop-in centre in Port McNeill. While not all women interviewed felt the need for such a centre, many identified the need for some place where women could develop connections with one another. According to many of the interviewees, a drop-in centre could help some women to break out of isolation, meet others, identify job opportunities, establish play groups for their children, and forge friendships for themselves.

Gender ideology and long-standing practices such as shift work schedules shape the extent to which women support forestry in their home work settings. In many cases, this work provides indirect services to the forestry worker and the forest industry, often precluding community work outside the home. One woman described her day like this:

> I get up in the morning, make his lunch, make sure he had the right amount of sandwiches and cookies. Then I send him off; then I clean the house; then I do all the errands. Then I make dinner, you know, have it ready when he gets home to sit down at. Then I do the laundry, everything, everything, even to making appointments for him.
>
> Even when I was working full time, on my coffee break I was expected to run over and do banking. Before he did none. I did the bankbooks, I did the banking, I did the paperwork, I did the bill paying, I did the grocery shopping, I did ... everything that ever needed to be done.
>
> That's because everything is closed around here when he's off work. He leaves at six-thirty in the morning or quarter to seven in the morning and comes back at five-fifteen at night. So if there is any banking or anything to be done, other than grocery shopping, he can't do it, because he is not here when it's open. He cannot even go to the building supply, I've got to go and buy a sheet of plywood and try and pack it home. Today, actually.
>
> ... It's very difficult because they come home really tired, some of the work is stressful, depending on what they are doing, they can come home very stressed. There will be grievances or something with the union, and they want to flop on the couch. Basically, it's not a normal forty-hour week, that's laughable, it's more like sixty.

Like women in the rest of Canada, those who juggled paid employment with domestic work experienced the greatest difficulties. Younger women, particularly those who had postsecondary educations, discussed greater equality in their personal relationships. Those without children expressed satisfaction and ease in establishing priorities between work and home. Women in their late forties and beyond expressed satisfaction with their lives, even if they were consistent with "traditional" relational forms. Children were out of the house. Where grandchildren were part of the equation, women shared "grandchild" care more equally with their partners than parents shared child care.

Women in mid-life appeared to encounter the greatest sense of imbalance in their lives. Preschool and adolescent children sometimes exacerbated expectations of domestic life. In some cases, the stress was imposed by domestic choices that the women did not fully support. In the cases of two women, activism began at home. The first woman began to reduce her home duties after she began working full time outside the home:

> It was like being wife, secretary, everything, as well as mother ... [Now] I'm working full time too, and I'll be damned if I'm going to be housekeeper and errand runner and everything, plus work full time. And I realize he works long hours and, as he has told me many times, makes much more money than I do. So therefore he has more status; it should be me, who brings in less money, who does the errands ... So I keep my money separate from him now; I have my own account. I don't use his money for anything except gas in his car.

The other woman described her acts of separation in this way:

> In spite of my lack of education, I would say I did pretty well. I have a financial worth of about $300,000 ... I did it all by myself. I had no help. I had no husband who buffered me through the tough times or whatever. I was divorced, but I got no child support from the man I divorced because I ended up adopting my own children ... But I felt it was the only option.

While many women reported being part of supportive and loving relationships, others discussed the negative aspects of forestry culture: drugs, alcohol, teenage pregnancy, emotional depression, financial disadvantage, and domestic violence. While these conditions are also common in urban centres, the social services and infrastructure that may encourage equal opportunities for women and men – access to higher education, social welfare, mental health services, programs to encourage men and women to change or leave unhealthy situations – are simply less available in rural regions.[6] For example, the lack of rental housing – affordable or not – was cited as a problem for women who want to leave their partners. If women leave, then visitation rights become a problem. In addition, the smallness of each community only added to the stigma and social isolation associated with admitting to, or obtaining assistance for, personal problems such as family breakdown, while opportunities for shelter, education, employment, and social services for women were extremely limited if they chose to make changes in their lives.

More specifically, changes in social services provided by the government affected women both as workers in services and as clients of service agencies. Census and other data reveal that social service providers and clients are much more likely to be women. During interviews conducted on the North Island in 1997, women in service positions documented reductions in the number of service providers. Female social workers experienced stress if they were laid off or if they remained in the work force. Those who remained were overworked, exhausted, and burnt out because of their chronic (and seemingly increasing) inability to meet local demands, even for simple services. As clients, women may seek help in their roles as primary caregivers for young, old, and/or disabled family members. The women interviewed believed that these roles had become more significant and stressful during transition while the public social supports had become less available.

Women also expressed increasing difficulty in understanding who was responsible for providing a range of social services. They were not always able to gain access to services that would have helped them. There were significant limits to services provided for a range of issues. These included health services, housing, education and training, financial services, employment assistance, supports for children and youth, seniors' housing, and other needs. For some women, activism meant supporting other women and families or lobbying for additional public services; for others, these issues constrained their material and emotional ability to act.

Almost all of the women interviewed in this study believed that they experienced more acute forms of sexism than women living in urban areas. They documented strong community attitudes that women's employment was not as worthwhile as men's as well as sexist attitudes in the workplace that continued to act as barriers to obtaining work and/or being promoted (Chapter 4). Many women, both those in the paid workforce and those working as unpaid homemakers, spoke of the sexist assumptions about women's skills or commitments when applying for work and of the sexist attitudes that they encountered at their work sites.

For some women, the division of household labour shaped their choices about activism. For women who experienced long and frequent separations from their partners, long-standing gender practices and/or personal desires compelled them to be available for the brief times that their partners were at home, reducing their capacities to act when their partners were both away and back home. For others, as the primary caregivers to young family members, the emotional and physical energy required for activism became too demanding, especially while their partners were away. One woman who had been extremely active in community affairs stepped aside almost entirely upon the birth of her second child. In part, this choice was made because of time limitations; in part, it was made because of the emotional drain of the activities. "It consumes you" was her explanation. She chose, instead, to be consumed by her children's needs.

Beyond the home, women's activism and influence in community affairs were shaped by prevailing attitudes of what was deemed appropriate. One woman stated that it was particularly hard to be a single woman in these communities since marriage conferred status, authority, and, most of all, trustworthiness: "Let's say I want to be the mayor ... You have to be married first ... You can't be single ... It's easier for me having Davis than it was four years ago when I didn't have [him] ... Women will let me go to their houses now because I have a man – I don't want theirs."

In the early 1980s, a women's centre was opened in Port McNeill. However, after three years of waning financial support, it was shut down. Several attempts to re-open the centre, even in the 1990s, met with resistance from male partners and the male-dominated local council, who argued that such a place was a hotbed for unwelcome radical feminists. In contrast, self-help programs that operated on an individual basis were deemed appropriate. For example, in Port McNeill two respondents were involved in providing food hampers and peer counselling to individual families. These activities were small in scale and publicly invisible. Yet the establishment of a public food bank was shut down after protests by the dominant woods workers' union. I am not arguing that food banks are socially progressive but pointing out how collective and public mobilization, specifically by women, was efficiently and effectively silenced by a union dominated by men. Similarly, women involved in economic development reported that, upon inviting local male entrepreneurs to their meetings, they were told that men were not interested in attending women's knitting circles.

In summary, policy changes during the 1990s affected land use and social services simultaneously, generating confusion, fear, and/or concern among residents. These changes had direct effects on forestry families. Within forestry towns of northern Vancouver Island, women were affected at work and at home. They became active in various capacities and from mixed perspectives in their homes and within their communities. These activities were welcomed so long as they did not seek to alter the dominant configuration of gender relations or community. Where women's actions might have challenged the authority of masculinist institutions (e.g., unions, municipalities), they were openly opposed and shut down. This dynamic resulted in a seemingly common front when a community faced threats from the "outside." The nature of this solidarity, crafted within the framework of "community," is addressed in the next sections.

The Solidarity of Community

The quotations used in Table 5.1 are deliberately provocative. To analyze them, I begin by simply observing the "presences" and "silences." There are remarkable convergences among them, despite the differences in the situations of the women. Some women were partners of waged or salaried workers, and others were employed in the new forestry economy as Ministry of Forests employees. Other women worked as tourist operators and relied on the region's natural amenities to attract clients. Regardless,

Table 5.1

Women support logging while commenting on community and consumer lifestyles

Women involved with or supporting logging	Comments about community and consumer lifestyles	Situation of interviewee
"[Hate] was a swearword in this house. That was worse than saying shit, is the word *hate*. But we hate the environmentalists. We hate Greenpeace."	"We're very, well, as you know, dependent on the logging … You know, like, I live here. This is what makes us become a town, stay a town, employs people … We're farmers. We're like a corn farmer. You know, they harvest the crop. They replant. A lot of the practices, years ago, weren't any good. But enough is enough. You know, we've changed."	Self-employed outside forestry, partner is a waged worker for one of the major companies (forestry family, "logger's wife"), long-term resident of the region.
"I'd say half the guys that work there anyway do care about the environment, and they want to see the changes. They just don't want to lose their jobs in the process."	"They are afraid that they can't do anything else, so they fight viciously to keep the good money and the high standard of living that they would have nowhere else … They had huge wages … It was a logging camp when I moved here … Now the old growth has gone, for the most part."	Community development worker, partner is a waged worker for one of the major companies (forestry family, "logger's wife"), long-term resident of the region.
"The resource industry is the backbone of this province … We are all environmentalists, we all want our environment to be sustainable … It's the preservationists that are doing the greatest damage … Urban people in Vancouver don't have a clue, they	"Young women who have come up from the city, the guys love it, … but these poor ladies sit in their apartment, and they are so unhappy because there is nothing for them. Social services, I find that we really lack here … support groups for young adults, counselling, support groups that you would	Self-employed outside forestry, partner's work is not related to forestry (forestry community), long-term resident of the region.

haven't got a clue, about what actually goes on in a working forest. We've planted trees, ... we are tree farming, a tree-farming country."

[referring to new regulators:] "You just can't make them happy. What really makes them happy is just don't log."

"People forget how they get their parks. You know, ... if you come up here to learn firsthand, instead of taking what you see in the papers and what you hear on the radio, what you see on TV, you're more than welcome."

have in the city for people with depression ... There is very little help here for people like that."

"People are way overextended on the North Island. Nobody here suffers. Have you noticed all the boats, all the trailers? It was the biggest shock when I came to the North Island, is people have what they want here ... They live well ... I think you'll see a lot of people affected by strikes, so you can imagine if they start losing their jobs ..."

Homemaker by choice, partner is a salaried employee for one of the major companies (forestry family, "logger's wife"), medium-term resident of the region.

"When you're twenty, in your mid-twenties, to get $80,000 a year, and you get people in Vancouver working five jobs so they can pay their rent, there's no relationship between the two, and I often wonder whether that's part of the process of the high impact here ... These people live payday to payday, even on $80,000 a year."

Forestry employee with the Ministry of Forests, married (forestry family, "logger's wife"), long-term resident of the region.

▼ *Table 5.1*

Women support logging while commenting on community and consumer lifestyles

Women involved with or supporting logging	Comments about community and consumer lifestyles	Situation of interviewee
"[Environmentalists] don't have the information to make a decision. Half the time, they are unemployed hippies or whatever. They got nothing better to do, and the other half, they're bleeding hearts with only half the information. A forest is recyclable, harvestable ... It's vegetation. You have to cut down the trees; otherwise, eventually, they decay, and they don't give off oxygen or anything ... And a healthy forest is a good thing. And it's a crop."	"To tell you the truth, we've been spoiled up here, because a lot of us were on the gravy train, like everybody else, thinking it was going to go on forever, and you learn to live a certain lifestyle, and everybody seems to have one or two cars and a boat, and ... all of a sudden your boat is valueless ... And then the end result is you still need a car to get around because even if you're going to go working ... somewhere else you'll have to leave town, but you need a car. You need a place for your family to live. And pretty soon you feel like you're back against the wall, and you don't know where to go."	Woods worker, common-law relationship (forestry worker), long-term resident of the region.

"We have our own business now ... I do all our bookkeeping."

"I think this part of the island has been spoiled for many years because they had such a rich resource of forests and fishing. And I know kids could graduate from high school and go get a big-paying job in the woods and, as opposed to people going to university for many years, ... then coming out broke and owing money, you know."

Self-employed in forestry, married (forestry worker, forestry family), long-term resident of the region.

"Everybody thinks that it's just a big bald patch up here and that, you know, nothing's happening. And there's no deer, and there's no animals. And that's not the way it is at all ... The companies are doing their very, very best to keep the industry working and sustainable."

"These guys up here, they're men's men ... They're not putting on a suit and going down to the bank. They're going into the bush ... They come home to the little women. I really do believe that it reinforces the traditional roles ... There have to be more services in place so that women can learn to identify their own identity, and they can learn to be happy with themselves."

Self-employed outside forestry, married, partner works for Ministry of Forests, short-term resident of the region.

Note: To protect confidentiality, years of residence have been classified as short-term (from zero to five years), medium-term (from six to ten years), and long-term (more than ten years).

they all spoke out in support of the industry. These are some of the anti-environmental sentiments expressed during interviews; they are the stuff of which yellow ribbon campaigns have been made. Taken out of context, these quotations can be used to demonstrate the nature of anti-environmental rhetoric and the solidarity of positions of people within forestry communities. For example, women with variable ties to the industry spoke of forestry as primary and renewable. They likened forestry to farming. They considered forestry workers to be environmentalists. Forest companies were seen to be in tune with the changing times. Many women viewed government regulations as stressful and unnecessarily bureaucratic. And sometimes women from these places shared the inflammatory rhetoric that has been exchanged between (primarily male) workers and environmentalists about forestry and land use practices.[7]

The silences, however, illustrate important differences among women. First, there was a remarkable silence about industrial restructuring and historical forest practices as causes of the challenges currently facing the industry and the landscape. Many women, both from wage-earning and from professional families, discussed technological change as inevitable or at least as a battle that had long been lost. One respondent pointed out that technological change had restructured logging practices "twenty years ago," whereas now job losses could be directly attributed to changing public land use policies. A recent review of historical harvesting and employment data lends some support to her analysis (Marchak, Aycock, and Herbert 1999). But contrary to the official union position that opposes new technology, some women discussed how technology had improved working conditions in the woods for their partners. However, most women with partners in logging had experienced the death of a friend or family member on the job. These safety concerns are rarely part of the public environmental debate.

Second, upon review, there are no "choice" comments from women whose partners were employed by the Ministry of Forests (MOF). Women with partners employed by MOF[8] were reluctant to speak out against new regulations. Many interviewees recognized that new employment opportunities for their partners had come about by the creation of these new, locally unpopular regulations. They remained silent about whether environmentalism was "good" or "bad" for their communities.

Women employed by MOF were more vocal in interviews than wives of MOF employees. The two women in administrative positions discussed the problems of speaking up for logging when their jobs were located in regulatory practices. Faced with this dilemma, one woman, young and single, became active in a letter-writing campaign under a pseudonym. The other woman remained silent. As the wife of a logger, she said, "We do have our standards of conduct, and we have been reminded that even as private citizens you can never divorce yourself from the fact, in a small town, you work for the Forest Service ... You still have to be aware that, if somebody sticks a microphone in front of your face, your employer still deserves a little loyalty ... Everybody knows who you work for, and it's pretty hard to stand up in a crowd and carry a placard and yell and scream, because we do have strong feelings as logging wives."

Women working as foresters and surveillance officers also raised the issue that forestry supports the local area and the province as a whole. Yet they tended to provide such comments within a much broader discussion of how forestry practices have changed. Environmental activism was seen not as a target but as one of many challenges facing the industry.

By producing a string of such quotations, there is the temptation to consider these women as part of a collective identity, in which forestry-town women really do provide unstinting support for conventional forestry practices. While some small differences are evident, the prevailing sentiment is strongly pro-industry, pro-community, and anti-environmental. However, this form of analysis alone is problematic because it takes the context out of the words. In the next section, I document the range of organizations in which women are active. By this analysis, one can see women holding multiple positions and places in the community, and their voices and concerns are worthy of further consideration and debate.

Women "Managing" Forestry Communities

Many women in this study undertook front-line protests at the BC legislature, in Clayoquot Sound, and/or during local events. But these activities were not their only or most important forms of community activism. Indeed, forty of the women interviewed were active across seventy-four organizations (Table 5.2).

As Table 5.2 reveals, across all types of reliance on the forest industry, there was a high level of involvement in community development activities.[9] Almost half of those employed in forestry and 36 percent of those in forestry families engaged in community development. Fifty-six percent of those with only a "community" dependence on forestry were involved in community development activities. Environmental and land use planning held the smallest number of women. In part, this was because of the women whom we selected to interview. However, during the course of the research, it was clear that there were few local environmental organizations to which women might have become attached. Those listed had very limited mandates and involved the work of one or two people. Both forestry family and forestry community members were active participants in resource and land use planning committees. The women who participated on these committees had direct expertise through their professional training and work experience, and they sought to apply an "integrated resource management" perspective that included logging. Table 5.2 reveals multiple sites of activism, both across categories and within categories. This is important because it illustrates the ways in which women have used both their work experience and that of family and community life as bases for their attachments to particular organizations. Forestry-related activism attracted people with all levels of reliance on forestry, suggesting that for some, at least, such activism might well be classified as community development.

Employment for some women was an important entry point into their volunteer work. For example, women foresters sought to influence others through mentoring (e.g., as junior forest wardens), public education/promotion (e.g., under the Forest Alliance), and supplemental activities such

Table 5.2

Number of interviewees classified by type of organization and relationship to forestry

Type of organization[2] (number of organizations [74])	Number of interviewees involved in organizations, classified by relationship to forestry[1]			
	Forestry employee	Forestry family	Forestry community	Total persons
Forestry-related (13)	4	7	3	14
Environmental/land use planning (9)	1	2	2	5
Economic development/ community development (13)	7	9	5	21
Health and social services (17)	4	6	1	11
Service and social clubs (7)	2	3	1	6
Miscellaneous/personal development (15)	9	10	5	24

[1] The number of interviewees involved in organizations will appear to add up to more than forty. This is because some women were involved across several organizations.

[2] The list does not include all groups or agencies in the region, only those reported by interviewees. It does not tell us how many people volunteer overall or what their levels of commitment are. The table also excludes several community events, first Nations organizations, organizations related to children and sports (e.g., parents' advisory committee, Brownies, sports clubs). Finally, the table does not tell us the number of organizations in which individual women are active. For example, if four forestry employees are active in forestry-related organizations, then they could be involved in all those listed or in one each.

as salmonid enhancement. Their affiliation with the Canadian Institute of Forestry was an entry point for some but also a place where they could engage other foresters in debates about "good forestry practices" and sexist attitudes in the workplace.

Several organizations were related to habitat protection and/or salmonid production. Originally, I placed these as "environmental" organizations but was "corrected" during the workshop in November 1998, being told in no uncertain terms that these were forestry activities. Here, then, was the most acceptable form of environmental action locally. It was also a site where forestry families, employees, and general community members could work together. For some, the entry point into salmonid enhancement and stream restoration work was employment, where women first saw the connections between forestry and fishery activities. For others, it was family. Activities were viewed as opportunities for all family members to have outings, to enjoy nature, to keep fit, and to enjoy quality time together. Others described the critical role of activities in community development, particularly among teenagers seeking meaningful work with chances for socializing. Of course, many who participated did so for these reasons in combination. For example, stream restoration work allowed for participants to involve family and other youth while learning about nature's life cycles. An appreciation of nature and a love of place were also present among forestry-town women.

The source of family income was not a good predictor of the kind of activism that would arise. Women of forestry families (i.e., the classical definition of loggers' wives) reported more activities in community development and social services than in forestry. In this study, only professional foresters clustered around direct employment-related actions, including forestry-related mentoring and "public education" activities. One might infer, then, that women who are most likely to be involved in *forestry* debates have direct experience in the industry. This interpretation challenges the precept that social mothering is appropriately the primary root of women's perspectives. Many women in organizations undertook front-line protests, including letter writing, direct action in Vancouver Island land use planning protests, Clayoquot Sound, and/or local protest events. By examining affiliations with varying organizations, however, we can render visible the multiple sites of activism beyond the front lines. While the above discussion reveals that women were active across a variety of organizations, it does not tell us why they participated and retained a focus on public activities. In the next section, I uncover the meanings that women attached to their activist work and present both private and public activities by developing more detailed profiles of nine women.[10] All those profiled were classified as members of forestry families who, superficially at least, presented a convergence of attitudes in support of forestry or loggers. Yet, in the context of this discussion, these women present markedly different ideas about forestry culture, how to support it, and how to challenge it.

Betty Has Always Been a Canadian Woman in Timber
"Betty" is in her mid-forties.[11] She has lived on the North Island for a few years but has spent several years in other logging communities. Her partner is a professional forester in one of the major companies. They have several teenage children. She describes herself as a housewife and mom. Here we see the classical stereotype of the logger's wife. While trained as a health care worker, she followed her husband's career through small logging camps, back to the big city, and then to the North Island, where he holds a senior position with one of the major forestry companies. She quit working early in their life together because "there was nowhere to nurse." When her children were young and she was living in a large urban centre, she chose not to nurse because she was "just too busy volunteering." She has continued to volunteer in her children's affairs, and at the time of the interview she was the chairperson of the parent advisory committee for both the school and the district. And, she reports, "I've always been a member of Canadian Women in Timber" (CWIT).

CWIT is a pro-industry group. Chapters in British Columbia formed after similar groups from the American-based chapters of Women in Timber warned of the social dislocations that they had experienced in the logging communities of the American Pacific Northwest. In British Columbia, however, the strong links often attributed to groups across the border were not evident in the study period or location. CWIT was described by other respondents as a traditional women's group. Of the sixteen women employed in forestry occupations, only two remained members of CWIT. Many others had initially contacted CWIT, but as an organization composed of "loggers' wives" it did not meet their professional needs or personal expectations. It does not challenge gender relations in the home or in society; rather, it stems from a desire to protect those traditional norms and the places that practice them. Long-term members of CWIT defined their involvement through their actions distributing leaflets at trade show booths, writing letters, and participating in elementary school programs that presented information about the "working forest." However, these actions were seen as educational and not political.

So why did Betty get involved in this organization?

> You keep reading [pro-environmental] stuff and saying to your husband, "How can you read this stuff? There's such garbage that they're writing. Why don't you write a letter back?" And you're saying, "Oh, you're too tired. You've worked your ten or twelve hours a day and can't be bothered

with it." If they want to say that crap, it was sort of just ignore it, it will go away, and it wasn't going away, it was getting worse. So the women kind of said, "Well, if we've got a little bit of time, why don't we do something? And if the general public seems to think that the men that are logging are all these horrible, unfeeling, bad people, just out there with power saws and dollar signs in their eyes, maybe if we say we're wives and moms and raising kids and stuff it would put a little different perspective on it a little bit." And we would have the time.

Importantly, Betty describes CWIT as a community-based activity, not just as a forestry-based activity. She describes her activism in CWIT in tandem with other activities associated with community management. When asked "What first led you to become involved?" she stated, "I've always been interested in health because I'm ... [a trained professional], so having to do with that sort of thing. Always been interested in forestry and logging because that was my husband's job. So. I don't know. You just sort of slide into things, I guess. Family. I would say family involvement. Things that touch your family."

Betty speaks from a financially secure situation. Her partner has a salaried position with enough seniority that they would simply move if the need arose. Thus, her desire to protect forestry is based on a need not to protect her own family but to prevent the potential downward spiral of diminished opportunities and life chances for residents left behind. Betty and her family live out the stereotype of the "traditional" family life. She has been involved in a range of activities for her children, ferrying them from skating to swimming lessons, attending parents' committees, et cetera. She asks several times in the interview why it takes a three-year study to determine women's perspectives – surely all women share the concerns that she and her friends have. She has accepted "traditional" norms and appears to be content with them. They have served her and her family well.

Recently, her activism has turned to other things. In her words, "I think my energies have been going into other directions instead, so that you start frothing at the mouth at the education and the health minister instead." In a traditional configuration of appropriate activism for women, then, forestry work is one part of the picture of building community in which education, health, and other commitments form parts.

In this case, feminist researchers of resource towns have accurately pegged the basis of Betty's activism. Family, "social mothering," and community management are good fits for her work. But as an explanation of the meaning attached to Betty's activism, community management fails. While her activism is rooted in community management, this position has led to her lobbying for conventional forestry rather than support for more pro-environmental positions. This finding represents a contradiction within the ecofeminist literature; however, for Betty at least, there is no contradiction. Her forestry work is an extension of, and entirely consistent with, her identity as mother, caregiver, and nurturer of family and community. She views these consistencies in terms of what she deems the appropriate division of labour within her family (her availability to undertake volunteer work), her community work in other spheres (e.g., public health), and her desire to protect her family's interests. Her convictions are further reinforced during the interview by a continual questioning of why we (researchers) need to talk to so many others and why it takes three years for an academic to determine the obvious.

Donna Goes on Strike

"Donna" poses significant contrasts to Betty yet shares many outward features of a logger's wife. She has been part of forestry culture for many years yet remains apart from it. She is in her early forties, with one grown daughter. Over the past twenty-five years, she has had two relationships with loggers. She has held several low-paying, full-time jobs in different businesses in the past several years. At the time of the interview, she was working for a community development agency and was heading south after the summer to continue her postsecondary education. She has made her relationship and household dynamics sites of activism in addition to her more "public" work.

Donna gives a long and detailed picture of the history of logging on the North Island. She discusses the huge profit and waste of the early years, the decline of old-growth stands, and the grudging changes in the practices of logging companies. She talks at length about the fears and concerns of loggers for their jobs, their health, and their local environments. Her partner has a grade ten education. He sits on an environmental committee within his company. She is concerned that loggers have increasingly been forced into adversarial positions with environmental organizations, yet she is also sickened by the stark, red-neck, anti-environmental attitudes of some individuals. She shudders as she recalls the "bugger a hugger" T-shirts that some people wear. Having said that, she has compassion for loggers. She discusses the generational expectation placed on male youths to "go to work in the woods like a man." For those in the industry, she believes that loggers now have to work under increasingly dangerous and stressful conditions and have few options or incentives for retraining. She talks of men who have tried retraining options but have returned to logging for the money.

Donna speaks of her own brief encounter with the forestry workforce. One year she worked as a cone picker, a highly seasonal occupation, lasting only a few weeks. She described women hunched over baskets, sorting cones, their nimble fingers and sharp eyes making them prime employees. "You can make good money at it if you work quickly," she explains. Yet she describes her own experiences very negatively because of the treatment she encountered on the job. She also describes her own environmental work. She has worked in a limited way for a local organization and promoted recycling projects on the North Island. She says that there is more status for women in volunteer work than in most paid jobs. Furthermore, she considers that women, on balance, are more "environmentally caring." When probed, however, she does not attribute this caring philosophy to women's roles as mothers or community managers.

Despite living most of her adult life within the culture of forestry, Donna describes it as profoundly negative for women. She provides many examples – drugs, alcohol, physical and emotional abuse, simple inequality both in the household and in the public sphere. She began writing letters to challenge particular sexist and degrading activities in the community – letters for which she was publicly intimidated. She has feared for her personal safety as a result. In addition to this individual activism, she has established a writing club for women, believing that women will become empowered if they can begin to tell their own stories. In her mind, communication – both literacy and public speaking – are important elements of empowerment for women. She recently became a member of North Island Women, an active organization dedicated to promoting education and training for women on the North Island. Her interests also lie in promoting women's entrepreneurship as a means out of financial dependence on men.

Donna states that women's traditional roles at home have been reinforced by economic practices that keep men in the jobs long hours and shut down community services early. For example, men's shift work schedules make it impossible for them to share equally in child care, home maintenance, and financial arrangements. For the past couple of years, she has, in her own words, "gone on strike" from being errand runner and housekeeper, refusing to continue to be the "wife-secretary-support worker-mother" for her partner. This strike (not coincidentally) has converged with her return to school for postsecondary education. Yet her ambivalence is clear: "I do try to coddle him a little bit, because when I'm away at school he does it all ... There's nobody there to cook his dinner, to rub his shoulders when he gets home. He needs a wife, I need a wife. We all need a wife ... I say we need to go and hire a wife."

As a further act of defiance, and to her financial loss, Donna has separated her bank account from her partner's and lives with her daughter while school is in, commuting back to the North Island whenever possible. She credits her continued relationship with her partner to her decision that they live apart. She does not want to return to the North Island on a full-time basis. She agreed to speak to us so openly because in a month's time she was returning south.

In this case, we see someone whose allegiances conflict. Donna supports her partner, a logger, on a personal level, though with increasing hesitation. More broadly, she is critical of the way in which the forest industry has set up the dichotomy between workers and environmentalists, and she recognizes that many workers also take actions to protect the environment. She also rails, however, against the unwillingness of loggers to change. She recognizes that workers will not continue to enjoy high salaries and associated lifestyles much longer. "The logs coming in are smaller now," she observes. She sees workers caught between expectations handed down over generations and new realities, so that the culture of forestry no longer serves male workers particularly well. But if the culture of forestry is not always positive for men, it has been profoundly negative for her. After working against sexist, racist, and violent attitudes toward women and environmentalists alike, Donna realizes that she cannot stay in the North Island any longer. After over twenty years in the region, she no longer feels that she belongs there.

Carole Lives with Poverty

I was most nervous about meeting women in the SHARE organization Coalition for Shared Resources on Northern Vancouver Island. I had set up a focus group with women in forestry families who were active in supporting the industry. Based on the individual interviews, I had anticipated meeting strong-willed, hard-hitting women who would have harsh words for an academic researcher from British Columbia's largest clear-cut: Vancouver. Instead, I met women of compassion and concern for the people living in their communities. It was a consistent challenge to bring the focus group back to discussing trees and land use; every woman spoke, instead, of her experience of living in a forestry community. One woman remarked during the session, "I'm a feminist." She then launched into a commentary about local social relations, in which "drugs, violence, and debauchery" were characteristic. Other women nodded their support. One of them was "Carole."

She was active in the coalition. At the same time, she openly discussed the challenges of forestry culture that remained hostile to women living in forestry communities. Having been married to a forestry worker, Carole now has her own job, earning a marginal salary. She describes the community situation as follows:

> Now one of the things that is affecting a lot of the families in this community are marriage or family units ... breaking apart because of the financial stress ... And this is what's happening, and they're [the women] going

to social services, getting on the program. They have a month wait before they can get in to get on the program until they can find something, not knowing, not educated, not having any focus of where to go. They have Band-Aid revenues here and there: "Okay, we'll get you trained into this." For what? ... They have to leave, move their families ... The women have to leave. And a lot of times for continuing on with their education, to get a job, or whatever, or they only offer so much, and then you have to leave. And so they leave.

Her situation was one of many similar stories:

I was in an abusive marriage, and it took me seventeen, eighteen years to get out of it. I came from ... [a large urban centre] up to an isolated place here. I did not drive ... I had jobs and that, but I got pregnant right away and stopped working. I was trapped in a situation, could not see any way to get out of here. And my outing was once every year, or once every year and a half to two years, at his choice, ... when we would leave the North Island.

And the only way to make it stop was to end the marriage, and he couldn't see it. And that's something else that is happening. A lot more abuse is happening in the relationships in town here. A lot of it is closet abuse, because now the women are having to go out and get work and that, and some of the men are feeling threatened. Because when the woman gets a job, it gives her independence.

Carole describes a culture that is extremely isolating for women. She speaks of the fear of change and the lack of control that women and men have in the current economic and social situation. The alternatives, for her at least, were bleak:

I grew up in a poor family myself, ... and I *could* go back to that ... Now I'm watching these same women, the women that I know, deal with it. Watching ... the effect it is having on their children and seeing what it's doing in the community, what it's doing to these families. And even with my own daughter, watching what she's going through, and [I] have to step back ... You have to do this, you have to restructure your life to live it ... And how threatened are ... [the men in forestry]? The guys are feeling very threatened by all of this; ... it's been a male's domain, and this, the north end, is a male community.

Carole attributes much of her hardship as an adult to a forestry culture and lifestyle. According to her, this culture is male dominated, and incomes and job opportunities are highly segregated. Men have maintained a high level of control within the home and the community. But despite personal hardship, Carole remains involved with SHARE. Her motivations for working with SHARE appear as she talks about the loss of economic and social well-being in her community:

> There have been many extended shutdowns, and then they'll go back to work for a week, two weeks, and then the shutdown again pending stumpage rates, et cetera, and things don't come across as they had promised ... And watching news media as the government stands there ... saying, "Well, we have nothing to do with what's happening in the forest industry." Well, the bottom line is they're making the final decisions here, and it is affecting, and it will affect, all of BC with the taxation dollars, the stopping of spending, the loans, banks, et cetera. This is just the top. It starts going down and starts going down there. There'll be less for spending for all ... The retraining programs, the money's gone. Everything is gone. The social services programs, they're going to be cut back there. And so it goes. For many years, the logging industry has been one of the biggest tax-making dollars for the government, provincial as well as federal. Now it's going.

Like Betty, Carole sees her activism as critical to maintaining the lifeblood of the North Island and of the province as a whole. The threads that have bound the community are starting to unravel. Carole expresses concern less for the money derived from forestry than for the loss of social services in the region. Her work is directed toward maintaining government programs to assist workers during economic transition. Obviously, Carole is not blind to the negative elements of life in her community. Unlike Betty, she has not been well served by forestry. Indeed, in leaving her relationship, she took a very direct and personal stand. Yet her concern for community lead her to become a spokesperson in support of forestry – the industry, the workers, and even the lifestyle with which she is no longer directly associated.

Faye Helps Others to Find a Voice

From a very different vantage point, "Faye" has worked to build social capital within the community. She and her partner arrived in the region sixteen years earlier, drawn by a new job for her. She held a great deal of responsibility in her work, for which she earned a good salary and remained the primary wage earner in her relationship. As a long-standing employee in the public service sector, she saw the needs of her community through the needs of new workers entering it. Despite her intention to support forestry families and spouses in particular, Faye's community service was not directly related to forestry per se, but to the community at large, created in party by the forest industry.

At the moment, I'm involved with North Island Women, which is a group of women that have come together in a coalition to network and to address some of the interests and concerns of women in the North Island, and looking specifically in training and employment. I became interested in equity issues in the North Island, partially from work, and being responsible for equity, and also recognizing that there were so many women coming into the North Island extremely isolated. And we were losing people ... because of the wives. Because there weren't the jobs for the wives. There wasn't the support for the wives. They felt isolated and ... couldn't get the work. And maybe a professional came here and couldn't get work, and then they were isolated ... I'm involved with [several community-based organizations that provide] training and education on the North Island [as well as] a literacy program, health issues, ... and the church, ... and I hope that we can help some women as well through the church and different services through the church. And then I belong to Toastmasters.

Toastmasters was another [area] where I saw ... a really significant gap in the community that, from work, so many people needed education and communicating. They just couldn't communicate their ideas. A lot of the problems they get into is because of communication, and there just wasn't any communication training. And self-esteem is so tied to communication. If you can't communicate, if you don't have enough respect for yourself or recognition of yourself, if you can't communicate or don't have the confidence to communicate, it just causes you more problems ... I just sort of kept tenaciously to it over the years.

In addition, other female participants who worked for Faye credited her with their current occupations. She attempted to upgrade the skills of women as the demands of forestry changed job classifications and tasks. Consequently, several women who had entered the ministry as secretaries and clerks had become more highly skilled in administrative work and had established fulfilling and responsible careers. In 1999, Faye was granted an award for her service in the management of communities on northern Vancouver Island.

Her work in the community first arose from needs that she identified in her paid work. Her efforts have been directed toward empowering women so that they can continue to challenge their positions in forestry communities. She has no children and does not extend her domestic skills beyond the home. Rather, she has used insights and skills from her paid workplace and applied them to the needs that she identified in the community. Consequently, the explanation of social mothering falls short in identifying the roots and tactics of Faye's efforts in supporting her community.

Marilyn Tells a Love Story

"Marilyn" is a middle-aged schoolteacher. She has lived on the North Island for twenty-three years. Her partner does not work in the industry. She, too, has been working in the rivers, involved with a nonprofit organization called Stream Keepers. She began working on stream restoration because a small stream ran next to the school. She saw it as an opportunity to work with children and learn about local ecology. But her motivation was stronger than that. She was asked to clarify her motivation during the interview: "You were involved with Stream Keepers because it originally began in your classroom?" She responded, "Yes, it grew out of that ... And my love of that stream."

Her explanation of the local ecology is detailed, almost sidetracking the interview protocol. She also loves to talk about the work itself:

> The organization didn't start out as Stream Keepers. It started out as a group that was going to clean up ... [a local river] on River's Day. And we did that. And we cleaned up part of it and got a pick-up load full of stuff, amazing stuff, bike frames, chairs, parts of heavy equipment, plus all the, you know, plastic bags and that kind of thing, and we only went halfway to the high school. So a month later we did it again ... I'm hoping that this year there'll be another cleanup around River's Day. Because it could be done several times a year ... Because many, many people, I think, don't realize that it is a salmon-bearing stream, except the youngsters who catch them.

When asked about her time commitments, Marilyn recalls the time spent in meetings and planning. However, when she talks about working in the river itself, she can't tell us how long she spends: "But then we had these marvellous days where, just give me a creek, and you lose track of time ... It's marvellous. You get down in the creek, and you'd never know that you were in the middle of a community." Marilyn speaks of the vulnerability of the stream and documents two accidents in which local toxins were dumped in the water. These events were reported by local children and required many hours to restore the stream and many educational activities to prevent similar accidents in the future.

Marilyn's interview is a love story. Her story is one of a long-standing commitment to protecting a particular physical and emotional place, both for current residents and for generations to come. Her activism remains local and focused on this particular place. She lobbies local officials about land use practices that may affect water quality. She educates local school children. She provides physical labour to improve habitat conditions for the small population of Coho salmon that spawn in the stream. These are acts of maintaining community and place that are not glorious. They are not captured in headlines or yellow ribbon campaigns. Rather, they speak of how particulars of place and person grow together. Marilyn's activism is in community management, but, as with Faye, attributing its source to social mothering does not fit well.

Annie Makes a Stand

When still a teenager, "Annie" ran away from home. A few years later, she began working in the industry on the North Island. She says,

> I've been dealing with men since I was nineteen. You know, I had to prove myself as a truck driver first. So the guys go, "Don't mess with Annie, she knows what is doing out there ... She's not scared of nothing." ... My father could not believe it when I started to drive a truck; I'd have my sandwich and gear dirt all over me ... My mom would go, "Do something else – how can you do that? You're out in the rain, the wind, and the storms, and you're dirty." I said, "What? Sit in an office all day, no, thank you, mom. I love it, mom, I'm free, I'll make it. Here's my picture ... I'm going logging."

For four years, Annie was a single parent while working in the industry. At the time of the interview, she was in her early forties. She has run the forestry centre, and she now works as a tour bus driver for one of the forest companies in the summer. She manages a local fish hatchery on a volunteer basis. Her partner of about twenty years works as a heavy-duty mechanic for the forest industry. Together, with their children, they work at the hatchery most weekends. Annie characterizes herself as a free spirit, hard worker, and lover of the outdoors.

Annie finds affinity with male logging identities and separates herself from the "victimized status" conferred on many women in forestry communities. These characteristics shape her current attitudes and work in managing the forestry community. She tells a story about how women have let men tell them what they are "allowed" to do:

> One day I had some big, huge boulders that I wanted to remove. So I borrowed a backhoe from my company ... I brought it up and started to move rocks, ... and they [female neighbours] are going, "How did you learn to do that?" I go, "Well, I just jumped in and played with the gears, started digging." They go, "Yeah, but can we do that?" "Get over here, of course you can do that. What makes you think you can't?" "Well, you know, the kids, the husband, blah, blah." I said, "You see that fence that's broken down over there, get your hammer, get your nails, and I'll show you how to put it back together."

It appears that Annie has chosen her partner well. "Whatever I do, he says, 'Have a good time, honey.' He does not say, 'Oh, who's going to feed me? ... Who's going to be home when I get home every night from work?' I've never been held back. I mean, when I was sixteen years old, seventeen years old, I was on welfare getting help. I thought, 'Oh, my God, how can anybody live like this?' I thought, 'Not me, it's not going to happen ... I can look after myself, and I'm going to do it. Everybody just get out of my way.'" Annie resists the interpretation of women as victims or servants within forestry communities. In her words, "I think women have to start making a stand ... You know, I think women are capable of doing anything."

Annie illustrates her frustrations about the contradictions of environmentalists by telling a story about a recent trip to the home of an environmental advocate. She drove tourists to her house. According to Annie,

> we drove into her yard that was clear-cut. She had an acre of grass, beautifully green grass, with a little wooden bridge over this pond, and they are all going "Oh, this is beautiful," and they are all hugging each other, "Oh, this is beautiful, this is what we want." We walk into her house, and she has everything made of wood, actual log trees, every picture frame is wood. They cooked on the barbecue with wood, they cooked fish out on a fire with wood, and they are all going, "Oh, this is beautiful, this is what we want. Yes, we want to do this." When I got them back on the bus, [I thought,] "They are mine now, right?" I turned around, and I looked at them; I said, "As we drove through her clear-cut, and you walked over her wooden bridge, and went into her wooden house, sat on her wooden furniture, looked at her wooden pictures, and we walked outside and s[a]t on the wooden furniture, while they cooked your dinner with wood," I said, "I want that deal, and so does everybody on this planet. How do you propose to get it? That's my question to you." They go, "Oh, that's not a very fair question," and I said, "Well, I'm sorry, but I know I have to work for it."

Her frustration is evident when she talks about how changes in forestry practices seem to be invisible to outsiders. Annie argues, "They don't want to just see changes [in forestry practices], that's the hardest part to take. Everybody knows what they are trying to do ... Okay, if you did that, what are you going to wipe your butts with tomorrow?"

Annie's knowledge of forestry is based on "common sense" praxis. In this sense, I refer to the importance of "practical action in the discovery of knowledge" (Satterfield 2002, 125). Working first as a truck driver and more recently at the hatchery has provided Annie with ample opportunities to observe and appreciate "nature at work." Her work in nature reinforces her understanding of natural processes, and it modifies those processes. Her experiences also provide her with a level of authority and authenticity when she acts out. Annie rightly argues that forestry provides material benefits that society requires and that loggers are necessary elements in the production process. She shudders at the moral arrogance of environmentalists who talk about the spirituality of nature without having had any direct working relationship with nature. So she inverts this arrogance and returns it in individual exchanges with visitors. Annie is active on several fronts, never missing an opportunity to engage in a political exchange.

But her work in the forest is an act of nature appreciation, of sustaining livelihood; furthermore, it is an act of sustaining community. Her work at the hatchery encourages young people by giving them job skills, getting them out of town, and moving them away from the temptations of drugs and other social "ills." It also begins to pass down practical knowledge directly through physical experience. Thus, it becomes a way to reinforce cultural identities for residents of forestry communities. These identities are characterized by hands-on experience in which loggers care about the forest and are active stewards of the land.

Danielle Is Burnt Out

"Danielle" is in her late thirties. She has several children and has been living in the North Island for fifteen years. Born in a large urban centre, she still finds the North Island an isolating place. Earlier she worked for a government agency, in part responsible for retraining of forestry workers and in part providing social assistance to those in need. She quit because government restructuring of social services would have moved her two hours south, away from her family. Besides, restructuring had already made it impossible to serve her clientele adequately. She was burnt out from trying.

Her partner is a log scaler, a waged worker for one of the major companies, educated in a prestigious private boys' school on southern Vancouver Island. He does his job because he loves the outdoors. Danielle sees him and his colleagues as environmentalists. Yet she understands the structural changes occurring in the industry and the need for the community to diversify if it is to survive. Influential community members have invoked an unhealthy silence about the changes before them. Danielle discusses her horror at finding out that teachers were not allowed to discuss the Vancouver Island Land Use Plan in schools because it was viewed as a threat to the local community. She is concerned that there is not much that men (loggers) can be trained for because there are few other opportunities. Neither loggers nor residents at large are ready to embrace other economic activities necessary for community survival.

Danielle has been involved, over the years, in several community service organizations, including the women's centre that was open for about three years. Her primary concern now is for the youth of the community, and her current activism reflects this concern. She worries that youth have few services available to them and suffer from a narrow perspective on life. She hopes that her own children will leave to pursue their adult lives elsewhere. She herself wants to leave the North Island, having long served her part of the bargain that she and her partner remain there for five years only.

Barb Gathers the Pieces
"Barb," another "logger's wife," is a self-employed woman who undertakes inventory work for major companies and the Ministry of Forests. She is married with children and has lived on the North Island for twenty years. She is active primarily in lobbying, educational activities, and land use planning committees. Barb cannot determine where one activity ends and another begins. She has visited the Greenpeace offices in Germany, kept track of changes in Washington and Oregon, and was a major organizer for forestry interests at the United Nations Development Conference in Rio de Janeiro in 1992. In her words,

> I think I realize that you're really an island [when] you're in the rural communities and there's a big ocean called urban development out there and urbanites that don't really understand what's on the island. And looking at it on a global scale, which I'm starting to look at, I've been to Germany as a representative of the forest industry. I've met face to face with Greenpeace in their head office in Hamburg, and you begin to understand. And I've followed very, very closely what happened in Washington and Oregon, where there's been major, major socioeconomic studies done ... And I think, on a global scale, the world needs wood, and are we going to do it here or let Siberia do it with no environmental concerns? It all relates to the environment and what you want. Sustainable forestry or what they're doing in Siberia.

Barb denies that women have any particular challenges either for working in forestry or for living in the community at large. She roots her activism in the concerns that urban areas no longer understand or respect rural places. She told me, "Somehow or another we've lost the respect of the basic industry of this province ... Either the resource industries have lost touch or the urbanites have lost touch, and, you know, we've got to gather that back somehow."

Barb also poses a challenge to the notion of social mothering. Although she made it clear during her interview that she has particular ideas about appropriate activities for a "good mother,"[12] she did not draw on this metaphor to describe her activism. Instead, she drew on her continual surveillance and professional expertise, keeping abreast of international developments in both forestry and environmentalism. Most of her activism focuses on issues of fisheries and forestry. In her mind, the issues are linked. "When I fly up [the] coast, I have to phone ... [names a researcher] and let him know when I see whales, because they're trying to figure out patterns, and I fly all the time, so I'm the one who sees them." So while Barb does not ally herself with environmental organizations per se, she does express an affinity for, and support of, nature protection. She attempts to mediate her forestry, fishery, and environmental interests through her participation in integrated planning initiatives designed to establish a rational means to resolve disputes.

Ferron Sticks to the Facts
Finally, I describe "Ferron." She is in her late thirties and has lived less than ten years in the region. For most purposes, she is an outsider. She was university educated in Vancouver. She bucks the (social) community norm of early parenthood, with preschool children.[13] She is committed to breastfeeding her children long after most women have quit that practice. In outlining her daily tasks, she allocates three to four hours a day to breastfeed her nine-month-old son. A few weeks after the interview, seeing that I was pregnant, she engaged me in a discussion of the benefits of natural childbirth and herbal teas suitable to prepare me for the birth. She is classified here as part of a forestry family because she quit her job after the birth of her second child. Now she sees herself as a mother first. In her words, "I'm doing a transitional change between working and being very active in the community to becoming active in my daughter's community."

Nonetheless, Ferron is a strong, unambiguous supporter of forest companies. Articulate, outspoken, and committed, she has become a spokesperson for community interests. But it is not motherhood, family, or community values that motivate and support her attachment to forestry. She comes to this position as a registered professional forester with several years of work experience. Her training comes from a school and a time period in which the "scientific expertise" of professional foresters was largely unchallenged. Her attachments come from professional training, work experiences, and the abilities and knowledge that she can bring to local issues. Her targets are external to the community: she has put together public education programs through the Knowledge Network and undertaken countless interviews.[14]

Ferron is not blind to the problems of forestry culture. In her opinion, these problems include individuals and families who are overextended on credit, women who lack education to undertake jobs, women (and men) who lack confidence to engage in community development and promotion, and a reluctance to face the fact that forestry practices are undergoing important structural changes. In addition, while she has adopted unequivocally the practices and vision of professional forestry, she speaks candidly of the sexism within the forestry profession. She believes that because she is a woman her prospects for promotion had been exhausted before she quit.

Despite these negative characteristics, Ferron has been active across a range of activities that promote the interests of forestry and forest-dependent communities. She is frustrated that companies must now engage in "political" forestry as opposed to "scientific" forestry, arguing within her scientific understanding that the blanket requirements of new forestry regulations do not fit local ecological conditions. She speaks of the increased stress on professional foresters, of whom her partner is one, of the fear of new legal sanctions if they make mistakes, and of the increased paperwork and decreased ability to undertake proper field analysis. Ferron has worked hard in mentoring and public education, and she speaks with pride that community members have seen her as a spokesperson for their interests despite her relatively short residency on the North Island. On this basis, she was asked to be a speaker at the rally on the steps of the provincial legislature in March 1994. At that time, she was six months pregnant with her first child. In that image, we saw her as just another logger's wife (Chapter 1).

Rethinking Women's Stories
These profiles illustrate how characteristics of place, community, and identity are interconnected to shape the perspectives and activism of women who live on northern Vancouver Island. For women such as Betty, Barb, Carole, and Ferron, forestry, as both a livelihood and a rural lifestyle, is in need of protection. While forestry was a primary focus of their activism, Betty and Barb were also heavily involved in improving the quality of life within their towns, lobbying, and/or planning for better education and health services. Faye, whose work experience has been firmly in forestry, focuses most of her energies on improving social services and local capacity for women to become full participants within their communities.

It is tempting to explain these interests in terms of their dependent economic position within the household or traditional family norms. Betty clearly fit this depiction. Ferron, too, was at home with her children. Yet Barb, who obviously shares the perspective of and membership in CWIT, was the principal of a thriving consultancy whose business has grown steadily because of the new requirements of the Forest Practices Code. In her paid work, Barb hired young women with undergraduate degrees in the hope that some of them would remain in the community. Yet her lobbying work did not challenge the gender relations of the community, and she did not believe that women needed any "special treatment" (her words).

Carole worked with Barb in the SHARE group. Yet Carole painted quite a different picture of her forestry community. Identifying northern Vancouver Island as a man's domain, she talked about how changes in forestry challenged male identity and local culture. She feared for women and children and was worried that the government had not thought through the social repercussions of changes in forestry policy. Barb and Carole came to SHARE with similar concerns for community but with very different understandings of the problems that the community faced. While Barb was able to bring international experience and expertise about environmental demands and forestry practices, Carole brought her life experience in social and family life. In comparing interviews, it would have been difficult to ascertain that these two women, of similar age, came from the same place. Yet neither woman could be considered to be blindly devoted to "her man" or "her community." In fact, neither one drew on her situation as partner or mother to explain her motivations.

Like Barb, Annie believed that women could do whatever they set their minds to do. Both denied that forestry communities held challenges for women specifically. Rather, they thought that the problems lay in the (lack of) ambition of individual women. The resolution of any challenges, therefore, would be found in changes in attitude and activity. While both shunned the dominant strictures of mothering as excuses for inactivity, they also used this rubric when deemed potentially effective. Both had been involved in community protests in which women and children were strategically placed to demonstrate community solidarity against employment losses in the forest industry. In these efforts, they sought to protect a dominant, male identity characterized by the domination of nature with production-oriented practices.

Ferron subscribed to a different set of household and community relations. At the time of the interview, she was financially dependent on her spouse, with the interests of two young children to protect. Yet her support of forestry came from her professional training. She began to withdraw from her activities after her children were born. At her most active, her income was approximately equivalent to that of her partner, and she had no children. CWIT had never attracted her activist interests since she viewed it as a group of less informed, more "traditional" women (her words). She held this view even though one of her best friends, also employed in the industry, was very active in that organization.

Donna and Danielle also illustrated superficial similarities. Both were the same age, having come to the North Island at least fifteen years earlier;

both were partnered with waged workers in the industry. Both also spoke of their strong support for forestry workers but were more critical of the forestry culture, which they described as serving both men and women poorly. Donna came to her position after her longtime residence in the community, her personal relationship, and her attempts to fit her personal experiences within academic debates that she had recently encountered during her postsecondary education. She spoke of personal stands she had taken in her relationship and drew attention to challenges that she had confronted in the community at large. Much of her activism she did alone, in the home and in letter-writing campaigns. Danielle's perspective on changes in the forest industry came from personal observation of her partner and from her paid work, in which she tried to find new training options for men in forestry. Her sympathies for individual men were strong; she spoke of their long-standing employment, their lack of viable work options, their legitimate fears of change, and an apparent disdain by the dominant (provincial, urban) culture for their work. Yet her criticism of forestry culture in her community was harsh. She spoke of a community that resisted open discussion about changes in forestry, that was very tightly knit and hard for women – both at home and at the paid work site. She spoke of a community that intentionally and unintentionally limited women's economic, social, and political mobility. In identifying these negative elements of forestry-town culture, Danielle's activism included securing safe places for women, advising some women to leave the region, lobbying for better access to social services, working on issues related to job training (both in the public schools and in the college system), and more recently becoming involved in community economic development.

Through their community-based activities, Danielle and Faye had become friends. Faye's job in the government depended on forestry. For Faye, as for Danielle, paid work, not family circumstances, informed her of community needs. Her initial community was located at her work site and place of worship. In these places, she attempted to meet needs among her staff by providing opportunities for training, access to good jobs, recreation facilities, basic communication skills, and so on. Realizing that the ministry had moved from being a paternalistic agency to being a regulatory one, she ensured that women who worked for her would be able to maintain their technological competence and thereby retain their positions. But she saw beyond her work colleagues as well and worked with women who lacked basic tools for communication – literacy and speaking skills.

Forms of environmental activism also emerged among women who supported forestry. While admittedly some of this activism was "pro-production," such as in fish hatcheries, other activities were more ecologically based, such as work related to stream restoration, ecological education, tracking of endangered species, promotion of community forestry, and participation in anti-pesticide and recycling campaigns. In fact, the work of Barb, Marilyn, and Annie in stream restoration was couched in their love of nature. Initial efforts to understand the stream ecology expanded to include young people in stream restoration and maintenance, ensuring that a small ecological legacy would remain for future generations. As mentioned when I documented community organizations, for many women stream restoration was work that could be done with their families as a means of connecting with each other in nature. Some women engaged in several of these activities in addition to gathering "in solidarity" at the picket lines.

Many of the women interviewed had appeared on protest lines at Clayoquot Sound or other places on the island. Nonetheless, many of the women documented that the impacts of changes in the industry were significant because of the lifestyle to which forestry workers and families had become accustomed. The women were divided, however, over whether or not they were entitled to maintain this level of consumption. All agreed, however, that the repercussions of loss of income and paid work would have devastating and long-lasting effects for large segments of their communities.

In addition, some women involved in protest activities expressed to me acts of violence and oppression in their home lives that they attributed, in large part, to "a forestry lifestyle." It is significant that these women identified the culture of forestry as male dominated, a culture in which women were subjected to physical, psychological, emotional, and sexual abuse. Some women opposed specific acts of violence on the domestic front by leaving the abusive relationships and supporting other women who faced similar circumstances. Nonetheless, some of the same women continued to support forestry, even serving on local committees created to support conventional forestry practices and workers. Other women supported loggers and foresters with whom they had loving relationships, but simultaneously they engaged in individual and collective acts that challenged local forestry culture. Some women did both. They undertook letter-writing campaigns (both for and against environmental activism), attended pro-logging rallies, organized workshops on women's health, and supported economic transition measures to aid displaced forestry workers.

Notwithstanding this diversity of activity, women's activist agendas were contained and inscribed for them by local norms and practices. Activities that supported forestry culture found easy expression and support within the local towns. For example, celebrations of "forestry days" always gained official local sanction. However, activities that challenged the dominant community culture were swiftly and dramatically silenced. These challenges included individual acts of defiance (e.g., letter writing, relationship breakdown) as well as collective activities such as the food bank or the ongoing struggle to establish a women's centre. The failure of these initiatives was both a cause and an effect of women's limited abilities to inscribe their own identities and agendas. So successful were supporters of the dominant ideology in quelling dissent that a very small minority of women argued that there were no challenges that women specifically faced, only their own lack of motivation – a perspective that was vehemently opposed by the majority of those interviewed.

Interpreting these actions and political agendas is tricky. Community work is the hallmark of "women's work" in small towns, maintaining social relations to nature within the home and the community. Where women's community work is viewed as a "natural" extension of their home responsibilities, it is frequently viewed as conservative. If women lay claim to family life, then they reduce their authority to "traditional" ascriptions of gender roles and relations that are politically feeble. By engaging in community work, women gain some of the benefits of paid employment, such as improved social and technical skills, greater self-esteem, and a sense of place within the community; these efforts are acceptable because they do not threaten male employment opportunities. On the contrary, where community work and forestry overlap, women's community work actually supports male employment and the dominant male culture. The local authority that women may gain by this community work is diminished by strong negative typecasting of appropriate jobs for women. In short, they become, merely, "good girls."

This conservative attribution is made for another reason. For ecofeminists, women who protect employment are seen to be protecting the dominant male identity built on exploitative relations with nature (Merchant 1995; Warren 1987, 1990). Ecofeminists argue that a female-centric ethic of care would break the cycle of male domination and contribute to building a more egalitarian society. In a female-centric ethic, "women are regarded as more capable of caring behaviours; their reproductive roles and experiences as mothers are believed to represent them more fully than men for becoming 'nurturers' of nature" (Satterfield 2002, 200). If these assumptions are applied to women in forestry communities, then by logical extension women who use their nurturing skills to protect industrial forestry would be seen to go against their true nature.

Not all feminist scholars fall into this trap. Yet, as noted in Chapter 1, even scholars who do not identify with this singular and essential character of women have set women's work into narrow codes of appropriate behaviour. For example, much has been made of tree hugging in the Chipko movement, India, and the Greenbelt movement, Kenya (e.g., Merchant 1995; Mies 1986; Shiva 1989), feminist peace camps in Greenham Common, Britain (Seager 1993), Clayoquot Sound, Canada (Berman et al.

1994; Boucher 1998; Wine 1998), and the Nevada Nuclear Test Site, United States (Sturgeon 1997). These foci have led to the celebration of the woman-nature association. For example, Joni Seager (1996) argues against women's predetermined biological affiliation with nature, yet she suggests that women's *social* location as mothers and caregivers transcends boundaries of race, ethnicity, and class to favour environmental protection. Those who do not fit such determination appear not to "fit" with feminist theories of women's environmental activism and therefore have received little empirical attention.

The possibility that women might hold multiple subject positions has been debated among poststructuralist feminists who have drawn attention to the partiality and situatedness of women's knowledge (including that of researchers), linking such partial "knowings" to a range of social actions (Feldman and Welsh 1995; Haraway 1991; Sachs 1994). Ruth Liepins (1998) applied this idea to environmental activism by considering the possibility of multiple subject positions for women involved in agricultural issues. However, despite the theoretical attempt to recognize multiplicity, she empirically recognized only two: "businesswoman/farmer/partner" and "mother/carer." In the second position, Liepins found that "attributes of nurturing, cooperation, foresight, communication, and education ... were all associated with the subject position of mother/carer" (1191). She argued that these two positions were in sharp contrast to one another. She did not consider the possibility that women who were businesslike in their approaches to the environment (i.e., emphasizing economic prosperity and resource exploitation) might also come to these positions as mothers, caregivers, and community managers. Thus, Liepins concluded that the nature-care ethic was derived from traditional forms of femininity and conventional community care (i.e., maternal explanations), while businesslike identities were correlated with exploitive relations to nature. The implication is that women connected to their communities through community management activities would act in favour of environmental protection, while those disassociated from community work would not. The link between community management and pro-environmental action, therefore, was safely retained.

In contrast to these approaches, I have illustrated women's participation in multiple facets of managing forestry communities. While I agree with other feminist scholars that the gendered division of labour within forestry communities grants women responsibility to "manage" their communities, I suggest that women, rightly, choose or support *many different perspectives and activist strategies*. Using different presentation strategies, I illustrated how women's activism to "protect forestry" crossed over lines of community development, social services, forestry and land use, as well as environmental initiatives. Even activities directed toward environmental stewardship passed on family and community values of physical work, self-help, nature appreciation, and social interaction. Hence, activities associated with environmental protection, such as stream restoration, became acts of community maintenance as much as acts of landscape restoration.

In short, women's identities can be seen to arise from multiple positions and differing understandings of their situations. These differences lead women to take multiple positions along the continuum of perspective and activism. For example, women may simultaneously support their partners who work as loggers but publicly speak out against the industry and the community. They can speak with authority on the impacts of changes in forestry in their roles as mothers, residents, forestry workers, community leaders, et cetera. These multiple positions make the job of fixing women's identities and perspectives very difficult. Furthermore, linking motherhood to community and earth caring is a chain of logic that does not fit circumstances found within forestry communities of the West Coast. Rather, networks of meaning cross conventional boundaries: community care may be found in women who gain their strength through their employment affiliations and spiritual beliefs (Faye), their scientific knowledge (Ferron), or extensions of their maternal roles (Betty). Notwithstanding this diversity, as forestry-town women confront outsiders, lines of difference harden, and the fissures of difference solidify into a more unified and acceptable position of community solidarity. This closing of dissent at the local level and the increasing separation between an inside community of "us" and an outside group of "them" is explored in the next chapter.

"Forestry feeds our businesses and families: This is a Greenpeace-free zone!" The yellow ribbon campaign greets visitors arriving at Port Hardy airport, 1997.

6
Communities Confront Outsiders

> And if we get one more park, I personally will vomit in the premier's office, on his shoes.
>
> My view of the future ... looks pretty good, as long as the environmentalists stay out of it.
>
> I think one of the difficult things is the change in status of working in the woods from what it used to be to now with the environmentalist movement. It's got to the point where you don't want to say what you do, what your occupation is.
>
> Every forester is an environmentalist. It's the preservationists that cause all the problems. The problems are the extremists that just feed off of emotion. They don't really have the facts.
>
> – Interviewees, 1997

It is not surprising that there are strong anti-environmental sentiments among residents of the North Island. These sentiments were often expressed baldly, without the dressings of polite prose. Women on northern Vancouver Island had participated in a range of events and activities that could be classified as "anti-environmental" protests. Many of the women described in this chapter had attended the 1994 rally at the steps of the provincial legislature and protested the new plans for land use on Vancouver Island. Others had attended or been involved in the Clayoquot Sound protest in 1993. We also interviewed women who volunteered for Canadian Women in Timber (CWIT). These women set up information booths, organized various public outreach events, and provided educational materials and talks to school children about forestry. The women in this study also volunteered and/or worked for pay at the forestry centre near Port McNeill, providing information and arranging forestry tours for visitors to the region. Many of the women interviewed endorsed the bold yellow sign on the hangar of the Port Hardy airport declaring "Forestry Feeds our Businesses and Families: This Is a Greenpeace-Free Zone!" In 1997, Greenpeace obtained a barge making its way up the coast to another protest location. It attempted to land on the North Island to refuel. While it found a place to tie up, local residents refused to allow Greenpeace demonstrators to come ashore. A small group of women was solicited to participate in the protest. While the incident did not materialize in the manner envisioned, it became known locally as "the barge incident."

Yet there is more to these actions and rhetoric than oppositional tactics. In this chapter, I illustrate how specific protests and more general symbols and rhetoric have been used by forestry-town women in these debates. These tactics are not the exclusive purview of these women. One could undertake similar analyses of environmental organizations or social justice movements (e.g., see Pulido 1996; Satterfield 2002). Women expressed common feelings of marginalization, anger, and animosity toward outsiders – be they environmentalists, public policy makers, or even industry representatives. In this context, though, moral exclusion helps to explain how women linked their circumstances to those of other rural communities.

Moral Exclusion and the Hardening of Difference

While the forestry debates along the North American West Coast have been classified by some as conflicts between parties struggling for control of economic assets, they can also be viewed as struggles over the legitimization of competing moral and cultural communities (Proctor 1995; Satterfield 2002). As described in Chapter 2, moral exclusion refers to the means by which some groups or communities may be included in or excluded from shaping a political agenda. Groups compete to dominate others and influence public sentiment and policy makers by manipulating cultural symbols through popular media. In the case of forestry, one moral community is articulated by the coalition of leaders in wood products corporations, independent contractors and local entrepreneurs, community elites, and organized labour. The other moral community is an environmental coalition composed of leaders who are mainly found in regional and national organizations.

Moral exclusion can occur when a set of shared cultural values is used to help designate to whom and to what we owe restraints and obligations. These values help to establish rules about socially appropriate forms of behaviour and ultimately to identify which political actions and actors are considered legitimate and/or worthy. Women and men in forestry communities intersect within this cultural dynamic in different ways. Cultural themes deemed worthy of action are not simply beliefs and attitudes of individuals; rather, they are shared, taken-for-granted assumptions about how to think or act with respect to a set of situations. Hence, they influence how individuals form their more specific beliefs and attitudes concerning their social and natural environments. In the findings of the Rural Sociological Society of America (1993), the moral exclusion from mainstream society of those believed to "harm or abuse the environment" has been one cultural theme associated with the greening of America.

Moral exclusion takes place when the views and experiences of some groups become stereotyped and marked as "other." This construction serves to exclude some groups by processes that consider the experience and culture of the dominant group as the norm or standard against which others are judged. Excluded groups are then placed into a network of dominant meanings by people who are outside their personal experience. This placement is usually marked as inferior to those meanings associated with the dominant society. Those excluded may then be forced to react to the behaviours of others influenced by those images.

In the battle of woods and words, the process of moral exclusion has been dialectical. This means that both environmental organizations and rural residents have been engaged in tactics that include stereotyping and marking the other in their battle for the moral high ground. The stakes are high. "Groups who gain benefit from these myths gain both legitimacy and rights of access and use of the resource" (Rural Sociological Society of America 1993, 159). Prior to the rise of environmentalism, the moral authority of "putting nature to work" served to legitimate resource extraction (see Chapters 2 and 3). Contemporary environmentalist perspectives on forests and wilderness have posed a direct challenge to this way of viewing nature and to the people who hold these views and engage in "resource work."

Partly as a response to their increasing marginalization, residents of forestry communities have begun to solidify the boundaries of community life. The crafting of stories of their rurality is a strategy to illuminate a common identity. As described in previous chapters, for residents of the towns that I studied, forestry was more than an industry. It was more than a job. It was a way of life, a way of living a rural lifestyle. Women identified with common elements of rural life, which included a slower-paced lifestyle and limited infrastructure and services. During interviews, several women joked that they were glad that their children had grown up without traffic lights.[1] Others pointed out that urban-style entertainment could be found by riding Port McNeill's only elevator, located at the offices of the Ministry of Forests. In these anecdotes, I was being told that rural life in a forestry town had some distinctive, even desirable, characteristics. Rural life was also connected to a broader story of the province, a story that included resource use. I was told again and again how much "we" – that is, British Columbians – continue to rely on forestry to build our homes, to provide the paper and pencils at our children's schools, and to reap the economic and social benefits that we enjoy as a society. These stories sought to build a common interest and a shared sensibility of *provincial* political culture.

Women also expressed strong attachments to their individual towns and to the traditions of forestry communities. For many of the women interviewed, forestry was part of a personal family history. Fathers, friends, partners, and siblings had worked in forestry. Among the women I interviewed, the feelings of belonging, of having one's livelihood shaped from within the community, and of participating in the culture and traditions of forestry were real and strong. Sometimes these feelings gave rise to resentment of and alienation from one's partner and the broader community; sometimes they gave rise to actions for change. Often these feelings brought women together to speak out about forestry and land use disputes and to display solidarity against outsiders. The previous chapter illustrated that, within the cohort of forestry-town women, women were associated with different groups, their specific goals varied, and they had differing levels of commitment to their identities as "loggers' wives," "forestry workers," "forestry-town women," and/or "members of forestry communities." Yet to admit these differences to outsiders would be to risk a rift in the social solidarity of the community and to jeopardize their identity and authority as forestry-town women.

This solidarity was forged, in part, by setting boundaries and determining who could be counted in and who could clearly be counted out. As I entered these forestry communities, then, I discovered boundaries and openings within and across them. Boundaries and openings were established by occupation, length of residence, local mores and codes of conduct, and actions and rhetoric used to celebrate shared perspectives and to separate "selves" from "others" (however these terms were defined). Simple acts such as being wary or welcoming of strangers established or maintained boundaries. Woven among the stories of family, lifestyle, community, and province were subtle and pointed ways of distinguishing "me" or "us" from "them." Every woman I interviewed told me "You can't have your first child up here." And women in their late thirties were automatically considered high risk and sent to a southern locality to await the birth. Given my advanced stage of pregnancy during the research period, I believe that the intention of these messages was to make clear how different my childbirth options were compared with those of women in these rural communities.

When communities were threatened, the boundaries between us and them began to harden. In some cases, hardening occurred through positive formations of forestry culture; people spoke of being citizens of their local community when celebrations of "forestry days" became focal points of local pride and when forestry centres became important sites of education in and promotion of local values. Hardening also took on negative elements in language and local activities, such as when strangers were described as foreigners, when singular community codes of conduct were established and enforced, and when local debate about changes in forestry was effectively silenced. Three particular circumstances were the nuclei around which boundaries were drawn. First, the protest events at Clayoquot Sound, held almost four years before my arrival in northern Vancouver Island, had left their mark upon the women I interviewed. Second, the planning process of CORE that followed the Clayoquot protest was another focus for discontent. And third, the introduction of the Forest Practices Code reinforced distrust, fear, and anger between forestry communities and the government as well as within those communities. These emotional responses then formed the raw materials from which the boundaries between us and them became so firmly crafted.

Legacies of Protest

Clayoquot Sound Left Hatred and Mistrust

Many female environmental activists marked the Clayoquot Sound Peace Camp as a source of empowerment for women and for the environmental movement (e.g., Berman et al. 1994; Merchant 1995). Women were prominent spokespeople throughout the campaign. Young women headed up campaigns by Greenpeace, the Sierra Club, and Friends of Clayoquot Sound. Older women who formed part of the "Raging Grannies" were sentenced to jail for their part in the event. Approximately two-thirds of the 800 people arrested were women. All these efforts were applauded by women's organizations and the popular press. In 1998, a feature film, *Fury for the Sound*, made the international circuit; its release was advertised widely on the Internet for any and all who cared to share in the power of women's collective protest (Wine 1998). The popular (and freely distributed) women's magazine *Homemaker* featured five of these women in an article in 1999 (Bossin 1999). Yet, while publication of the protest event at Clayoquot Sound brought empowerment for, and valorization of, some women, it also left a legacy of alienation, heartbreak, distrust, and exhaustion for others.

The Clayoquot Sound protest mobilized forestry communities across the province. Men, women, and children who relied directly on the continuation of forestry attended the peace camp. For some, it was a chance to show and celebrate community solidarity. Communities based on attachment, interest, and geographic location banded together physically and socially as they made their way "south" to witness the peace camp. In the words of one woman, "I went to the Clayoquot rally with my oldest son ... That was a long day ... [A forest company] donated the bus, and they picked us up here at seven in the morning. And we drove all the way down to Port Alberni. We got back, I think it was one o'clock in the morning. And there was [sic] still ones from Port Hardy and Port Alice that had to get home. That was fun, I enjoyed that." But for most women, Clayoquot was anything but fun.

One woman, who had lived nearby at the time of the protest, described the stresses that it had brought to her family and her community. Acting within the umbrella organization SHARE BC, she wrote letters directly to the premier protesting the blockages and asking for support from the government to help with the crisis and the stress that the community was experiencing. Her husband, a senior manager with one of the major forestry companies, was involved daily with protesters. He received special training to ensure that he was prepared to address the protesters peacefully and without personal offence. But after the demonstrations, he requested a transfer. He continued to work for the company for a short time and then took a year off to help alleviate his stress. After persistent requests from the company, he returned to work. He had his pick of places to live. They chose to move to the North Island. In her words,

> Kennedy Lake Division [the forestry division in which Clayoquot Sound is located] was a big division; we had twenty-two staff members at that time. When the problems started out there, there were a lot of protesters out for Clayoquot Sound, and they were putting blockages up so that the guys couldn't go to work. Our staff members were cut from twenty-two down to ten ... We didn't know whether we'd have a job or not. They [company officials] came in just after Christmas, January, and they cut them. It was like a firing squad. Everyone was sitting at their desks, and they were called in one by one and were given five minutes to clean out all their stuff, and somebody drove them home. It was the first time, I think, that I ever saw my husband come home and cry ... over his job, because it was so stressful. And then they still had to go ahead and do the same job ... And then he'd have to drive them home as well. You know, he had to drive them home with their stuff and drop them off at the door. It was horrible. And since then, it just got worse.

In the wake of Clayoquot, residents of forestry communities feared that environmentalists sought to shut the industry down completely. For those on northern Vancouver Island, Clayoquot was one of a chain of public demonstrations moving from south to north. In the 1980s and 1990s, all along the West Coast of North America from Oregon to Clayoquot Sound, ongoing protests left a legacy of weariness and wariness among forestry-town residents. Several perceptual strategies were used by these women to explain the actions of environmental organizations in terms that they could understand and accept.

For some, the impacts of the Clayoquot protests were not direct, but nonetheless they instilled in forestry-town women both bitterness and resentment:

[The news] ... showed what they [environmental protesters] left behind. Like trucks and trucks of garbage. And they're going down and collecting their welfare cheque[s]. Cut them off. We're the ones that are paying their welfare system, you know. Cut them off. So, you know, before you would see somebody that was a hippy or who looked a little different; now you look at them and ask, "Are they involved with Greenpeace? Are they involved with trying to destroy what we do for work?" You look at them different, you know, instead of "It's only a hippy." Now it's different.

Many women told me that urbanites (of whom I was clearly representative) should stop telling others how to live. For these women, anger and hatred were the sparks that animated them, as illustrated by these comments of an operator of a tourist establishment:

Q: Now what about forestry, what are some of the changes that you've seen?
A: Hatred.
Q: Hatred?
A: Yes. A lot of hate.
Q: Towards government? Towards the environmentalists?
A: Towards both ... You know, Greenpeace, who cared about Greenpeace before? We didn't. Now, all of a sudden, they're in Port Hardy on a barge, you know, like hatred. We hate them, and one of the things is we don't use that word in our house. We never have. My kids weren't allowed to swear. That was a swearword in this house, that was worse than saying shit, is the word *hate*. But we hate environmentalists. We hate Greenpeace. We hate, you know, those type[s] of people that [are] dictating to us people who live here what we should do. I mean, it's an awful thing, but that's what the change in the forest industry is.

Others sought distance from environmental protesters by classifying them all as foreigners. For example, one woman said, "When I went down to Clayoquot Sound, ... I would say maybe only one of them had a Canadian accent. All American. German. A few of them couldn't even speak English, but I didn't see any people from Canada there. They're all, you know, they're all foreigners." Several interviewees selected Germany as the home country of the protesters, and this choice may reflect the dominance of German tourists in these landscapes. But Germany has had a profound influence on forestry in Canada. Ideas about sustained yield discussed in Chapter 3 were introduced from Germany. It was believed that even aged stands would literally provide the raw materials for sustaining incomes and forestry communities in perpetuity. Today Germany is the first country to be governed by a green party and has an active division of Greenpeace, which ran a successful "markets campaign" there.[2] That Germany has served as a model in shaping forestry rhetoric, strategy, and policy in British Columbia was not lost on me.

Environmentalists formerly considered quaint anachronisms had more recently become dangerous for forestry-town residents. Danger was felt in the fear of loss of livelihood, well-being, and basic respect. Women spoke freely of the environmentalists' ignorance of local conditions and the hypocrisy of their positions, and they defended the right of rural peoples to "the good life" that they believed was enjoyed by their urban counterparts. Much of the rhetoric that we heard during interviews had been formulated during the Clayoquot rallies, while subsequent events, such as the CORE planning process, had reinforced it.

CORE Reinforced the Boundaries between "Us" and "Them"

CORE's efforts to establish a land use plan for Vancouver Island (see Chapters 3 and 7) reinforced divisions associated with rural and urban and northern and southern residents of the province. Due to the rapid pace of new legislation and policy in the 1990s, residents of forestry communities began to feel bombarded. CORE was supposed to integrate several new government initiatives into its land use planning process even though the policies and regulations had not been finalized. While these initiatives were diffused among different government ministries and divisions (e.g., Ministries of Forests, Environment, and Human Resources), the commission's requirement to integrate them made its mandate appear to be pro-environmental. This funnelling of government initiatives into CORE's central mandate provided some tangible focus for community concern – and a target for women's political frustrations. In the words of one woman, "At that time, we got together and acted as a unit, and we were able to be activists, ... but right now there are so many things assaulting us from all sorts of different directions. It's very hard to focus."

The months leading up to the CORE rally in March 1994 and the months that followed were filled with fear, misinformation, rumours, and closure of local discussion. For example, one woman whom we interviewed was a staunch supporter of forestry. She was a university student who funded her studies by working at the local forestry centre in the summer. When CORE representatives visited northern Vancouver Island, she attended the meeting. Her own position on environmental issues was mixed: "There are special places, and they should be protected, and they should be reserved for enjoyment ... There should also be places for public access." She did not support the positions or actions of environmentalists and believed that her position at the forestry centre compromised her inclusion in land use debates: "I attended the CORE meeting they had here in Port McNeill ... I thought it did not fairly represent the youth ... I wore my forestry centre jacket, ... and the youth sector was going around passing out their little brochures; the young people in the CORE totally avoided me. I'm pretty sure it was because I had the forestry centre on my jacket." While she was clearly a supporter of forestry, she was not willing to accept the industry position and tactics unchallenged. She discussed the lack of accurate information that circulated around the community and fed the fears of residents:

> There was so much fear instilled in a lot of communities. The information was a bit obscure. Not all the information was let out. So people were coming up with their own assumption of what things meant ... So the companies utilized that a lot to almost feed fear ... I think the companies did that ... The big thing was saying that 22 percent of Vancouver Island was going to be protected, and it's only, I think, 11 percent that's actually protected, the other section of that was put into the low-intensity areas, ... basically [where] there's more careful management of the ... forest. But the big companies just lumped that all up together ... So then it was 22 percent of Vancouver Island was to be protected, and that's what all the signs said, 22 percent. I talked to most people, and they said, "Oh, you know, 11 or 12 percent, no problem." But 22 percent, when I look at all government documents, it said only up to 12 percent. Where's this other number coming from?

Fear was reinforced by closure of debate locally. One woman recalled, "I remember when CORE was going on it was forbidden to be spoken about in the school here ... They [teachers] couldn't talk about it in school ... That to me was just horrifying. I really do think there's always two sides." Organizations such as Canadian Women in Timber and the SHARE coalition were instrumental in ensuring that local dissent was silenced. The result was a high level of anxiety within the communities. This woman went on to say, "I thought when this CORE was happening maybe we should sell our house now, ... a real feeling of insecurity."

When CORE made its recommendations to the government, the verdict of the forestry communities was swift and loud. In March 1994, men, women, and children descended on the steps of the provincial legislature to denounce the plan. They rallied to say that too much land had been put into wilderness protection and that not enough had been reserved for logging. They called for stronger measures to protect communities during times of economic transition. They broadcast their betrayal by the government. They argued that the (social democratic) government was responding to only one part of its constituency and turning a deaf ear to its traditional constituents – the workers who had built the province.

If Clayoquot was the rally for environmentalists, then the "CORE protest" on the steps of the legislature belonged to the forestry workers. Its numbers were impressive. While news reports of the Clayoquot Sound protest claimed that 10,000 people attended the protests over the summer months, newspaper reports of the anti-CORE event suggested that 15,000 people attended the one-day rally. Like Clayoquot, the CORE rally was an opportunity to celebrate solidarity. As one woman put it, "All the family was there and family friends and stuff. It was kind of neat. For me, it was more like a big family reunion than a protest."

But it was a reunion with a sober side. Representatives at the rally spoke of losses to individuals, families, and communities that would attend the recommendations. A "logger's wife" also spoke out against the plan, arguing that the community impacts were too great and unjustified. The mayor of Port McNeill, who had become a spokesperson for forestry communities, wrote a commentary in one of the main Vancouver newspapers. In it, he denounced the government, saying that the plan "would give the preservationists almost everything they wanted ... [and thereby] would decimate resource communities" while catering to "multi-national" environmentalists (Furney 1994, A23). This rhetoric was a deliberate attempt to reclaim the moral high ground in forestry debates. If CORE gave forestry communities an outside target on which to focus disaffection, then the introduction of the Forest Practices Code brought the battles and anxieties directly into communities and homes throughout the region.

The Forest Practices Code Made the War in the Woods Personal

The new enforcement regime associated with the Forest Practices Code also altered the perception of workers in industry, in the Ministry of Forests, and in the relationship between them. Women in this study argued that the government no longer believed in logging and that the Code undermined the integrity and authority of forestry workers to do their jobs. For these women, it imposed political solutions to political problems based on superficial aesthetic sensibilities instead of applying appropriate scientific principles of forestry and land management.

New government jobs were created in the areas of surveillance and compliance, and employees were recruited from across the country. Those who were hired to enforce the Code were doubly excluded from the community. First, while many "outside" jobs in the ministry were as demanding physically and intellectually as jobs in the industry, they did not confer the same status. Ministry workers had a long-standing reputation as being "soft" and "not too bright." For example, one woman said, "Anywhere you can travel in the world doing forestry ... Anybody that doesn't do well in the industry always finds a job in the government, which is a standing joke ... When you're working for a private industry, you work very hard and fast and do it ... And it is a joke that people that don't make it in the industry always get a job in the government – they end up in the Forest Service. Then you're dealing with those people."

Second, beyond this long-standing prejudice, there was a heightened concern that the new enforcers did not belong in the communities. Recruited from outside the province, many were new to the region. Their salaries were a fraction of the salaries paid to industry workers. Therefore, in some towns, government workers were unable to purchase houses, particularly if they were the sole wage earners. They literally could not fit in. Some of the women interviewed believed that officers had obtained their training from ex-police officers and lawyers, contributing to an adversarial position toward industry workers. Consequently, the Code introduced a new dimension to the war in the woods. The Clayoquot Sound and CORE debates targeted government policies formulated in a distant location. In contrast, frustration with and anger at the Code were focused on compliance officers located within the communities themselves. Whereas forestry communities had previously banded together against regulations, new battles were now being waged *within* these communities and threatened to tear apart their social networks and cohesion.

Those women who worked for the ministry or had partners in it indicated high levels of stress due to understaffing and the pressure to perform their new functions. One woman, the partner of a ministry official, said, "If your husband works for the Forest Service, then the forestry people outside of the Forest Service aren't really keen on you because you're the bad guy." Some women did not want to discuss the implications of the Code for this very reason. But one woman described the tensions in great detail. Her partner had recently got a job working in compliance for the ministry:

> When the Forest Practices Code came in, they gave my husband a badge, you know, in a leather pouch, just like LAPD [Los Angeles Police Department] ... So I was really, really nervous ... When they originally brought in the Forest Practices Code, they said that it's going to be tough enforcement, and, you know, we're going to change the way, you know, the rules and the regs [regulations], and, you know, they've got these pink tickets that they give out. And everybody was all freaked out because the industry thought that they were going to be fined, you know, fined, fined, fined, and end up in jail and out of business. And I thought to myself, "Now wait a minute now, my husband hasn't been in this forestry industry very long, and here they are telling him to go out and tell this guy that's been driving a cat since he was sixteen years old, you know, and he's supposed to go out, and, and I thought, hmm, this is the makings for a war." Like he's going to get a stick of dynamite up the tailpipe of his truck. And, you know, I thought, "This just does not seem right to me." ... [My partner]

was all gung ho because they were giving these seminars ... They were bringing in ex-cops and lawyers telling them how they should be out there, you know, instant cop training ... And I thought, "Hey, this is not right. This is going to lead to absolute war in the woods." So I said to ... [names partner], "Look, the forest industry has been going through transition in BC since the Forest Act and probably long before then, so I think you should probably decline from taking a stance, and you should observe." ... I said, "Just hold back. Don't go out there and push your weight around, and remember that these guys have been around for a long time." You know, you can't change something that's been going on for thirty years in three months, you know ... Industry has been working with these regulations anyway. It's just that all of a sudden now it's in gold lettering ... Because you give somebody power, and it's very human for them to want to wield that power. But you've got to remember that a sword cuts both ways. You know, you can use if for carving something out, or you can use it for cutting something up, at the same time as you can use it for doing war, because there are people in the Forest Service that are going out and throwing their weight around, and ... it's not working. It's not working.

By the time that I arrived in the late 1990s, many of the dramatic protest events on Vancouver Island had passed. In some cases, the government had moved toward new negotiations and planning initiatives. In other cases, the fire of protest had been spent. Speaking about her disappointment with the results of the CORE protest and her withdrawal from activism, one woman described her situation in this way:

> I don't get involved usually unless I feel really strongly about [the issue] and because I don't like politics just for something to do ... A few issues that came up after that, I really put my heart and soul into it, and ... it didn't make a bit of difference. And I saw my brothers go through it with the fishing, with the Mifflin Plan. They took over the office in Port Hardy, you know, DFO [Federal Department of Fisheries and Oceans], the whole thing. Nothing. It made absolutely no difference. So I just felt kind of like, like, well, it is really stressful to me, that stuff. It ages you. You're not having fun. So why do it?

One woman withdrew because she wanted to focus on her children's lives and priorities:

> I think you can let it control your life, if you're not careful. And the objective is not to become like the other side ... After I finished [one set of activities], ... I really went through a period where I didn't want anything to do

with forestry. It sort of eats at you, it drains you, and it obsesses you ... It takes you over. And it becomes really hard to be objective. You know what I mean? I think we have to understand how intense this is, how emotional it can become.

But despite the passing of the Clayoquot Sound protests and the CORE planning process, the story continues, just as the yellow banner continues to fly on the hangar at the Port Hardy airport. In keeping with my expanded definition of activism, I found fertile soils in the rhetoric and sites of "acceptable" activism. The first was in the rhetoric of the working forest.

Pushing Back: Action Sites and Rhetorical Strategies

Taking a Tour of the Working Forest

> I'm a firm believer in special places being preserved, but I certainly believe in a working forest.
>
> – Interviewee, 1997

Countless promotional brochures available on northern Vancouver Island promote "the working forest." According to members of Canadian Women in Timber (CWIT) whom I interviewed, it is an educational organization, not a political one. It is dedicated to educating the lay public and children about the working forest. Yet surely such a statement is political. Are trees that grow unimpeded not hard-working? Are forests that provide ecological services such as oxygen and clean water not productive? How have these people imposed ideas about their own labour onto living, growing, reproducing biomass to produce this metaphor? While I piece together the narrative of the working forest, I puzzle over the suitability of this image.

The working forest is associated with specific sites of political activism and particular rhetorical strategies. Locations that promote the working forest include hatcheries, information centres, classrooms, and guided tours. This part of the working forest is contained within ideas of production, family, and community. Here the work of loggers, foresters, and families establishes and maintains the capacity for resource production. One woman, a forester, stated, "We have a salmon hatchery ... And we go out there and feed the fish every day ... If we're out there, it'll get done during work, but if we didn't make it out there we'll just go after work and do that. Feed the fish." Other women spoke of similar experiences. "Both my sons do the Marble River [an official hatchery] and my husband ... Wherever a little logging camp was, you always started a fish hatchery there." As documented in Chapter 5, these efforts reinforce a sense of family and community that extends to the natural world. They also contribute to how forests work or remain productive for the next generation of harvestable products.

As a rhetorical strategy, the idea that the working forest is productive lies in stark contrast to the forest as "wilderness." Reinforcing the divide described in Chapter 2, women described the working forest as "productive," not "pristine," as trees "farmed" rather than "free," and as having been created through human labour and stewardship. Forests are improved through activities that boost their productive capacities for timber harvest. Hatcheries help to replace the fish lost due to habitat alteration and direct harvesting, just as silvicultural practices help to replace trees lost by logging.

Part of the rhetoric of the working forest is its contrast with urban ideals of wilderness. One woman expressed the contrasts in these words: "Most of the population is an urban population, and there's an urban mind-set that's out there ... They like to think of some place they can go to that's calm and peaceful and always stays the same, and so for people increasingly it's been 'Out there is the wilderness, the pristine forests,' ... and they have an idealized vision of what wilderness is and what the animals are like and what goes on." According to many of the women interviewed, the working forest is not beautiful, but it is authentic. Women returned the

"Take a tour of the Beaver Lake Forest." The tour is used as a means to promote the "working forest."

outsider's gaze by pointing out that most urbanites in British Columbia live in clear-cut landscapes. Ideas about the working forest, urban values, and hypocrisy came together in the frustrations of residents:

> It's just a big domino thing ... I don't think that a lot of people who live in the – how shall I put it – the largest clear-cut in British Columbia – Vancouver, Victoria – have got to get out and start looking at the trees, because all of the decisions are made in these places. And yet, I mean, a lot of us who are in the forest industry left [those places] because they do live in the biggest clear-cut there is. And not only that, they've never even planted a single tree back down there, you know what I mean? All they do is put down cement or pavement or whatever else. They don't even allow a tree to grow back. So if the population keeps cutting down the trees in those clear-cuts down there, maybe they're going to lose sight pretty soon of what a real forest looks like.

Illustrating its authenticity, the working forest also "fed" families. For example, "It was ugly for a little while. What, you might not think it's pleasing to the eye, but I have always thought, 'Look at that, a family is being fed.'" Many women reiterated this sentiment.

Those who employed the metaphor of the working forest made links to farming practices and agricultural landscapes. As in agriculture, the working forest requires the application of labour and technology to create a "working landscape." The current portrait within logging towns is of loggers as tree farmers. In Port McNeill, small flags can be purchased locally that insist "Port McNeill is a tree farming community." These small flags fly proudly in shop windows, beside tourism establishments, and outside the homes of ordinary people. One woman in the forestry industry described the metaphor in this way: "We're farmers; we're like a corn farmer." Many women, within and outside forestry families, also drew attention to this analogy (see also Table 5.1):

> I'm a farmer's daughter, and what we did on the Prairies, you go out and plant your crop, and you take it off, and then you turn around, and you plant the next one, and you just keep going the cycle. I mean, it's no different than the trees. It's just that the trees take a little longer in the cycle, but it's the same theory ... I'm not offended when they cut all the trees down. And I am in tourism. But I am not offended. Because it's just like a wheat farm to me ... And if they're doing it right and planting, the trees will come back again ... I'm glad they cut the trees down; now I can see the ruddy lake. I never saw the lake for twenty years. I didn't even know it was there until they cut the trees down for me. Now why would I be unhappy about that?

Another woman told me, "What really annoys me is people [who] say, 'You can't cut down a tree, a tree is a beautiful thing.' But yes, they are, but it's like a crop, it's like farming. Nobody tells the guy in Saskatchewan, 'Stop planting grain,' you know, my goodness." Both women were involved in tourism; both drew heavily on the analogy to agriculture to describe the working forest.

For residents, the showpiece of the working forest is the forestry tour.[3] Here pride in forestry communities and forestry culture emerges as women narrate the tour. It begins by exposing urban and frequently foreign ignorance:

> I went to [Vancouver] where ... there was a protest group, and there were two young lads, university age, and I went over to talk to them, and they informed me that we didn't have any bears left, and, you know, and what the logging was doing. I said, "Where are you from?" Well, they were from West Van[couver]. And I said, "Well, I haven't seen a bear on Granville Street ever, and [laughs] well, come on up, come and visit."

> We had one German fellow actually come into the [forestry] centre, and he said he had gone on a forest tour and loved it. He could not believe it, he learned so much ... Everybody that comes, they all say, "We are here to see the other side of the story." ... Well, come on out!

Recall (from Chapter 5) that one woman used her role as a tour bus operator to "educate" tourists about the hypocrisy of environmentalists in forestry debates. But the tour is not just for outsiders. As forestry families have been mobilized to protect themselves, forest companies have been actively involved in educational activities that promote the interests of industrial forestry within the local community. These activities provide the rhetorical tools that may be used to confront pro-environmental sentiments and perspectives. For example, one woman discussed how

> one company especially realized that, holy cow, you know, here we are getting all these people saying we are terrible people, and the kids are coming home going, "Dad, what are you doing? ... You are killing all the trees, and there won't be anything left, and you are a bad guy," and Dad goes, "You're kidding, right?" ... So they decided it would be a good idea to take the families out. There is a lot of women who don't get to see where their husbands work. So they took all the wives and children and loaded them on the bus, spent the week, took them out, let them get on the machines with their dads. Let them just see everything and answer all the kids' questions about wildlife concerns and everything. "This is what we do, this is how we have to do things, we are not out here killing

things." It was really good; I think it was good for the wives and good for the kids ... They are sick and tired of their husbands looking like the bad guys, right, and they are not. And everyone should be proud of their spouse and what they do ... You have to be proud of your husband, and the kids are going to be proud of your husband, and they are also going to be proud of you as a mother, because you have maintained them all these years.

In this way, the tour becomes an act of self-affirmation, a way to bring family members together socially and physically in an excursion that nurtures forestry culture. In turn, this culture provides broad-based support for and contributes to the social cohesion necessary to create unity of purpose for view by outsiders.

The family connection is an important element of these bonds. For some of the women interviewed, protection of family and community is an obvious and appropriate motivation for becoming involved in forestry protests. Documentation of the wise use movement in the United States suggests that workers there have used the rhetoric of family to engender sympathy for their position (e.g., Switzer 1996). In British Columbia, pro-forestry rallies have highlighted women who have warned of social dislocation and family breakdown if environmentalists are successful in their campaigns. And the notion of protecting families has run through several actions described in these chapters.

While protection of families and communities motivated some women to act, the use of family members in protest events was controversial on Vancouver Island. For example, during one of the focus groups, one woman asked others in the group, "Last summer when Greenpeace was active, were any of you contacted to come out if Greenpeace showed up on the north end of the island?" Others nodded in agreement. She went on, "Women and children? ... [The organizer] came to me and said, 'If Greenpeace comes here, women and children are coming out to meet them. No loggers, just women and children. Are you in?' I said, 'Oh, sure.'"

This strategy, however, was highly contested by others who were equally active in pro-forestry demonstrations. In the words of another activist, "Women up here have to become more political. And I don't mean doing what the environmentalists do. I'm totally against kids under twelve being at rallies. [Impersonating an environmentalist] 'My child will do what I want her to do, not because she knows what to do.' I don't mean for women to do that. I mean they have to get involved with what's happening."

Here the us/them dichotomy is applied to strategies used by the other side. No doubt young children have been involved in both environmental and industry rallies and protest events. Typically, environmentalists who have used young children do so to illustrate the needs of future generations.

Forestry advocates have used young children to draw attention to immediate concerns of social dislocation. And for some activists at least, the willingness to involve children directly separates those who seek a rational (and appropriate) means to resolve outstanding issues from those who seek to draw out emotional and less helpful responses among government policy makers and the general public.

Residents use other rhetorical strategies as well. Both forestry-town residents and environmental activists use the same rhetoric in defence of themselves to point out the differences that separate the two camps. For example, corporate funding and sponsorship of the wise use movement have been denounced by environmentalists to discredit their opponents (Rowell 1996; Switzer 1996). Residents of forestry communities also point to the large pool of funding that drives environmental campaigns. Thus, the lines between us and them are drawn by contrasting, long-standing stereotypes of environmentalists and loggers.

Rhetoric about Environmentalists

Part of the rhetoric of the working forest is intertwined with the rhetoric of work in the forest. Loggers, like farmers, are seen to be hardworking, honest folk whose physical labour has cultivated the forest and created the tree farm. This rhetoric is then contrasted with environmentalists themselves, who are allegedly supported through a multinational movement with enormous financial resources. For example, one woman argued that environmentalists can afford not to work because "The only reason they stay in existence is because people give them money. How do you think people can afford to go up to the mid-coast? Can you afford to go up to the mid-coast for a four-weeker? Yes, for a four-week holiday. How many of them are going there for the thrill? You know, they've got this big organization funding them." For some of the women, environmentalists are religious rather than rational: "The really, really heavy-duty right-wingers, you know, the extreme environmentalists, where it's become a faith. You don't argue religion. Those people are religious. That's what they believe. And it comes from something inside. It has nothing to do with common sense or anything like that. And you can't argue with those people. And for me, it was really important that it didn't become, that I could remain objective, keep it to technical, you know, instead of it becoming some spiritual thing, you know, it's them against me. Because you're a lot more believable, especially when you're telling the facts."

This woman recognized that the environmental movement has many parts. The "faith" component was identified at one extreme of the movement. Interestingly, it was characterized as an extreme of the right, not the left. And yet she believed that it was the extreme that had captured the attention of policy makers when, for the most part, negotiation was not an option. In contrast to the emotional and irrational character of her counterparts, she claimed her own contribution as one of objectivity based on her expertise as a professional forester.

Rhetoric also inverts stereotypes. For example, the media have drawn attention to threats and/or incidents of violence toward environmentalists by loggers. In contrast, on the North Island, the women in this study spoke of loggers as peaceful people who had experienced threats from environmentalists.

A: There are foresters, I know, who've had threats at home. Threats, where their parents have received threats.
Q: Really?
A: Their family members have received threats. You know, we talk about the environmentalists being threatened by the loggers. Well, hey, there's documented proof that it's happened the other way round ... You don't see a lot of documented proof of loggers doing it, other than hearsay, but there's people who have tape recordings of it happening. And in the [United] States, there was machinery being wrecked, and, well, let's wreck a piece of machinery. What happens when a guy gets on and he doesn't know? And I think you would see that is a real fear for some of the people here.

There were fears that their participation in protest events could lead to vandalism and injury: "Because there was a lot of fear, with all these people going down [to various rallies located to the south], leaving all these communities basically empty. Perfect for vandalism, theft, and robbery. I mean, a lot of us were also thinking, WC Squared [Western Canada Wilderness Committee], Sierra Club, they might be in there playing with the machines or something ... The thing is you always hear the kind of bad stories; you never know whether they're fully the truth or partially the truth." These fears helped women to place loggers and other forestry workers safely within a moral community. Clearly, this community was concerned for the safety of its members – the workers and families who inhabited forestry towns. But as the rhetoric about loggers attests, it also incorporated ideas about the love of nature that informed workers and residents more broadly.

Rhetoric about Loggers

Part of the rhetorical strategy is to reclaim the environmentalist position of "nature lovers." Indeed, the women interviewed expressed how those in forestry began their work with a love of the outdoors and the multiple ways in which their actions have supported good forestry practices over the years. Women explained how professional and waged workers in forestry worked in the woods because of their love of nature:

> You get tired of trying to explain to people; it's difficult sometimes when your husband's trained for many years and goes into forestry because he likes the outdoors, and we like nature and living where we do. And you're suddenly the bad guys and don't know what you're doing and don't care about future generations and don't care about your kids and stuff.
>
> We had one guy, an IWA [union] worker, who was actually out counting owls, surveying owls ... He really enjoyed it. We would run into him, and he'd say, "Oh, yeah, got a great horn today." There's so much knowledge, like those guys know the woods.
>
> So when we started, you know, my husband's office was a little closet, and we were the joke of the division ... He created selective logging down south island, ... and he went to Germany and kept bringing ideas back. And he was always leaving marshes where the birds were and leaving natural seed trees and trees where the owls were in. He was doing that without all that publicity. And as he ventured forth into that, guys did follow him.
>
> A lot of these men, they take pride in their work ... These guys are environmentalists. You know, they really care about their job and how they do it.
>
> People don't have much idea of what you're doing. You're not there just to make money. I went into forestry, you know, because I love the woods, and I always have.

In relating these stories, the women resisted the label of "blind supporter." In some cases, the concern for future generations was highlighted. Practising good forestry meant taking care of family. Some women spoke of the years of experiential knowledge that men acquired in their work, knowledge that was used to protect species and ecosystems. Other women, particularly foresters, were highly informed about forest ecology. One woman spoke in great detail about why the regulations associated with the Forest Practices Code were unsuitable to local conditions: "We're seeing books and things being written that may not even be applicable in the field, or they may not be applicable here. It may be fine down in Chilliwack, but it doesn't work in Port McNeill ... That's not providing a chance for the technical people up here to use their experience of what they should be doing." Finally, women outlined how they had tracked the work of environmental organizations, had travelled to other countries, and/or had undertaken research about the potential impacts of environmental positions on local communities. Nonetheless, while these stories spoke of a serious social divide between forestry workers and others, they also illustrated a marked spatial divide between regions of the province.

Creating Community Identity

Reinforcing the Rural/Urban Divide

Conflicts between loggers and environmentalists are social conflicts attributed not only to people but also to the places that they inhabit: "Well, I think, a lot of times, in larger centres, people don't really understand what happens in the logging community, and there is a stigma attached to being a so-called logger." Considerable scholarly research points to permeable boundaries between rural and urban regions (e.g., Bryant and Joseph 2001; Fitchen 1991). But for women living on the North Island, boundaries between the two are real and fixed. Despite their apparent proximity to and love of nature, rural communities are not considered the locus of environmentalism. More radical environmental sentiments are attributed to people living in urban environments, while more rational and informed environmental sentiments are located more firmly in rural settings.

The isolation from urban life has particular sites associated with it. One woman described her separation from an outdoor sporting goods store because it was viewed as a supporter for urban-based environmental values. When asked if she had ever been part of a conservation group, she replied,

> You have to really watch before you join. I remember years ago we went to Vancouver, ... [and my husband and his friend] went to Mountain Equipment Co-op. They went in there, and for five dollars they became a member. So they did. They thought, "What the heck?" because it's like all to do with outdoor gear and stuff, till we got the letter from them ... And I looked, and I said, "I don't believe it; they donate to groups that are trying to take our jobs away from us." So I won't have anything to do with Mountain Equipment Co-op now.

This "location" of environmental values in Vancouver is consistent with research elsewhere. For example, Thomas Dunk's (1994) research related to forest workers' culture revealed that, among loggers of northern Ontario, environmentalism was specifically located in the south. Perspectives of loggers and environmentalists were associated with other aspects of "region" and long-standing political relationships. Thus, there arose a spatial understanding of the categories of "environmentalism" and "environmentalist" that added a contemporary component to the ongoing sense of "northern alienation" from sites of economic and political power in the province (see also Weller 1977). Women from northern Vancouver Island also expressed this sense of alienation across a boundary that divided the North Island from its southern counterpart.

Universities were singled out as particular sites of environmental prejudice. One respondent in her twenties grew up in one of the logging camps on the North Island. During two summers, she worked near Port McNeill. She stated,

> I fully believe without our economy we will have no environment and without our environment we will have no economy ... Actually being at the university was very interesting ... I had heard a lot of horror stories ... about the faculty in the geography department being very green. In fact, I heard a story where a girl from a rural community ... up here, and she was in a geography class at [names university], and they were talking about social structure on rural settings. Being at the university, there should be freedom of speech. She said she did not believe what the prof said; she had grown up in a community, and this was how she thought. And the prof basically harassed her. "Oh, here's Miss Rural Community" from then on ... She eventually dropped out of class.

The woman indicated that her own experiences were more positive than those that she reported. Yet she remained wary about disclosing her own geographic origins: "I rarely get anyone in class saying I was from a rural community or from a small community from the north end of the island ... It's because you know what you're up against. You just want to get in there, get your marks, and get out. Fortunately, I didn't have any bad profs at all. There is one in environmental studies. I made sure I did not say where I was from. When I did on a trip, he really did not want to talk to me much."

This woman also described an experience of reverse discrimination in which one of her teaching assistants became infatuated with her experiences of being raised in some place other than an urban environment:

> But then the TA [teaching assistant] was infatuated that I had come from a rural community. She was the one part of WC Squared [Western Canada Wilderness Committee], dragging Stumpy across Canada.[4] She was totally fascinated that I had grown up in a logging camp. She wanted to know all about it. Like it was the most unique thing in the world. For myself, I'm

like, "It's just a place I grew up," nothing really unique about it ... One time we went to the bunkhouse, and we had the cook cooking for us, ... and she [the TA] was looking around at all the pictures saying they are so neat, can't you just imagine a big, burly logger walking through the door, going ga ga. I'm looking at her. I said, "You sound like a pirate, not a logger. You know, you're so much against log cutting, you have no idea about the people." And that's really frustrating, just like you see all these people from Germany and Belgium.

During a focus group, I asked women to respond to issues raised during interviews. I asked them to help me interpret different pro-industry organizations and sentiments. A log scaler who had dropped out of school at the age of fourteen described a conversation with a university professor from greater Vancouver:

I was in Vancouver at that time, and I had an interesting conversation with a university professor at [names university] ... And it was real comical because he taught history ... So we got talking ... We got sort of into a general discussion about the forest industry, and he painted a picture of the poor dumb logger being victimized by the big bad company and how they're [the companies] endangering our livelihood and our clean air and our clean water and our trees and blah – he went on and on and on, and basically the big bad forest company was responsible for every bad thing that ever happened to the environment. And I came along with "Well, I don't think that's necessarily true, because the loggers all have training in Forest Practices Code, and they know that they're liable to some degree for any infringements or whatever that are in contravention of the Code, and they're all given training." ... They gave us those courses through the company so that we would know all the classifications of all the streams and our rights and the regulations ... I said, "They're way more informed than you think." And I said, "They're way more aware because it's their backyard." I said, "People that live in the city don't understand what is going on there because all they're doing is feeling an emotional reaction to something." ... Anyway, he thought I was some kind of, ah, humanitarian studies teacher ... He had a name for it. And I said, "No, I'm a logger." And he went [makes a surprised face]. Anyway, it was kind of comical. Well, he thought I was something to do with ... teaching ... But I'm not educated. So I didn't know. I just knew that he thought I was something I wasn't, but I straightened him out pretty quick.

In confronting the stereotype of the logging dupe, this woman also challenged the site of knowledge. She challenged the notion that only those with university educations can understand the dynamics of ecology, economics, policy, and regulation. However, she also played up stereotypes herself, identifying urban environmentalists as those who respond emotionally rather than rationally to logging.

Later during the focus group, I said, "The forest is a provincewide resource. So you could argue that environmentalists have as much right to say whether it gets cut. Environmentalists from Vancouver even have as much right to say whether or not to cut it as people living here. Do you want to respond to that?" Thus, she responded, "They don't have the information to make a decision. Half the time they are unemployed hippies or whatever. They've got nothing better to do, and the other half, they're bleeding hearts with only half the information." In this case, "the other" was uninformed and emotional, in contrast to her rational and more knowledgeable position. She was not immune from applying a simple stereotype of the other to those who might have opposed her position.

Another woman suggested that the segregation of rural and urban people has arisen because they have lost touch with one another: "Hopefully, people will start to appreciate the forest industry ... The resource industries are the only true generator of wealth that we have ... Somehow or another that has been lost ... Somewhere the resource industries have lost touch. Or the urbanites have lost touch, and, you know, we've got to gather that back up somehow. Develop the appreciation, get them in touch with the farm, the forest. There's the Bambi approach ... My kids would eat Bambi." These women emphasized that on both sides of the debate participants operate on partial information. Resolution will require moving beyond the stereotypes and toward an honest appraisal of the current circumstances and future possibilities.

Cracks in Community Consensus
But to leave this chapter before illustrating other sentiments would be to paint a partial picture. Cracks in community consensus could be found in both the rhetoric and the activity of these residents, many of whom were long-term members of forestry communities. While stream work dominated among environmental activities (see Chapter 5), loggers and other residents engaged in other activities. One case was a campaign against the use of aerial pesticides in the industry that was taken up by a local environmental organization: "They [companies] were going to spray pesticides on the island ... And there were a lot of loggers who are really not interested in pesticide use, herbicide spraying. But they couldn't really say anything because they're afraid they're going to lose their jobs or whatever if they oppose it. So they [individual loggers] affiliated with us, although a lot of them never bought memberships because they didn't want their name on anything, but they talked to us about what was happening out in

the woods ... We did win on the aerial spraying issues." A small number of women interviewed were involved in other successful environmental campaigns ranging from opposing the location of a ferrochromium smelter in the region to initiating local recycling programs.

Some women simply refused to accept the rhetoric that has insulated and comforted residents of forestry communities. In the exchange documented below, activism occurred within the interview itself. The exchange took place between one of the community researchers and her subject. The interviewer was a local person with links to the industry. She went beyond the bounds of appropriate protocol in an attempt to lead her interviewee in a particular direction. The result, however, is instructive.

A: You're going to see fifty-five-year-old men who've never done anything but log have to be retrained. It's going to have to be dealt with, and it's going to be very big. Everybody knows this is coming. It's either going to end up that the IWA [International Woodworkers of America] is going to give people early pensions and only the young people will be working, or it's going to create a huge catastrophe. It'll be the catalyst for many problems within families because the province has permitted these tree farm licences to be logged at such irresponsible rates that there will be a cause and effect to it. There is going to be a domino effect ... It's going to be very impacting on these people because they are very sedentary in their ways. They don't look. They have tunnel vision, many of these old-time loggers. They've been doing the same thing since they were fourteen years old. They don't know any other way.

Q: It's who they are ... It's their identity.

A: Yes.

Q: You know, ... we were talking about changing the word *logging* ... We're not a logging community, we want to be a tree-farming community ...

A: I'm not into semantics very much. I mean, it is what it is. And they are being responsible to a certain degree now. I think there's a lot more that could happen. They're still logging too big of a clear-cut in some places. People just aren't being able to see where they're doing it, unless you're flying over it, and believe me I have, on the North Island. And there's a lot of stuff that goes on under the table that still has to be dealt with. And I think the logging companies are very good at getting away with whatever they want to. So there has to be a better catch-all mechanism to stop this from happening. And it will happen. It will happen in our lifetime too. And there will be such a huge effect to it that it will be a question of either you shut down permanently or you fix this stuff. No more oil spills in our watersheds, no more this and that. It's all dangerous stuff ... Environmental issues should be dealt with up here, even by the forest companies. I don't think they're dealing with them well enough. That's something that I personally feel. I feel the environmentalists are doing a good job by being their watchdogs. I really do.

The interviewee had lived in the community for most of her life. Her partner was a heavy-duty mechanic who had worked for the forest industry for nineteen years. Her whole family – including her father, father-in-law, and husband's family – worked in the forest industry. She also had a close relation on the provincial executive of Canadian Women in Timber. Yet she refused to be led along the acceptable community pathway. She continued to affix responsibility on the government and companies for practices that were not environmentally sustainable. She recognized that the industry would require wholesale restructuring, even while she explained that those who would bear personal costs would be the workers themselves.

Another woman, partnered with a logger, also pointed out cracks in the shield of solidarity. She expressed relief when she found a local group that held similar feminist and pro-environmental viewpoints. This woman said, "I used to feel that I was the only one. I felt totally isolated because I did not fit in. Now I know there are a lot of people here who feel the same way. Not everybody follows the popular line." Later she told us, "There is not a lot of critical thinking going on here." Then, turning to the work of the Forest Alliance (established by and for the large-scale companies) specifically, she said:

It's a propaganda movement; they have hired huge publicists, and you see the results here, because everyone is getting behind it. There used to be mixed feeling about North Island Citizens for Shared Resources, because we used to call it Share the Stumps. Everyone did it jokingly because most people here had the perception that they really did not want to share. They were for logging it all, burn it all, but now everyone is getting behind them. The publicity by the Forest Alliance is working, that's real sad to see, I don't know what to do about it.

But she refused to lay blame with the loggers themselves. Rather, she argued that forest companies have failed to meet their commitments to stewardship:

The Forest Practices Code has never been enforced up here; now I don't think it ever will. The companies have made changes, but they have made it sound like they did it on their own. They've done it under pressure from their own men partly ... Now the old growth has gone, for the most part ... And whatever is left of the old growth are in areas where the people are fighting trying to save it. So the companies are now playing a political game, where they are pitting the loggers against the environmental movement and are constantly working to that end.

Moreover, this woman suggested that not only had the relationship between government and industry been changing but also the "social contract" between company and worker had been dramatically altered:

[My partner's company] ... used to be run by an old-time logger. I remember ... [names logger], an old-time logger. He knew logging inside out, men respected him for it. Even if they did not like him, they knew that he knew what he was doing, and he cared about the men. Now they are run by the accountants, accountants who care about bottom line, you know, how much have we spent on operations this year. "How can we make it look like we give a shit about the guys, without spending any money?" You know, and finally the morale was so bad a few years ago they have finally come back to spending a little money. Like having picnics and Christmas. When I first moved here, the guys would get a toy for each of his kids and a turkey every Christmas. They would have a Christmas party thrown for them, and they were taken care of ... The logging itself has changed, the jobs have changed, because the wood, for the most part, the wood has got so much smaller.

Her position was clearly not allied with a singular position of community solidarity. Nonetheless, she continued to support her partner and other workers, placing responsibility on the shoulders of the industry rather than on the individuals who worked within it. Any attempt to classify her support, therefore, is muddied by the crisscrossing lines of allegiance and defiance.

Community, Identity, and Complexity

While the history of settler occupation on northern Vancouver Island is short, the culture of forestry contains traditions that have provided the matrix for a community identity. Although women have not been strongly represented in waged work in forestry, social networks of family and friends as well as the social contract between company and community have extended the range of forestry communities beyond the payrolls of individual workers. Kinship networks linked women to forestry beyond the geographic communities in which they lived; many women had lived their lives in many locations, their fathers or partners leading the way (Halseth 1999). For a generation after the Second World War, companies were known for their paternalistic practices, such as providing company-owned housing (e.g., Woss), recreational facilities (e.g., Port McNeill), and family assistance programs (all communities) as well as sponsoring specific community activities and events (e.g., little-league teams, forestry centres, forestry days). All these activities extended the common interests shared by employees beyond the wage relationship and forged social cohesion among family and community members. These activities also extended the notion of forestry communities to include workers and families who shared in a culture that reached beyond individual geographic locations. These collective activities and institutions, then, created the stuff – the matrix of forestry culture – from which dogged loyalty was crafted. They also became the stuff that women shaped and defended when they took stands to support forestry culture despite their multiple exclusions from it.

When communities appeared to be under threat, forestry culture rose in determined opposition to changes in land allocation and land use practices. The lines between them and us were drawn most obviously between environmentalists on the outside and community residents on the inside. Environmentalists were considered outsiders both physically and philosophically. But they were not the only outsiders. Unions, firms, and even government administrators and politicians made decisions in Vancouver and Victoria on the basis of industry and provincewide considerations. The outsiders also became targets of local animosity.

Specific protest events – notably at Clayoquot Sound – highlighted divisions between insiders and outsiders. Outsiders came to organize, manage, interpret, and simply be part of the dispute. Police officers, judges, and lawyers were required to contain and adjudicate it. Environmental and union spokespeople along with journalists and photographers interpreted and displayed the event in ways that their distant audiences might appreciate. For women on northern Vancouver Island, Clayoquot demonstrated an unequal dialogue and exchange between forestry families and the broader urban culture in which the provincial government and international environmental interests were entwined. The experience set the tone for smaller-scale protest events and the ongoing rhetoric that followed. Smaller-scale demonstrations (e.g., the yellow flag at the Port Hardy airport or the barge incident on the North Island) maintained the separation between rural and urban, local and global, inside and outside. Once the issues were represented in this fashion, there was no going back. Local issues had become global ones. Sentiments had hardened. There were few mechanisms to bring the controversies back to the local level and to reconcile them through negotiation.

In addition to sharing an identity related to working conditions and forestry practices within the local community, women shared values, norms, and perspectives related to forestry beyond their geographic communities.

In this study, many women expressed a strong sense of identification with loggers in other places in British Columbia and the American Pacific Northwest. Many shared the perception that the public did not appreciate the importance, danger, or difficulty of forestry work. They saw the predominant occupation and the associated culture of forestry as maligned and embattled. Their fight was one of "insiders" and "outsiders," with these notions holding particular social and geographical connotations. Outsiders were specifically urban environmentalists who simultaneously demanded use of forest products (e.g., for home building) and access to pristine wilderness. While women acknowledged that forestry jobs had changed due to economic and societal developments outside environmental activism, they still saw ENGOs as a visible target, for which there was a clear political constituency, and an apparent "common enemy." These perceptions shaped women's activism and were clearly intertwined in their shared understandings of, and attachments to, the paid work and the local culture of forestry.

These attachments have contributed to clear demarcations of us versus them. Or have they? In the last two chapters, I attempt to illustrate that forestry-town women can lay claim to multiple identities. Therefore, they can speak with authority on the impacts of changes in forestry on their lives in multiple arenas and relations – as workers, mothers, residents, and community members. In this chapter, I have shown how solidarity has been constructed, but I have also illustrated cracks in its composition. As I review this chapter, I realize that researchers never uncover complete identities or perspectives. It is likely that, while this research has unearthed multiple roles, relations, identities, and ideas, other elements of forestry-town life have been obscured or removed from view. It is with this understanding of the partiality of the researcher's gaze that I begin the next chapter.

"21 percent of the island means 32.5 percent from the North Island." A protest sign, used during protest at the BC Legislature, is planted in the front yard of a research participant.

7
Fitting In: Making a Place for Gender in Environmental and Land Use Planning

> On Vancouver Island about 95 percent of resource workers are male, and about 80 percent of them are married. This suggests that there are about 15,000 women on Vancouver Island whose spouses work for resource industries. In many, if not most, cases *women* carry the brunt of family stresses associated with economic trauma.
>
> – CORE (1994a, 205; emphasis added)

> What should we make of the demonstration this week by thousands of loggers *and their families* at the legislature in Victoria?
>
> – Stephen Owen (1994, A23; emphasis added)

> Why are you here now, one and one-half weeks *after* CORE has been announced?
>
> – Leah F. Vosko and Lynn Bueckert (1994, 17; emphasis added)

Engendering Land Use Planning

In Chapters 4 through 6, I argued that policy makers, academics, and even community leaders have been slow to identify and respond to the issues and concerns attributed to and/or made by women in forestry communities. While government agencies have recognized that the social impacts of changes in land use and environmental policy are significant for both women and men, most efforts to assist communities during transition have been directed toward supporting male workers through employment adjustment and (re)training programs. While this is a laudable and necessary objective, it is entirely insufficient. Social concerns about transition that have been ascribed to women (e.g., those related to women's employment and training, family stress, and other social services affected during land use change) are considered "women's burden" and frequently not addressed. In short, planning initiatives and transition programs first segregate issues into gender categories and second assign the greatest need for and support of the interests attributed to men. The Commission on Resources and Environment (CORE), and the response that it engendered, were no exception.

Paid employment has become the primary focus of transition strategies proposed by government, community, and public interest groups alike. By focusing on paid employment while simultaneously reducing access to social programs, government policies have reinforced a gender bias that has permeated forestry communities. In the first epigraph above, CORE counted only those women who were connected to male resource workers as spouses. This ideological bias has real material effects on women and their partners who suffer job losses. In the second epigraph, CORE Commissioner Stephen Owen reflected on the broad-based community opposition to his recommendations a couple of weeks after his report was submitted. Women figured only indirectly in this rumination by virtue of their dependent relation to loggers or primary wage earners. This bias was reflected in the individuals and groups invited to participate in the planning process that led to the recommendations. The third epigraph reflects the frustration of women living on northern Vancouver Island when two consultants were hired two weeks *after* the final report was submitted to identify the potential social impacts of the plan for women in that region. As a consequence of opposition to the gender blindness of CORE's process and recommendations, consultants were brought in to engage in "damage control" even as the provincial government approved CORE's recommendations. Although the consultants identified a range of social issues that affected women and to which women might contribute, the government failed to provide any additional services or supports to address these concerns.

Perhaps the chronology of the quotations is not surprising. Planning, as an academic and a practical exercise, has been slow in general to adopt feminist perspectives, perpetuating current representations and priorities and helping to obscure their male bias (Eichler 1995; Little 1994; MacGregor 1995). According to Sherilyn MacGregor, by being locked within rationalist frameworks, "planners have adhered to theories and conventions of practice that assume gender neutrality ... Planning efforts ... have either failed to recognize the specific impacts of ... plans on women or have made assumptions about what would be best for women based on narrow and rather stereotyped understandings of women's lives" (28). MacGregor developed a three-part framework that describes the deepening understanding of feminist scholarship related to planning issues. This framework provides a useful strategy for evaluating the gendered dimensions of the CORE process.

First, feminist critiques of planned environments focus on the impacts of planning on women's lives. Here analysis of planning decisions can illuminate differential issues and remedies accorded to women and men. Second, feminist critiques of planning processes draw attention to how, and with whose participation, decisions about the planned environment are made. Attention, then, to the planning process can identify which interests had the power to be heard and addressed during planning initiatives. Third, feminist critiques of planning epistemologies question planners' values and underlying assumptions with respect to the forms of knowledge that have been admitted into planning practice. In this case, analysis of language and society is necessary to situate planning exercises within broader norms and values of society. Each element identifies a deeper layer that illustrates how planning processes themselves are embedded within and perpetuate structural biases of the broader society. In this chapter, I examine the process and recommendations of CORE in light of this three-part framework.

Planning as a Political Process

To claim that CORE was biased in executing its mandate is to contend that environmental and land use planning is not merely a technical exercise but also a political one. Environmental and land use planning is political in two senses. First, planning requires the articulation of choice among different alternatives. In the mainstream, it is an exercise based on the peaceful resolution of conflicting values and interests, so it requires politics to reconcile these differences. Second, planning involves addressing issues that are often highly contentious and open to public debate, particularly where changes in the status quo are proposed. It is important to note that conflict is a normal, even desirable, element of environmental planning because it arises from legitimate, differing values, interests, hopes, expectations, and priorities of individuals or societal groups (Mitchell 1997). Conflict brings these differences out, often contributing to new and original ideas for their resolution.

One perspective on planning suggests that, in mediating conflict and developing consensus among competing interests, planning agencies should be considered "referees" (Painter 1991) or neutral regulators of conflict operating to organize, regulate, and mediate in the public interest (Cloke and Little 1990). This dominant conception is frequently tied to pluralist assumptions concerning the power relations among groups involved in planning processes (e.g., Jamal and Getz 1995; Jordan 1989). Pluralists argue that the interests of any one group cannot dominate a process because power is widely distributed, fragmented, and dispersed (see Cloke and Little 1990; Dye 1986). In contemporary land use planning processes, these assumptions about power and the role of state agencies have frequently been married to idealistic visions about the desirability and ability of interest groups to work cooperatively to reach consensus about mutual problems. According to researchers, planners, and managers, the search for and/or attainment of consensus will lead to solutions to environmental and land use problems in which conflicting objectives and interests are "balanced" (Brown 1996; Mitchell 1995).

In contrast, I view planning agencies as much more than neutral arbiters. Assumptions about the equal distribution of power ignore how the interests and participation of groups are influenced by structural and procedural conditions used in the process. These conditions can act as constraints to effective and equitable participation, for example, through the types of criteria set to determine access to participation or through the inclusion or exclusion of certain types of data. Consequently, they ignore the extent to which interest groups have varying access, and unequal capacity, to influence decision making. Furthermore, they do not explicitly address the nature of relations between the government and specific interests (for discussions specifically related to forestry in British Columbia, see Cashore et al. 2001; Hayter 2000; Wilson 1997). Consequently, I view planning agencies such as CORE as purposeful and influential players in determining the nature of the processes and the outcomes (in line with Dye 1986; Hollinshead 1990; Reed 1997b; Rees 1990). When viewed in this light, CORE's work – either intentionally or unintentionally – reflected, reinforced, and/or reproduced social norms and inequalities in the dominant structure of power relations.

When first established, CORE adopted a broad perspective on land use and planning. Its definition of "land" included all "aquatic lands, natural resources, natural processes and people and social systems on the land," while "planning" was recognized as "the process that attempts to integrate the interdependent parts of sustainability: society, economy and environment" (Brown 1996, xxi). CORE also explained land use planning as a social process that incorporates concerns for both natural and social systems (Brown 1996). This broad perspective was consistent with academic perspectives on planning that emphasize its fundamental political character (e.g., Briassoulis 1989; Friedmann 1987).

CORE developed a Land Use Charter (the Charter) that embraced these premises and provided a set of principles to achieve social, environmental, and economic sustainability in the province as well as to guide decision-making processes (CORE 1994b). CORE also viewed its commitment to social sustainability broadly, incorporating elements associated with social equity and quality of life (see Chapter 2).

CORE attempted a breakthrough in the adversarial context that characterized land allocation and management in the province. Its vision of integrating social, economic, and environmental considerations into land use planning was progressive. CORE made important advances toward the objective of participatory land use planning through the establishment of new procedures for shared negotiation and consensus-based decision making. Despite its progressive efforts, though, CORE reinforced inequalities within Canadian society. One of them related to gender relations and stereotypes of forestry-town women. These effects were neither intentional nor the work of one or two individuals or recommendations: Rather, CORE's planning *model* reflected and reinforced dominant gender stereotypes of women and men living in rural, forestry-based communities.

CORE's model was based on shared or consensus decision making among sector interests (BCRTEE 1991; CORE 1994a; Pinkerton 1989), with CORE acting as a (quasi-) independent agency to facilitate the process.[1] The argument for use of the sectoral coalition model was that it allows for broad public participation, while government provision of resources (e.g., data or expertise) facilitates consensus decisions (BCRTEE 1991). CORE organized these interests into coalitions (or sectors) based on its assessment of their common interests, attitudes, and priorities (Brown 1996). Each sector, or coalition of groups, developed a common statement of the interests that it sought to have addressed during the planning process. A spokesperson was then elected by the sector to represent those interests at the negotiating table. This spokesperson was accountable to the constituency that formed the sector and was obligated to carry forward group views and promote specific interests during negotiations. Figure 7.1 illustrates how spokespersons and sectors were brought together.

The Vancouver Island CORE (VICORE) process was the first of four regional processes conducted by CORE in the early 1990s. For the VICORE process, fourteen sectors were formed to serve as the negotiating table. The mandate for the VICORE table was to prepare a set of recommendations for CORE to present to the BC government (the province). Specifically, this mandate included the "allocation of resource lands through development of a land use designation system" and the "development of transition and mitigation strategies for all those, including communities, affected by land use allocations" (CORE 1994b, 11). The table met for forty-seven days over twelve months, from November 1992 until November 1993. In February 1994, after the VICORE table failed to reach consensus on a set of recommendations in the time allotted, the commissioner, using the work of the table, completed plan recommendations and presented them to the government (CORE 1994a). This proposed plan increased the amount of land for conservation purposes and contained a transition strategy to assist forestry workers in dependent communities to adjust to reduced access to timber resources. With minor modifications, the plan was accepted by the province, and new initiatives were set in motion on the basis of its recommendations. In June 1994, the province approved a land use plan adopting most of the substantive decisions made by CORE (Government of British Columbia 1994). Actual land allocation was a much less publicized process. After the CORE recommendations were accepted, years of individual negotiation ensued between the province and private and public interests. In February 2000, the Land Use Coordination Office announced that the Vancouver Island Land Use Plan was finally complete.[2]

The most contentious recommendation of the CORE report was an increase in the proportion of protected areas from 10.3 percent to 13 percent of the island's land base. The main impacts of this allocation would be felt within the rural resource communities dependent upon forestry. CORE estimated that timber harvest would be reduced by about 800,000 cubic metres (or 6 percent) per year for four years, with about three-quarters of this reduction attributable to newly protected areas. This reduction in volume was estimated to reduce employment in harvesting and processing by about 570 person years of employment annually (239 and 331 in each sector) and a further 331 indirectly.[3] The revenue lost to the province would range between $15 and $18 million annually, excluding potential costs of additional provincial income support payments and compensation costs for timber rights (CORE 1994a, 194-96).

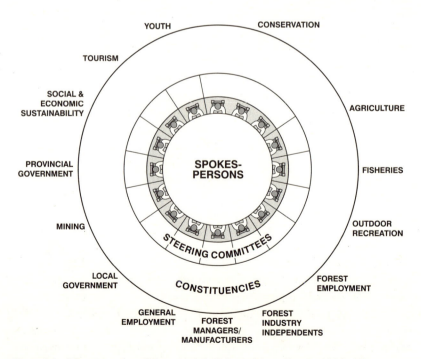

Figure 7.1 The sectoral coalition model. (Adapted from Brown 1996, 46.)

The transition strategy proposed by CORE to address these impacts contained four substantive initiatives. First, it suggested that increased employment opportunities could be realized from enhanced forest management, including more sensitive harvesting practices, enhanced silvicultural practices, and forest, stream, and logging road rehabilitation. Second, it recommended ways of assisting older employees toward early retirement. Third, it suggested training for forest workers related to new silvicultural techniques, forest ecology, new regulatory requirements and harvest systems, as well as value-added manufacturing. And fourth, it encouraged the province to increase support for economic diversification by focusing on opportunities for value-added manufacturing by direct investment in community development banks or by financing new plants and machinery or forest-related research (CORE 1994a, 212-17). The government's response was to announce new program initiatives to reflect the employment and training components of the transition strategy outlined by CORE.

A Gender Analysis of the Vancouver Island Land Use Plan

Despite the appearance of comprehensiveness, CORE's representation of women's experiences of land use changes omitted and/or marginalized important elements of women's lives. The recommendations made by CORE illustrated that it produced static, dated, even "traditional" interpretations of forestry-town women. At the heart of this analysis is the way in which the social component of sustainability was conceptualized and made operational. In this regard, one can trace a continued narrowing of focus in CORE's plan. Although rather vaguely defined, the social component of sustainability was clearly identified at the outset. Its main components appeared to be concerned with social equity and the quality of life for people living in rural resource communities, suggesting a concern for both employment and broader social contributions to community life. Despite identifying the importance of "the social," CORE's operative definition of it became more narrow. Its efforts became focused on employment, particularly on the jobs lost in the harvesting and processing sectors. This focus had at least two consequences. First, the social and cultural contributions to community life became excluded from any serious analysis, and thus considerations for the transition strategy were missing. Second, women's productive roles within the economies of these places were once again marginalized (see also Chapter 4). In the discussion that follows, my purpose is not to develop a detailed analysis of the plan but to generate a broader understanding of how the recommendations accounted for, and sought to address, the changes that the plan would bring to the material conditions and social positions of women within rural resource communities.[4] By doing so, I suggest that CORE reproduced dominant stereotypes about women's dependent positions within forestry and their attendant social and community interests.

Identifying and Defining the Social within Sustainability

To its credit, CORE noted that "the social impacts are not experienced by 'average communities' or 'average individuals', but are unevenly distributed through communities and among individuals" (CORE 1994a, 201). The commission noted that "the social issue associated with this re-allocation of land is not so much the gross magnitude of impacts but the fact that they will be concentrated in forest-dependent communities and among their residents" (200). In recognition of this concentration of effects, CORE concluded that, "as a matter of equity and in order to reconcile environmental with economic and social sustainability, a transition strategy is essential to respond to the needs of those communities and individuals who will be affected by the implementation of this plan" (209). Here, in the identification of impacts and the preamble to the transition strategy, social sustainability holds equal footing with economic and environmental components. These statements lead the reader to believe that the transition strategy will be broadly conceived, dealing with the multiple dimensions of change affecting people's lives. Yet, despite a broad identification of "the social component," two strands of social sustainability emerged as worthy of CORE's attention. The first was the concern for the family and community stresses associated with the economic dislocation of workers. The second was the concern for job losses associated with the proposed plan.

At the outset of the social impact analysis, CORE attempted to calculate the magnitude of the social problem,[5] in part, by counting (some) women in. As noted at the beginning of this chapter, CORE identified about 15,000 women on Vancouver Island who might be affected by its recommendations by virtue of their relationships with partners in resource industries. This estimate only considered women connected to male resource workers as spouses and did not acknowledge women's work within the forestry sector or in support of forestry. Therefore, the figure not only underestimated the number of women living in the region – that is, it did not include widows, single women, women with same-sex partners, or even women with spouses in the nonforestry sector – but also illustrated how CORE placed women, in its conception of the region, in secondary and dependent roles to the Real Workers.[6]

CORE noted that the disproportionate stress associated with economic dislocation would be felt by women. In this regard, the report suggested that its information about women might be "useful in designing social services support to better respond to the needs and roles of women in communities affected during economic change" (CORE 1994a, 205). Thus, while the impacts were potentially significant, they were not considered an imperative for government action. They did not form part of the recommended transition strategy, nor did they signal the need for specific policies or programs to address such impacts.

Beyond the family unit, CORE stated that, where communities (e.g., those on the North Island) are heavily dependent on forestry, the loss of forest industry activity would reduce the funding available from employment and tax revenues for locally financed community services. Here CORE quoted another study, which argued that under such circumstances community services become increasingly stressed: "A persuasive perception, voiced by people who administer mental health agencies, operate programs for the elderly, run youth programs, coordinate services to the handicapped, or provide emergency food ... is that there are more people with needs and more needs than there are services to meet them" (CORE 1994a, 202). Yet the obvious inferences were not made. First, the gendered division of labour leads more women than men to take up social service positions (see Chapter 4). This is particularly so in resource-dependent towns (Marchak 1983; Seitz 1995). As services are cut, it is (predominantly) women who experience the stresses as laid-off or remaining workers (see Chapters 3 and 4). Beyond the paid workplace, those who undertake the bulk of dependent care in the home are overwhelmingly women (Evans and Wekerle 1997; Jennissen 1997; Sachs 1994). Instead of fully considering the potential impacts on local caregivers, the report moves immediately to discuss patterns of out-migration and impacts on forestry workers left behind.

Thus, in CORE's recommendations, the social problem was not even properly identified, let alone addressed. To the extent that "the social problem," as defined by CORE as family and community stresses, was considered at all, specific recommendations were not made. Rather, they were considered outside the scope of land use planning. Clearly, CORE viewed these issues as sufficient cause for hand-wringing rather than action.

Eclipsing the Social within Sustainability

As one reads CORE's report, it is clear that employment became the operative definition of social sustainability. It also became the strategic issue to which policy attention was given and program recommendations were made. Yet this rather narrow definition of the social became even further attenuated by the assumption that, while all jobs were important in maintaining local income levels, only men's jobs in the harvesting or processing sector were worthy of transition programs. This focus is curious given that CORE recognized that women contribute economically to the survival of forestry communities that are currently organized around, but cannot depend on, forestry as the sole source of income.

Within the forestry sector, one might expect CORE to have examined the specific factors that inhibit or enable women's retraining and re-employment. Although women are fewer in number than men, women in production-related jobs tend to have less senior positions and are more vulnerable to changes in technology.[7] There is also some evidence that women are more likely to lose their jobs as a result of plant restructuring (Grass and Hayter 1989; Hayter and Barnes 1992). In the appendices of CORE's report, a report made to the Ontario government is included, and it documents labour adjustment for laid-off workers. The Ontario report documented that labour adjustment was more difficult for women than men, not because of family responsibilities, but because, when all other factors are controlled for in the analysis, "women ... take a greater cut in pay compared with men when they are displaced ... They experience significantly more long-term unemployment and earn less when they do land a job. Because of this, there is justification for special efforts to ensure that women have full access to labour adjustment services" (Ontario Ministry of Labour n.d., 75-76). Thus, despite an obvious awareness of the problem, CORE did not provide for any specific services that might have addressed these needs.

Beyond direct forestry jobs, women contribute to forestry communities through their involvement in indirect and induced employment (see Chapter 4). Even CORE (1994a, 195) calculated that 331 or 37 percent of indirect or induced full-time jobs would be lost as a result of its recommendations.[8] This is the same number of jobs as that estimated to be lost in the harvesting sector. Unfortunately, CORE did not attempt to identify the number of jobs held by women and men in indirect and induced sectors. However, its report did note that "there are a disproportionate number of women living in resource-dependent communities in lower paying service industry jobs. Such jobs will likely be among any indirect or induced job losses brought about by this Plan. Where that occurs, the loss of income to women, and in many cases to their families, can be very serious and difficult to replace" (205). Here is where CORE's analysis stopped. One need not expect CORE to have considered the consequences of this observation for family relations, decision making, or aspirations or even the importance of female support for maintaining the culture of forestry communities; however, one does expect CORE to have evaluated the economic dependability and distribution of these other sources of income and the effects that these losses would have on the economic and social fabric of these places.

Despite CORE's earlier recognition of both the economic and the social contributions of women to community life, recommendations for economic transition failed to address these contributions. Its short-term focus was allegedly placed on supporting individuals and communities in generating new jobs in forestry, while the longer-term objective was to identify means for greater value-added production and diversification of local economies. Yet all of the efforts of the transition strategy were directed toward workers (i.e., male forestry workers) in the harvesting and processing sectors. The de facto purpose of the planning exercise became narrowed just at the point where women become most prominent in the social life of rural resource communities. By CORE's own calculations, indirect employment impacts would be felt by women in large numbers. Why, then, were there no employment strategies directed toward them?

Furthermore, to the extent that land allocation had become a strategic environmental issue in the sense used by Maria Garcia-Guadilla (1995), the main concern was for "workers," defined in operational terms as workers directly employed in harvesting and processing. Not surprisingly, the transition strategy focused on these workers to the general disadvantage of women. In contrast, concerns for the quality of life within the affected localities were considered "community issues" outside the purview of the land use strategy. Beyond employment and production considerations, the social needs, as evidenced in stresses within families and upon social service agencies, were also considered beyond the scope of planning for transition. The social impacts were documented as family and community stresses; however, as the lead epigraph of this chapter indicates, these impacts were simply recorded as part of an information base. They were not used to develop specific elements of the transition strategy. As a consequence, women's needs were narrowly ascribed at best or completely omitted, resulting in an uneven distribution of potential impacts upon, and remedies for, men and women.

Analyzing the Follow-up Study of Women on the North Island

In this context, perhaps it is not surprising that, upon public announcement of the CORE report, women on northern Vancouver Island protested the exclusion of their interests. Almost immediately after the provincial government endorsed the plan, private consultants were contracted by the Ministry of Employment and Investment to determine the impacts of the Vancouver Island Land Use Plan on women, their homes, their workplaces, and their communities as well as to assess their proposals for economic transition and training (Vosko and Bueckert 1994). The report was intended to provide specific proposals as well as a model upon which to design research and policy programs applicable to other communities affected by land use plans and, more generally, communities facing economic adjustment. I turn to this report to identify insights about women's lives that were missing from the CORE report and to consider directions for future research about environmental and land use planning that includes the experiences and perspectives of women.

Leah Vosko and Lynn Bueckert (1994) met with fifty-two women in Port McNeill and surrounding communities between 4 and 12 July 1994, within two weeks of the government's final announcement. Women who participated included provincial and municipal government workers, teachers, First Nations, economic development officers, counsellors, day care operators, private contractors, wives of loggers (the report's terminology), tourism operators, fishers, realtors, and small-business owners.[9] According to Vosko and Bueckert, women in the region had diverse reactions to the CORE report. Some actually welcomed its recommendations. Others believed that it did not go far enough in terms of establishing protected areas, while others expressed concerns about the impacts that it would have on families. Some women expressed relief that a decision had been made so that they could plan for the future. Despite this diversity, there was a consensus among the women that they had not been consulted during the CORE process and that ongoing research about the needs of women in communities affected by land use policies was required.

The Vosko and Bueckert (1994) report revealed that, while CORE's definition of the social became narrowed in practice by CORE, women's perspectives on environmental and land use planning were wide-ranging. Beginning with employment, the authors argued that a transition strategy that incorporated the concerns of women of the North Island would have some shared elements as well as some distinctly different dimensions from those that were proposed by CORE. In common with CORE, the women supported value-added production and the investigation of niche opportunities for high-value-added products within the forest products sector. In addition, they recognized that the local economy would have to diversify beyond forestry, although tourism was considered with caution because of its propensity to create seasonal and lower-paying jobs. They also noted that investment in tourism would require greater investment in infrastructure to attract and retain visitors to the region.

In contrast to CORE, however, this post hoc assessment revealed that women themselves wanted to be counted in for the programs and benefits associated with an economic transition strategy. Women realized that their jobs in support industries were also threatened by the land use plan and expressed concern that retraining opportunities for displaced male workers would, in turn, displace current training opportunities for women. They wanted current training to give them access to nontraditional jobs (e.g., carpentry, mechanics, and forestry-related occupations), which could lead to "full-time, meaningful, well-paying, year-round jobs that provide benefits and security" (Vosko and Bueckert 1994, 33).

For women to take on such roles, the report noted, an effective transition strategy would also have to meet a variety of community needs. In particular, affordable, accessible, safe, and flexible child care and affordable transportation were considered necessary to allow women to undertake shift work, work full time, or go to school. Access to training and apprenticeship programs would have to be expanded. Existing programs were viewed as inaccessible for many women living in the region because of the times at which courses were offered and the limited eligibility requirements. In addition, access to credit for starting small businesses was also considered a problem for women in particular. While CORE discussed generic options in this regard, the women of the North Island recommended that a small-scale loan program be put in place that targeted women in the region. In combination, these programs would address some of the practical issues that women faced in their daily responses to the land use designations.

This post hoc assessment suggested, however, that a transition strategy should not merely focus on employment-related issues. Women emphasized their concerns over how the social aspects of community life would be affected by the new land use allocations. They pointed out that increased unemployment would place greater pressures on social services at the same time as these services were being withdrawn by forest companies and/or governments. In this respect, the women argued for improved health care facilities, counselling services, youth services and education, and affordable rental housing. They pointed out that limited availability of affordable rental housing made it impossible for female single parents to remain in the community after family breakdown. The prospects of compounding circumstances seemed to be more immediate throughout the uncertainty and fear that pervaded the CORE process. And while the limits of these services have been endemic to these towns even during times of economic prosperity, women noted that they would become exacerbated during economic decline.

These comments illustrated how the women linked the contradictory elements of environmental, social, and economic policies in their daily lives. These links indicated that the specific and narrow interpretation of environmental and land use planning was not shared by women of the North Island. Because of different material realities, women's perspectives about land use planning were revealed to be distinct from those of male workers. Women experienced land use change as a crisis of production, reproduction, and community caregiving, and they believed that transition planning must address all of the associated issues.

The Powers of Planning

Thus far, I have suggested that environmental and land use planning sets up a particular context that favours certain kinds of representations over others. More specifically, the definition of the social context, which has been narrowly ascribed as direct employment in the dominant resource sector, has served to marginalize women's perspectives in land use planning. While the overwhelming majority of people who have lost or stand to lose their jobs are men, the acceptance of this general pattern, coupled with the preoccupation of land use planning with direct stakeholders and impacts, has led to an inadequate conceptualization of the social dimension of sustainability. As a consequence, contemporary land use planning fails to include women's contributions through their multiple labours within forestry communities.

Part of the reason for this omission lies in how the process of participatory planning, unintentionally perhaps, reinforces dominant societal power relations to the general disadvantage of women. At least three forms of power relations are relevant in land use planning: command power, bargaining power, and influence. While theorists have developed these relations in terms of social class, differential relations of power are also gendered. First, command power is "the ability to impose one's will in the face of resistance" (West 1994, 415). It is limited to those groups with the ability to exercise direct control under conditions involving direct conflict. In contemporary society, legal, legislative, or economic rights and privileges underlie the institutions holding command power. In the context of land use planning, one can associate the ability of groups to gain direct access to the planning process as an indicator of a limited form of command power.

Second, bargaining power is associated with the ability of interest groups to participate in negotiations over issues affecting them. Successful bargaining requires gaining influence within the process to set and exercise the terms and conditions favourable to one's interests. Two qualities are necessary for effective bargaining. First, groups with bargaining power within the process require strategic knowledge of social transactions. Such transactions include both formal and informal rules, procedures, practices, agreements, and contracts that operate in the market, legal, political, and planning spheres of the social system (Stone 1986). Being knowledgeable about these rules and protocols allows groups to favourably structure the terms of social transactions. Second, in the context of participatory land use planning, the ability to act on this knowledge also involves securing access to the resources of government institutions. For example, the state has a major and influential role in setting land use priorities through its legislation policies and regulations, as well as through its coordination and allocation of the huge financial, informational, and administrative resources at its disposal. Access to government agencies may allow for a favourable dispensation of these resources as well as some consideration as to when policy and legislation are formulated and advanced.

Third, influence, as it is used here, addresses the outcomes of command power and bargaining power by focusing on how power is exercised indirectly.[10] By examining legislative and economic instruments, in combination with strategic resources and informal procedures, one can identify the relative influence of groups engaged in and/or affected by participatory planning exercises. However, just as all groups do not have the qualities that would provide them with command power or access to bargaining power, so too the possession and use of influence are unequal. Groups lacking strategic knowledge of social transactions, or the ability to act on that knowledge, are less powerful in acting to protect their interests. As a consequence, those who do not or cannot participate or are ineffective participants in bargaining will experience the adverse effects of planning decisions as more powerful groups act to protect and further their own interests. This classification can illuminate various ways in which power dynamics omit or marginalize community management issues attributed to women in forestry communities.

Access to the VICORE process was obtained by invitation from CORE. Three criteria were used to assess potential participants: (1) ensure that those who were interested have access to representation through a sector, (2) include those significantly or directly affected by land use planning issues in the region, and (3) include those who could impede plan implementation (CORE 1994b).[11] These seem to be justifiable criteria. The formation of sector interests implies that stakeholder groups can be readily identified and selected. Organizations that gain credibility and recognition for consideration have often been able to demonstrate long-standing competence and commitment to their causes. To this end, an organization needs to have a good track record and be able to communicate to its members and the broader local community. "Recognized" groups need to have basic knowledge about opportunities to participate and need to demonstrate their ability and willingness to cooperate with other public groups. Furthermore, in a world of male-dominated institutions, such recognition only reinforces unfair access to and influence over planning processes to the general disadvantage of forestry-town women and community issues ascribed to them.

Command Power and the Biases of Representation
The criteria for participation established by VICORE assured access to the planning process of well-organized, long-standing domains, such as mining, forestry, agriculture, unions, and government agencies. In addition, they encompassed organizations (e.g., ENGOs) able to exert increasing power to disrupt the planning process. However, these criteria assumed that people would understand in advance of the process how land use planning would affect their interests. They favoured interests that had already formed strong regional or corporate networks. In this context, "corporate" refers not to the private sector but to the ability to establish an effective collective entity. For example, institutions such as unions,

professional associations, and corporate business interests (which, in the case of the forestry sector, remain remarkably male dominated) can more easily gain direct representation at planning tables to ensure that their interests are met in the creation of transition strategies. Environmental organizations have also been able to establish their corporate connections through networks and coalitions. Labour, in the form of private sector unions, almost always gets a seat. Labour, in the form of public sector unions, almost invariably does not. By and large, women's labour is less organized. However, where women are represented, they are more likely found in public sector unions (see Chapter 4). These unions were not invited to the table. Alternatively, a search for local representatives from places such as women's centres may be futile because those centres simply do not exist. Therefore, the selection of appropriate groups favoured representation by male-dominated institutions (e.g., private sector unions) and interests (jobs). In contrast, institutions deemed to be female dominated (e.g., public sector unions, community-based organizations) and female interests (e.g., community care) were not systematically incorporated into planning processes.

Beyond this observation, many of the issues that characterize the social dimension of sustainability are often not amenable to being included in this type of planning process. They are often dependent on soft interpretations of social change that are dynamic and contingent on local conditions. For example, there are few uncontested measures of "adequate access to social services" or "vibrant social networks" or "sufficient elder care" or "affordable day care." In small towns, these concerns are bound by a loosely affiliated community of users. More likely than not, these values are held by or ascribed to women. As a consequence, CORE deemed the broader concerns of "social sustainability" and the remedies that might accompany required changes in land use as "women's community issues." These concerns and potential measures to address them became attenuated just as women became prominent in social life.

The marginality of women's issues arises not only due to biases in CORE's selection process. Dominant power relations *within* forestry communities also thwart women's efforts at organizing, rendering marginal, if not invisible, the diversity of women's issues that might legitimately become part of participatory planning processes. It may seem strange to talk of women from forestry towns in this way. As members of forestry families, many women enjoy the high incomes of their partners. Some women are quite vocal about local issues and downright colourful in their language. They are hardly timid victims. However, these more outspoken women do not represent the totality of women's experiences. Among the cohort of forestry-town women is enormous diversity of experience and location.

For some women, this marginalization became acute upon marriage breakdown, when economic necessity for work came into direct conflict with job availability (as described in Chapter 4). The women interviewed in this study expressed feeling disempowered because their perspectives on local issues were not accorded basic respect within the community. This was particularly true when their opinions were unpopular and went against the dominant community culture. For example, one woman was silenced through public intimidation after she wrote a letter to the local newspaper that questioned the appropriateness of a striptease act that had been used as a fund-raiser for the boys' community hockey team. She was labelled anti-community. She said that she will not speak publicly in *any* forum anymore.

Beyond the general category of "women," there is a multiple layering of marginality. Certain ethnic or social communities within forestry communities may also contain strictures on and limits to women's participation. For example, in some forestry communities in British Columbia, there are strong pockets of Indo-Canadians.[12] Older women from this ethnic community may feel very reluctant to speak out in public ways due to family pressures, language barriers, and social customs. Poor women of all ethnic backgrounds have significant challenges in coming forward. Poor women are most highly represented among First Nations populations and among single women of all ethnic backgrounds – all of whom live in significant yet often invisible numbers in forestry communities. How do we ensure access for these people and their perspectives in multistakeholder planning processes?

By referring to these examples, I have illustrated that there are structural biases within these communities that reduce the ability for social issues to gain a coherent voice and thereby be granted stakeholder status. So while participatory planning forums grant all formal rights to participate, many people cannot act on these rights and thereby cannot enjoy the substantive benefits (Wharf Higgins 1999). In short, because of structured inequalities in society, people have unequal opportunities to participate. The dominant planning model of multistakeholder participation has, unwittingly, perpetuated gender bias to the general disadvantage of women. And within the cohort of women, some are more marginalized than others.

A planning model based on interest representation exacerbates the social exclusion described by the women in this study. By focusing on interests organized at the corporate level (e.g., through umbrella organizations having regional or national significance), rather than at the community level, the resulting sector formation reflects narrow domains of command power. Institutions that were well protected tended to be male dominated, whether through worker unions or through private sector interests. There were no obvious stakeholder groups assigned to represent social concerns such as those associated with family breakdown, social services, et cetera. The sectoral coalition model consistently underrepresented the unemployed, small-business owners, and homemakers, yet the extent of social impacts indicates that it is these groups who will experience indirect or mediated effects of planning decisions. And in the gendered division of labour in forestry communities, these interests are frequently allied with women. Some of the women in this study believed that they were doubly excluded from planning processes, given their marginal position within land use debates and their marginal position within forestry communities themselves.

Bargaining Power and Influence
Beyond actual representation, those officially representing forestry communities at the planning table lacked bargaining power and influence. As gender and community are intertwined, both are characterized by marginality *within* planning processes. Bargaining involves the ability to participate effectively during the process. Successful bargaining is achieved through knowledge of social transactions and the ability to use that knowledge to one's advantage. In this regard, important bargaining factors included procedural items (table agenda, time, funding, and data requirements) and policy instruments. A lack of influence over these areas can be seen by the ways in which forestry-based community interests were addressed both by the negotiating table and in the commissioner's final report to the cabinet. For example, social and economic concerns were the last items to receive attention on the agenda. In the limited fourteen months assigned to carry the process through to recommendations, a substantial portion of the planning agenda was devoted to planning procedure itself. Before any efforts at dispute resolution were undertaken, much time was spent in lengthy and contentious discussions as sectors manoeuvred to gain procedural advantages during the planning process.

While some of this time commitment reflected a lack of experience by participants with these new processes, the consequences for community-based interests were serious. These effects were compounded by a lack of influence over other important resources. For example, funding represents an important factor in effective representation. Even though the planning process included a participant assistance program, the lack of funds presented a barrier to access for some groups representing community interests (Kelly and Alper 1995). While travel expenses were paid, some rural residents had to take time away from paid employment to attend meetings. Seventeen of twenty-two meetings were held at the south end of the island, several hours' drive away. This drive placed an onerous burden on many North Island participants of sectors with the fewest financial resources. One spokesperson, for example, stated that she had logged

30,000 kilometres on her vehicle and had spent two to three days every few weeks to undertake work for the planning table. Recall from Chapters 4 and 5 that fewer women drive their own vehicles and can afford to take time away from their home situations to participate in such a process. Another member from northern Vancouver Island had to step down since his private business was suffering due to the time required to attend meetings. Obviously, these were not simply women's issues but also community issues. Yet, with such high demands for participation, it is likely that those who might have the greatest understanding of social service needs are in the least favourable position to participate.

The shortage of government resources in terms of personnel time and funding allotments to the process was also an important factor that served to limit the amount and quality of data for analyzing the impacts of plan decisions (CORE 1994b; Kelly and Alper 1995). Only existing and available information on social impacts was collected due to the time constraints placed on the process. In addition, some requests for socioeconomic information were not met, not only because of the limited time, but also due to the limited resources supplied by the government to the process. On this subject, the table report stated, "In particular, specific quantified information on the social effects on communities resulting from land use changes was consistently not available" (CORE 1994b, 22). As a result of these procedural factors, a social and economic transition and mitigation strategy was developed by the commissioner himself, relying solely on existing and available data at the provincial level rather than obtaining current information directly from communities that would be impacted by plan decisions.

Finally, one can illustrate influence by examining the policy instruments and recommendations incorporated into the commissioner's final report. For example, the Land Use Charter developed by CORE in advance of the Vancouver Island process provided a set of overarching principles aimed at achieving environmental, economic, and social sustainability, as well as principles to guide decision-making processes (CORE 1994b). The principles were expressed in terms of provincial government commitments. Importantly, the Charter made explicit an environmental imperative that not only acknowledged the essential role that ecosystems play in supporting society but also recognized nature as having intrinsic value. This commitment was then more clearly articulated in the Protected Areas Strategy in terms of a specific environmental goal: that is, protection of 12 percent of representative ecosystems of the province.

While the Charter made explicit commitments to environmental sustainability that were supported by specific policy goals, no such goals were presented to support social sustainability. The Charter principles did recognize environmental sustainability as interdependent with economic sustainability[13] and did provide strategic direction for a strong economy through commitments to a strong (emphasizing economic competition and diversification) and sustainable (through waste reduction and sustainable resource use) economy. Support for these commitments was to be obtained by implementing both economic policy instruments and an economic regulatory framework (CORE 1994b). Although the rhetoric of sustainability was present in these principles, it is clear that the imperative of economic sustainability was to be attempted within the competitive framework of British Columbia's mixed economy. In the context of forestry, this economy includes incentives and regulations associated with tenure arrangements, royalties and stumpage fees, environmental standards, and planning requirements.

However, unlike the commitments for environmental and economic sustainability, supported by policies or regulations, the provincial commitment to social sustainability in the Land Use Charter was expressed, not in terms of any strategic goals for social or community well-being, but in terms of social equity. Social equity was expressed as a fair distribution of the costs and benefits of land use decisions and a commitment to support economic and social measures to address the economic effects of decisions. Yet there was no policy commitment that articulated how social equity might be attempted or achieved. Whereas a specific strategy was provided for achieving environmental sustainability (through the Protected Areas Strategy), there was no such strategy for achieving social sustainability. The social and economic well-being of forestry-based communities was thus defined not in terms of specific policies or pro-active strategies but in terms of the impacts upon community well-being caused by the plan.

The negotiating table failed to reach consensus on a strategy that would address these socioeconomic impacts of planning decisions because of disagreement over how "broad" the scope of the strategy should be (CORE 1994b). Some participants argued that the terminology of "impacts" had predetermined the nature of the final decision. This argument was viewed by environmental organizations as reactionary (Kelly and Alper 1995). And yet, as the government moved toward implementing its Protected Areas Strategy, it was also silently withdrawing or – euphemistically – regionalizing the delivery of health and social services. The results became increasingly clear. The government had made a political commitment to establishing a network of environmentally protected areas throughout the province. This commitment was supported, even demanded, by strong environmental organizations that had effectively garnered international support for change through a sophisticated and successful advertising and market-based campaign among individual and corporate customers of British Columbia's wood products. However, the social services had no comparable champions; the welfare state was under attack. The rhetoric of the political right held sway as media, politicians, and even activists began to talk of the "need" to turn to the market and to voluntarism to provide social services and community cohesion. The effect has been a slow but material draining of human capital from rural places.

Because the negotiating table could not agree on the appropriate level and means to deliver social services, the CORE commissioner was left to make recommendations for a socioeconomic transition strategy. Yet, despite the identification of significant job losses for women employed in the service provision for these towns, the transition strategy excluded ways to deal with these job losses. And, importantly, additional social services to address the multiple transitional needs such as financial and mental health counselling were not mentioned. The commissioner's report recommended that social programs and services be designed to address the problems identified by the social impact analysis; however, it failed to identify specific kinds of programs (either existing or to be created) to address these impacts. The social impacts and service requirements associated with family and community stresses were regarded as being beyond the scope of the transition strategy that was created. Consequently, the broader concerns of those living in forestry-based communities, and women in particular, were simply not addressed. Instead, specific recommendations were narrowly and more safely restricted to addressing impacts on employment in the harvesting and processing sectors of the forest industry. Thus, the transition strategy narrowly focused attention on direct forestry employment and shuffled indirect economic and social issues to other agencies without any compulsion that they follow up on them (Reed 1997b). Addressing these concerns then became dependent upon the limited resources of impacted communities and community organizations and upon the will of other government levels, programs, and agencies.

The planning process design reinforced conventional power relations between government and community and within forestry communities themselves. For example, it was the government that determined the conditions and criteria under which participating organizations could operate and the policies available to prescribe planning actions. Even though planning processes followed democratic principles, negotiation among only direct interests meant that those who could provide input into decisions that supposedly reflected the broader public interest were those who maintained bargaining power in negotiations. In the case of CORE's approach to planning on Vancouver Island, women in forestry communities were required to bear the social costs of plan decisions without adequate access to remedies to redress these effects.

Thus far, I have argued that environmental and land use planning is a political process in which public planning activities set up a particular context that favours certain kinds of representations over others. In the case of CORE, the social context was initially defined broadly but quickly became narrowly ascribed to include only direct employment in the dominant resource sector. I am not saying that jobs are not important. They are. I am not saying that women do not benefit from job strategies. In small part, they do – both directly as clients and indirectly as partners of male workers. But in the contemporary gendered division of labour, a focus on jobs is insufficient to deal with social changes brought on by environmental and land use changes. In addition, this limited conceptualization of the social dimension of sustainability has served to marginalize women's perspectives in land use planning and to omit women's multiple contributions to forestry communities.

This bias is exacerbated by the endemic nature of many community issues. Direct employment losses as a result of land allocations (or other production issues such as corporate restructuring) are often short term and newsworthy, drawing public attention and political heat. Community-based problems resulting from these losses include out-migration (particularly of the younger generation), erosion of the local tax base, family stress or breakdown, and closure of local and community services (see Chapter 3). These impacts occur over a long period. CORE recognized this time disjuncture by stating that "while impact analysis generally collapses direct impacts into a single time ... in the actual unfolding of events, the major economic and social impact of this Plan will be spread over some considerable period. The extent to which they can be spread out in time can be a crucial determinant of the experience of individual workers, families and communities ... The adjustment burden of land use change is sufficiently significant that other measures should be sponsored by society at large to ease the transition" (1994a, 208). Yet, as these problems become part of the social fabric of communities, they become endemic: that is, *commonplace*. Their saliency as strategic issues that draw media and public attention is lost. Without public attention, the support for social initiatives to address these repercussions is significantly diminished. The longer the period over which the problems are spread out, the less incentive there is for governments to act. Furthermore, as individuals choose to leave rural communities, these places lose political representation, and consequently their voices become either fainter or more shrill – and therefore less effective. The time disjuncture and the loss of political voice may help to explain why it is so hard to incorporate a social agenda along with land (re)allocation. And yet the time lag and the renewed interest in community self-help point to the need for, and an opportunity to, create alternative forums that can address a broader range of community interests and actors in processes of public deliberation and participatory citizenship.

Toward Participatory Citizenship

> Because science and politics are, in this arena, inseparable, public participation efforts need to emphasize competent communication, systems learning, and opportunities to work through different viewpoints.
>
> – Steven E. Daniels and Gregg B. Walker (1996, 80)

Researchers in political and feminist theory as well as students of environmental management have begun to offer fresh perspectives on long-standing issues associated with citizen involvement in public policy. For example, David Prior, John Stewart, and Kieron Walsh (1995) called for the restoration of deliberation to the democratic process, while Janis Birkeland (1993) argued for a new, relatively autonomous, social decision-making arena to ensure that social concerns can be specifically addressed and integrated with concerns for environment and economy. In complement, students of environmental management suggest that sustainable planning systems must be built on management institutions with strong learning capacities (Cortner et al. 1996; Daniels and Walker 1996; McLain 1993) and should draw on and develop a community's capacity (Cortner and Moote 1999; Kusel 1996; Roseland 1999). Emphasis is now placed on establishing a "civic science" involving citizens as researchers and striving to develop a contextual understanding of environmental problems and their resolution (Kruger and Shannon 2000). Efforts are placed on establishing tools for managers to inventory and monitor sociocultural meanings of places so that they can incorporate these meanings into planning processes. Attention is given to activities/species that not only carry instrumental values such as food or fibre production but also have symbolic (noninstrumental) values, such as those pertaining to self-identity, spiritual renewal, a role in local myth and history, ritual significance, and a sense of place and community (Berkes 1999; Jakes and Anderson 2000; Kellert et al. 2000; Martopo and Mitchell 1995; Pulido 1996).

All these considerations require more than citizen participation; in fact, they require the obverse. They demand the development of participatory citizenship in which opportunities to exchange values and experiences, and to discuss potential and desired futures, occupy a central space in planning processes. Such a form of citizenship requires planning processes that value and nurture the energies and capacities of local communities as well as external communities of interest when defining social issues and shaping their resolution. In short, processes that determine collective social, economic, and environmental goals in the long-term public interest are part of a vision that "is markedly different from current definitions (of planning) that emphasize guiding land use efficiently and/or distributing resources equitably" (Birkeland 1993, 30). In effect, forums must be created to engage in "anticipatory" and "preventative" planning.

This vision requires several strategies that differ from contemporary models of participatory planning. First, given the limitations of interest-based sector formation, more effective representation might be achieved by using a "values"-based, rather than an "interest"-based, model (Brown 1996; Hawkins 1999; Ness 1992). With this latter model, individuals represent particular values or points of view identified by communities in the planning area rather than an interest position of a sector or coalition. The advantage of this strategy is that representatives are accountable not to individual sector constituencies but to the communities of the planning area, they may speak as engaged public citizens, and they may cultivate a long-term perspective on pertinent issues.

Second, problems of access and effectiveness might be addressed through changes in the scale of planning processes. Part of CORE's failure to address a range of issues may have occurred because its planning area was too large geographically and too diverse socially. This concern was also raised in the subsequent planning process of the Central Coast. A reduction in the scale of regional processes might overcome communications problems by allowing group structures and networks to operate more effectively locally and regionally (Kelly and Alper 1995), eliminate perceptions of urban bias, and reduce travel time and funding requirements that reduce the scope of local participation. The challenge here is to determine a scale that would accommodate socially derived objectives with those desired for ecosystem management.

Third, drawing on researchers of environmental management, new measures for participatory process design may also be appropriate to consider. In particular, environmental "planners" suggest that forums must be built on developing communication competence (Daniels and Walker 1996) or good civic dialogue (Lee 1999). This is more than mere participation. Emphasis is placed on planning as a learning experience wherein interventions are considered to be a series of experiments from which new knowledge leads to continuous adjustments and modifications.

As this chapter has illustrated, identification of shared values is a significant challenge. Experience elsewhere in the province suggests that collaboration alone will not be able to address unequal distributions of power that circulate within and act upon local communities (Reed 1997a). By considering collaborative efforts as learning opportunities, one can explicitly examine and address power relations within community settings, and perhaps both the explanations and the experiences of collaborative environmental planning/participatory citizenship can be advanced. By introducing an active learning component, however, alternative models or scenarios may be used to illustrate different assumptions, values, and implications and thereby help to address power differentials. As Rebecca McLain and Kai Lee suggest, "with only one model, based on one set of assumptions, the assumptions and values of less powerful stakeholders are bound to be submerged ... The presence of multiple models may provide an appropriate forum for debating how social and cultural values affect both the discovery of consequences and choice of corrective action" (1996, 445).

Making a Space to Include "Others" in Public Deliberation
Thus far, I have suggested that "participatory citizenship" is qualitatively different from "citizen participation" as practised by CORE. Yet these suggestions are clearly not a model that is ready for application. Applied models and case studies can be found in many places (e.g., Cortner et al. 1996; Daniels and Walker 1996; Gunderson, Holling, and Light 1995; Lee 1999; McLain and Lee 1996; Reed 1999a; Susskind and Cruikshank 1987). I raise these ideas here for two reasons. First, these suggestions are intended to reinvigorate the politics of planning and to ensure that the relationships connecting individual, community, and the state do not substitute management – or activities associated with technical decisions – for moral judgment – politics. Second, I want to promote an alternative model of public decision making that is situated in the hands of broad-based social and geographical communities and avoids favouring individual preference and choice. Without continuous evaluation, critique, and re-creation, contemporary public involvement programs – even those whose express intention is to democratize decision making – may paradoxically transform what should be a public responsibility into a private interest.

My suggestions are not intended to replace other systems of democratic governance; rather, they are intended to enrich the lives of citizens who may wish to become active in inclusive and inviting forums. This entails organizing and delivering environmental and land use planning in a way that treats all people involved as responsible citizens. Part of the challenge of such an approach is to maintain interest and motivation during quiescent times and to expand and rotate membership so that processes of learning are truly collective. In this way, planning does not need to be elitist – that is, a process that entrenches insensitivity, paternalism, inflexibility, and local dependency (e.g., Reed 1995). Instead, it may be more inclusive of a range of citizens and the interests, *norms, and values* that they bring to planning forums. For example, planning might legitimately include discussions of local social practices, patterns of gender relation and family formation, work habits, and local celebrations. Understanding these relations can help us to understand why groups hold particular positions within society and to explain the links between cultural identity and acceptable practices associated with resource and environmental management. This understanding can help in the long run to develop strategies that will be locally and globally acceptable.

Those responsible for crafting public planning processes must recognize and affirm that society is composed of individuals and groups with contrasting ends and purposes in which norms and differences emerge both within and across communities. They must find ways to take collective action in processes that are just, accountable, representative, and responsible. This responsibility requires that practitioners, academics, and general citizens continue to promote and reinforce self-worth and capacity and to enable people to be active contributors to processes that shape both their own lives and the lives of their communities.

Planning decisions about the allocation of land uses and associated economic transitions can be powerful influences on the lives of all people living in forestry communities. Women, men, and children living in rural resource communities on Vancouver Island and likely beyond will continue to confront uncertain futures as they struggle with the loss of ecological diversity as well as economic and social well-being. In this context, the pursuit of sustainable and healthy communities requires us to reconcile persistent demands of economy and environment with obligations of social groups that do not automatically "fit" into forestry and land use debates. Addressing these issues requires the willingness to expand criteria for inclusion and relevance. Ultimately, we must consider new spaces and strategies for public deliberation if we are to take seriously human needs within specific geographical, social, historical, and ecological places. The time is ripe for considering approaches to an invigorated participatory and inclusive citizenship.

A broad horizon, looking out from San Josef Bay, Cape Scott Provincial Park.

8
Social Sustainability and the Renewal of Research Agendas

> [Achieving sustainability] ... now requires harmonizing the insistent demands of poverty and capitalism with the quiet obligations of the biotic community. Heeding those obligations requires an uncommonly broad perspective, one that takes seriously the social institutions, human needs and biogeography ... I do not propose that single individuals embrace all these qualities. But how to organize the skills and commitments of a diverse human community to strive for these uncommon aims is a challenge we are only beginning to address.
>
> – Kai Lee (1999)

Broadening Our Perspectives

The stories that I have told are intended to spark new ways of thinking about the social dimensions of sustainability. Policy changes in environment and land use invariably have impacts on and are accompanied by alterations in the broader society, hence the need, as Kai Lee points out in the epigraph above, for "an uncommonly broad perspective." Alterations in gender relations illustrate some of these dimensions. This research has attempted explicitly to bring the lives of women in forestry communities from their marginalized position to a more central location, both in their communities and in public policy debates. By using this analytical strategy, I have shunned the classical separation of environmental policy making from domestic, everyday life. Instead, I have illustrated links among changes in policy and in relations at regional, community, household, and individual levels. This effort is consistent with other feminist scholars who have challenged the public/private divide often used to characterize social life and who have applied multiscale analyses to explain individuals' actions, behaviours, and meanings.

My primary argument is that what seem to be environmental struggles played out in rural areas are not strictly environmental. Instead, challenges of the various elements of social and political life that produce conflict over politics, identity, and lifestyle illustrate the social marginalization of people living in forestry communities. Drawing on a four-part framework for social marginalization, I argued that we must simultaneously confront multiple issues that include economic exploitation, social and moral exclusion, and a sense of powerlessness that has begun to pervade rural communities. Environmentalism is mixed in and blurred with these elements. Emphasizing protection of forestry as anti-environmental simplifies and ultimately misrepresents the issues and overlooks how the complex economic, political, and social relations interact to shape it. My position is similar to that of Matthew Carroll, Steven Daniels, and Jonathan Kusel, who concluded that "Addressing displacement and retraining [of forestry workers in Oregon] will require policy that is cognizant of the social embeddedness of workers and their families and responds to the complex relationships between industry, environment, workers, and communities ... Our collective future will likely consist of choices that test our ingenuity, our environmental ethic, and our compassion for one another" (2000, 156).

When I began this project, I was guided by the question "Should the activities of women who resist new environmental regulations be considered part of feminist struggles for environmental sustainability and social justice, or are they part of the problem of resolving them?" Upon reflection, I believe that any direct answer to this question feeds the dualism of "progressives" and "laggards" that has inhibited understanding and creative actions in forestry and land use debates. The words of Sandra Harding, a feminist scholar of the philosophy of science, resonate instead: "What may be considered radical and progressive from the perspective of some women's lives may be too conservative, too dangerous, or just irrelevant from the perspective of other women's lives" (1991, 7). In my own research, acts of labelling and classifying became extremely difficult since some activities and perspectives as well as women themselves defied the theoretical explanations. I reiterate my claim that, in order to understand women's activism, we must examine how their perspectives and actions are embedded in local and extralocal social relations. As I draw toward a conclusion, I abandon my original question and its implicit assumption that I can identify inadequacies in the women whom I studied. Instead, I turn to describe the inadequacies of theories that have been used to describe and "support" these women.

Seeing the Trees among the Stories of Forestry-Town Women

I first tried to "fit" the situations and perspectives of forestry-town women into feminist theories of women's activism. I identified two stories that dominate the literature. The first was a labour studies story that tells of women's roles in protecting social class and community culture. The second was an ecofeminist story of women's role in environmental protection. Both labour studies theorists and ecofeminists first identified women's marginality from mainstream society. Both suggested that women who are politically active mobilize around practical-domestic concerns that affect the safety, security, and welfare of family and community, focusing on specific issues such as public health, education, morality, and environment of their communities (Garcia-Guadilla 1995; Merchant 1995; West and Blumberg 1990). Women's role as nurturers and caregivers in the family was extended to notions of community care and management.

As I attempted to apply these frameworks, I found that these stories did not easily apply to the women of this study. Women's roles and relations within these disputes form a complex identity that is difficult to summarize. Symbols of forestry, family, work, and community combined in unequal ways at different junctures. However, none was sufficient in the singular to describe women's identities and voices. For example, the home was both a site of political action and a place of strong political rhetoric. The home, like family and community, is an important value in Canadian culture. For forestry-town women, the home and its physical manifestation of the house represented the contribution made by wood products workers in providing the raw materials to build affordable homes for Canadians as a whole. The home was also an icon that illustrated the value and dignity of holding a job, a good job in which all family members could take pride. In some cases, the home was a place of domestic ambiguity and even violence. Changes in environmental regulations did not simply alter contemporary access to timber; they also threatened more fundamental values of family, community, hard work, and societal contribution, upon which forestry communities had developed. These were themes identified by the pregnant wife who spoke on the steps of the provincial legislature in protest of CORE's land use plan for Vancouver Island (see Chapter 1 and Chapter 5, "Ferron").

Among the women with whom I engaged, it was difficult to find the "forestry-dependent, politically conservative" woman. There were a few women like Betty, profiled in Chapter 5. These women could easily be depicted as classical loggers' wives. They were usually in their late forties or older and economically dependent on their partners' incomes. With tactics that bore a conservative mark, they openly supported the forest industry and their partners and families in "traditional" formations. But trying to align Betty's motivations and actions along an ecofeminist trajectory was unsatisfactory. I could classify her as a "social mother." She viewed her activism in the more conservative land use organization as an act of community preservation, and she applied her understandings and strategies as a mother to her actions as a protector of community values. Yet she sought to protect her family's interests against perceived incursions by environmental activists. Thus, in her case, acts of social mothering or community management did not lead to actions that favoured environmental preservation. Therefore, I had to reject the theoretical proposition of some feminist scholars described in Chapter 5 that the subject position of "mother/carer/community manager" (Liepins 1998) or "social mother" leads to activism within environmental preservation organizations (e.g., Liepins 1998; Merchant 1995; Seager 1996). Instead, Betty – at least in her efforts with Canadian Women in Timber – exhibited a "women's politics of resistance," as described by Sara Ruddick (1989), that was unpredictable.

The notion that these women opposed environmental preservation was also contested. Women's activities supported some forms of preservation and some forms of exploitation. While many women, such as Betty, protested against wilderness preservation groups, they did not interpret their own actions as anti-environmental. Indeed, many of their activities in daily life demonstrated their interest in protecting elements of nature. Barb, for example, kept constant watch for whales to support a scientific research project, while Marilyn and others worked tirelessly to restore natural habitats and ecosystem processes for future generations. Even Betty worked with other family members to undertake stream restoration as an act of family and community "communion." Many women spoke of a love of nature and a regular and ongoing intimacy with the nonhuman environment that helped to attract and hold them in their communities.

Within the labour studies story, many women in this study could, superficially at least, be seen to "stand by their men." Like Betty, most of the women whom I interviewed were strong supporters of the forest industry. This is not surprising since my research strategy involved seeking these women out. Annie, Barb, and Ferron, for example, were married to men in the industry and were active locally, regionally, and even internationally to protect the forest industry. Yet they spoke with the "local authority" associated with their current or previous employment in the industry. These women were not dependent financially or emotionally on their partners. Annie described the need for women to move beyond emotional dependence, Barb refused to condone "special treatment" for women, and Ferron discussed the financial volatility of working in the industry and spoke at length of the need for families to shield themselves from instability during the good times. Each had her own reasons for supporting the industry.

Furthermore, women's support was not blindly provided. Many women spoke of a logging lifestyle that had been built on big money and big spending. On this point, women agreed that the communities built on forestry were in trouble. They mused whether or not part of the impact of changes in the industry seemed to be dire because of the contrast to contemporary circumstances and the expectation of the good life within their communities. More than half of the women interviewed suggested that curtailing consumption might be a good thing, considering limited global resources and/or social issues related to equity. Some women returned the gaze of judgment. They pointed out the hypocrisy of urban residents with good jobs, lots of "toys," and time off who sought out large expanses of wilderness, with opportunities to play in nature, while they maintained their demand for the wood products extracted from it. They pointed out the impossibility of meeting these demands simultaneously.

Women also spoke of marginalization within forestry communities. Almost all of the women agreed with Carole that forestry had built "men's communities" on northern Vancouver Island. These exclusive communities were illustrated by the relative lack of paid work opportunities for women, particularly well-paid, career-developing opportunities. Women such as Donna also pointed to male bias at the work site – be it the office, the "yard," the field, or the home. Male dominance was expressed in what were deemed appropriate community actions, such as Logger Sports Day, long celebrated as an icon of forestry versus the ongoing struggle to open a women's centre. Women in one focus group linked drug abuse and male violence against women to "a forestry lifestyle."[1] Attempts to erase women's concerns were observed during local economic development meetings, in relation to provincial government policy making, and in the protests of women after the CORE decision on land use on Vancouver Island. These observations challenged the long-standing societal assumption "that what is good for the male breadwinner/wage-earner, his success in industrial struggles, is of benefit to the family as a whole" (Parr 1990, 243).

While a small number of women still upheld this assumption, most vehemently opposed it. They argued that there were many more struggles facing forestry communities than simply maintaining traditionally male income levels. In this context, women also spoke of issues that arose from outside their communities. They discussed their more general fears relating to the loss of rural identity, voice, and respect. For some women, protests at Clayoquot Sound, the provincial legislature, and smaller incidents on the island were signals that their own voices were not being heard. They feared erasure from the political agenda, increasingly dominated by urban (and "southern") interests. They feared that there would be no political place for their children in the dominant society of the future.

In short, I found that neither ecofeminism nor labour studies theories accurately accounted for the multiple layerings that shape women's lives or the multiple forms or sites of women's political activism. For people living in these communities on northern Vancouver Island, family, place, and lifestyle were intimately interwoven. They became sites of consistencies and contradictions. Factors such as physical and social isolation, ecological changes, and revisions to social policy all had varying but direct effects on the lives of women on northern Vancouver Island. As a result of these more diverse stories, I had to find other theories that might help to explain women's perspectives and actions. I began by following Lynn

Staeheli's (1996) suggestion to separate the content of activism from its location. I examined forms of activism beyond those visible in the making of public environmental policy, such as activities within the home and the community. Consequently, I found that women took political actions at home, in their workplaces, and in community development organizations that both reinforced and challenged their attachments to the forest industry and its culture. Recall Carole, who left her partner because she opposed "the violence of forestry" in the household; nevertheless, she worked on local committees to protect forestry and community identity. Had I simply examined her public actions, I would have seen her as a staunch supporter of the industry. How, then, might I conceptualize the perspectives and activism of women in forestry towns?

Because other theories did not fit, I argued that women's perspectives and choices for activism are embedded within local social and spatial contexts. In my case, details relate to local effects of restructuring of the forest industry, changing ecologies, reorganization of government environmental and social policies, availability of physical and social infrastructure, local labour practices, and community social norms. These factors inscribed women's identities and shaped their motivations for, and choices about, forestry and political activism. These elements of women's lives were explicitly documented. I found that women's support of workers, forestry practices, and forestry culture was not unified, conservative, progressive, or crassly material. Rather, women's activism, both individual and collective, could more accurately be identified as heterogeneous and contingent, complex, contradictory, and embedded.

Embeddedness offered a means to include "other" women in feminist theorizing without predetermining the status of women (i.e., marginality), political orientation (i.e., progressive or conservative), or sites of activism (i.e., public protests). The idea also opened up multiple lines of fracture and complications in women's identities and avoided the tendency of maternal explanations to dichotomize and render static the nature of women's lives. The more fluid approach adopted by embeddedness provided a space between polarized positions that frequently characterize heated political debates, of which environmentalism is one. Such an in-between space is critical as a means to generate a dialogue among people (including researchers) who frequently stand on opposite sides of high-profile public policy debates.[2]

I used the notion of embeddedness because I believe that it helps to explain multiple motivations, perspectives, and activisms of forestry-town women and that it avoids classifying activities into static dichotomies of pro- versus anti-environmental actions. This attempt is consistent with Geraldine Pratt's (1996) distinction between trashing and critique. Pratt pleaded for scholarly efforts that attempt to understand an argument more fully from a perspective of "partial insider" rather than exercises to illustrate moral or intellectual righteousness. In her words, "dialogue is likely to be more constructive if it is conceived outside the binaries of right and wrong, true or false" (254). Similarly, my emphasis on embeddedness attempts to maintain conversation and inquiry.

Embeddedness also tempers a tendency to assume that women freely choose particular political actions. Women's identities and activist agendas are not only continually open to choices but are also shaped by how partners, coworkers, community members, policy makers, academics, and/or other women delimit and constrain them. Thus, women do not only "play" their subjectivities and choices of activism but may also be "dealt" them within the confines of households, workplaces, communities, policy debates (e.g., environmentalism), and research agendas (Reed 2000).

Finally, the notion of embeddedness serves another important quality of feminist research. Embeddedness may help to maintain an engaged and sympathetic understanding of the complex and contradictory nature of women's lives attempted by feminist research methods (England 1994; Moss et al. 1993; Reinharz 1992). It allows one to avoid a preemptive stand on what is deemed progressive and glorious, and it attempts to avoid reinscribing exclusions that feminists have worked so hard to dismantle. Almost a generation ago, bell hooks argued that this was a substantial contribution of feminist organizing. She was commenting on political issues far removed in time and space from those of forestry-town women. Yet her words resonate for me today in relation to understanding and negotiating differences among those dealing with the implications of environmental and land use change for forestry communities: "Women need to come together in situations where there will be ideological disagreement and work to change that interaction so communication occurs. This means that when women come together, rather than pretend union, we should acknowledge that we are divided and must develop strategies to overcome fears, prejudices, resentments, competitiveness, etcetera" (1984, 63). By listening to and considering alternative viewpoints, feminist researchers can help to build an environmental movement that goes beyond ideological positioning and invites multiple others to take stands in ongoing debates.

Taking Stands for Forestry Communities

But if women's lives are embedded within social and spatial contexts, where are their actions located politically? First, as part of a rural society and culture, the voices of women are muted at two levels. As Chapters 4 through 7 illustrate, women's voices within forestry communities are restricted by male-dominated institutions and social norms located within those communities. Second, women's voices in rural communities are also muted by the rise to prominence of urban voices and ways of life in setting political priorities in Canada. According to Christopher Bryant and Alun Joseph (2001), most of this change is attributed to demographic changes as people have moved from the countryside to urban places. Thus, the prominence of urban society and its concerns can be attributed to the sheer numbers of people who live there. But this change is also evident because rural peoples have been relegated to a social location that is increasingly politically marginalized within broader, mainstream society (Buttel 1992).

To analyze this situation, I developed a four-part framework of social marginalization that included facets of exploitation, social exclusion, powerlessness, and moral exclusion. These facets were then examined through an interpretive lens that included uneven development, environmentalization and anti-environmentalization, and identity politics. I discovered that concerns about maintaining economic livelihood were real and ever present in the minds of residents of the forestry communities that I entered. However, these were not the only concerns. Rural residents also expressed concerns about the diminishing life chances in their communities resulting from a degrading economic status and urban and/or political indifference. I placed greater emphasis, therefore, on attempting to understand how processes of environmentalization and identity politics worked with one another to produce conflicts and continuities in the perspectives of women from forestry communities.

My investigations supported those of Laura Pulido (1996), who argued that environmental issues for rural peoples were bound up with issues of quality of life. As she points out, quality-of-life issues are awkward for "progressives" to discuss. Such issues are often construed to be apolitical or worse, to serve only to obscure the blatant class interests of the privileged. However, for those living in forestry communities, these issues included basic services such as access to educational opportunities, to medical care, and even to the peace and quiet of small-town or camp life that women sought to secure and retain. One person whom I spoke with informally told me, "If you want to examine hardships within these communities, focus on changes in public health and social services." His comment led me to engage more directly with these issues. I discovered that, at the same time as CORE was meeting with stakeholders to discuss redrawing the land use map, the provincial government was restructuring the delivery of health care and social services across the province. In combination, these activities threatened many aspects of basic services that formed part of the quality of life for residents of rural communities.

Women spoke about their concerns for the future of health and social services in a variety of ways. One woman, who worked for a social service agency, quit because she was required to move south in order to fulfill her previous role. She could no longer condone the long waiting lists and ever-dwindling resources. Women who worked in organizations that supported forestry lobbied the government for improved access to health care and educational opportunities. Some emphasized opportunities for women who did not qualify for many of the new training programs directed toward men in the industry. Women feared that without education, training, and opportunities that met the needs of all residents – male or female – more people would simply leave the communities, contributing to the decline of economic and social life.

What drew the strongest reaction was concern for the loss of forestry culture and identity that defined women of this study. The struggle to retain respect and identity is one of cultural survival. Only one to two generations ago, the basis of a "traditional" rural lifestyle was revered within the provincial culture. As a child growing up in British Columbia, I learned with great pride that forestry accounted for fifty cents of every dollar earned in the province. Those who laboured in the woods risked their lives and gained their identity as productive, hardworking, and honest workers. The myths of logging permeated even those who would never enter the woods. And the myths were positive. Today, however, public sentiment has turned unequivocally in favour of protecting wilderness for its aesthetic and ecological values, particularly if the costs of that protection remain far distant from the economic or geographic realities of the daily lives of urban residents. "West Coast environmentalism," with its focus on protecting old-growth forests along with their ecological structure and integrity, has gained moral ascendancy, challenging both local and global industrial elites who have traditionally benefited from access to, and use of, natural resources. Yet, as Bunyan Bryant and Paul Mohai point out, "to champion old growth forests or the protection of the snail darter or the habitat of spotted owls without championing clean safe urban environments or improved habitats of the homeless, does not bode well for future relations between environmentalists and people of color, and with the poor" (1992, 6). Nor does it sit well with rural people, who also claim that they have valid experience, knowledge, and love of nature and who observe the hypocrisy of urban consumer lifestyles.

The visions and goals of rural resource communities will vary in content and scope. In some cases, communities want economic diversification and funding for social planning; in others, they seek to block the allocation of new wilderness sites, to terminate specific projects, or simply to have a meaningful voice in land use debates. In all cases, it is an effort to work with and sometimes to challenge the prevailing power relations so that community members can live with dignity. The cases in this book present women's activism centred on creating locally appropriate economic change, maintaining ecosystems, confronting an exclusionary planning system, addressing local and systemic sexism within their communities, and affirming a local identity focused on forestry. Their actions to protest wilderness preservation cannot be separated from these efforts. I reconstructed the identities and actions of forestry-town women and loggers' wives to highlight their multiplicity. I illustrated that their activisms are many, crossing lines of community development, social services, forestry and land use, as well as environmental organizations.

In sum, perspectives and actions of women in forestry communities challenge both environmentalism and local social relations. Thus, women's identities, even within narrowly defined geographical or social spaces, can be seen to arise from and support multiple understandings of local situations. The problem, therefore, is not that we establish categories but that we make them too simplistic. Because of the multidimensional character of the lives of rural residents, the dichotomy of pro-environmentalism and anti-environmentalism as descriptors of people's political positions appears to be worn out, feeble, and simply inaccurate. The social movements and political struggles seek to improve material conditions, but they also emphasize issues of quality of life and rural identity. These multifaceted motivations and perspectives cannot be reduced to simple, singular explanations. A more complex understanding requires us to move beyond the environmental literature to marry insights about sustainability with theory and practice in other research contexts.

Second Growth: Renewing Research and Understanding of Social Sustainability

Before identifying future research needs, I want to reiterate disclaimers about my position. I am not arguing that environmentalism is a unitary ideology. Like other social movements and rural culture itself, environmentalism is composed of heterogeneous philosophies, ideologies, and strategies. Neither am I suggesting that environmentalism is the cause of social marginalization of rural communities. I do not believe that environmental proponents have "caused" the plight of resource workers and communities, nor do I believe that they wish ill of rural residents. Neither am I trying to generate sympathy for positions commonly described as anti-environmental. Many of the positions held by these women are problematic, and there remain environmental imperatives that must be addressed. However, as part of a system in which social, economic, and environmental relations intersect in complex ways, environmental organizations are caught up in the social problems now facing forestry communities.

Finally, I am not suggesting that rural residents are uniform in their social marginality. My approach considered both material distribution and cultural displacement as important elements in the marginality of forestry communities on the BC coast. Yet not all women experienced or expressed marginality in the same ways. There were important divides within these settings across class and ethnicity that situated some residents in a more privileged position than others. Some women did not see themselves as marginal at all within their communities. Furthermore, most residents of British Columbia remain far more privileged than workers in the tropical rainforests of "developing" countries. Notwithstanding these differences, all of the women I interviewed saw their communities and ways of life as threatened by the outside and dominant interests of urban society. By drawing attention to many facets of social marginalization, I have attempted to illustrate some of the social effects of changes in the regulation of forestry.

The work of conceptualizing social sustainability and learning how it can be advanced in rural communities is just beginning. There is a critical need to develop theory, debate implications, and put into practice actions to advance social sustainability. In research on sustainability, there has been far more effort given to, and consequently greater clarity in, understanding and advancing the links between environment and economy. By contrast, the implications of alterations in environmental and economic relations have been narrowly prescribed to jobs and citizen involvement. While these are important elements, they are wholly insufficient. Within each element, both research and policy practices have tended to privilege existing institutions associated with paid work and public politics, resulting in practices that favour men and marginalize women. Furthermore, jobs and citizen involvement simply do not begin to capture the breadth, richness, and complexity of everyday life that make up sustainable social systems. I will consider each element briefly.

As noted in Chapter 7, transition strategies introduced to cushion the blow of changes in environmental policy and land use have targeted jobs in the harvesting and processing sectors. These are considered primary sectors, both in the division of resource occupations and in terms of their contributions to forestry communities. In Chapter 4, I argued that many contributions by women do not fit within these job classifications, yet they remain critical to maintaining forestry communities. Thus, research must also attend to the distribution and stability of alternative sources of income during times of economic and social transition. Losses in timber harvesting and manufacturing will also have repercussions for the broader social fabric of these places. Development of the concept of social sustainability must also extend to how alterations in "primary" job sectors affect both community and household economies. Urban labour theory offers some purchase since it examines how household dynamics shape job prospects (e.g., Hanson and Pratt 1995; Morris 1990). There is relatively little that examines these dynamics in rural settings (see Halseth 2002; Preston et al. 2000). What little research has been done has not been concerned with issues of sustainability. These intersections must be developed and admitted into policy debates.

There is also a critical need to develop and apply models of participatory citizenship that are in contrast to current ideas about citizen participation. Current efforts that seek representation by known stakeholder groups reinforce unequal power relations that favour some groups over others. We must be willing to experiment with other models of representation and to search out ways to support alternative individuals and groups to become meaningful participants in these models (see Hawkins 1999; Wharf Higgins 1999). To this end, recognition of difference within communities and social groups requires us to think beyond conventional stakeholder groups when identifying participants who want access to participatory processes (Caragata 1999; Wharf Higgins 1999). Thus far, the emphasis on "corporate" forms of organization (e.g., unions, ENGOs, private companies) favours interests that are already well known and have established clear voices and positions in public debate. More diffuse interests – typically those that represent "social life" – have not gained coherence or clear representation. Yet they are key to developing a more inclusive and accurate conception of social sustainability.

I make this suggestion recognizing that there are significant challenges of implementation. The theoretical point that we must admit differences within communities and find ways to include multiple others comes with practical and ethical problems of implementation. Practically, it would be no mean feat for the state or other planning institutions to find, recognize, and agree on appropriate groups or individuals. Furthermore, it would be a challenge to provide logistical assistance to address power imbalances within planning processes so that all who take part can participate effectively. Ethically, when working within small geographical localities, a concerted search for appropriate individuals to participate according to differences such as age, economic status, gender, and ethnicity may expose those individuals to significant harm by separating them from their broader social groups. For example, acknowledging and addressing the practical and policy interests of women require a level of safety and trust that may only be found in aggregated categories. A focus on difference may only weaken the situation of women's collective interests in planning debates. Therefore, research strategies must simultaneously acknowledge differences among women and unite their diverse experiences so that women can forge alliances to advance a practical agenda for change. Such research strategies must work through theoretical problems of making generalizations with historically and geographically specific analyses in order to confront the moral issues and political choices that drive changes to public policy and social practice.

Conclusion: Toward a Politics of Engagement

Not long ago, to admit that wilderness is not, or should not be, a pristine, untouched landscape would have been to admit one's anti-environmental sentiments. However, the idealized image of pristine nature has more recently become a source of criticism for those concerned about social justice at international and local levels (Braun 1998; Bullard 1990; Buttel 1992; Cronon 1995; Guha 1989; Neumann and Schroeder 1995; Pulido 1996; Redclift 1987). It has even been an image worth challenging by environmental activists themselves. Tzeporah Berman was the lead campaigner for Greenpeace during the Clayoquot Sound demonstrations intended to halt all logging in the sound and to protect its wilderness character in perpetuity. In 1998, Berman announced Greenpeace's endorsement of new plans to begin logging in the sound. The decision to log was part of a pact crafted among the Nuu-Cha-Nulth First Nation, Weyerhaeuser (formerly MacMillan Bloedel), and the provincial government. This decision was given the official blessing of Greenpeace. I watched with interest as the news was announced on national television. Berman and Linda Cody, then vice president of Weyerhaeuser, embraced. Then Berman faced the camera with dignity and courage and stated, "We were wrong."

This anecdote is not provided to embarrass Berman or the movement that she represents. Her redirection of efforts in Clayoquot Sound did not gain the support of important elements of the environmental movement. The Friends of Clayoquot Sound refused to lend their support to the pact (Langer 2000). The anecdote is provided for a few reasons. First, it illustrates that, as with any social movement, the environmental movement continues to evolve. Its strategies and its understandings of issues are likely to change over time. Individual organizations may change tactics and directions in subtle and appropriate ways to navigate an agenda for social and ecological justice. Berman's final statement was one of courage and dignity, inviting new forms of collaboration and understanding. Organizations such as SHARE or Canadian Women in Timber might learn from this example.

Second, the story illustrates the power that people in international movements have in defining and redefining the agenda for change. Where moral exclusion is at work, such an admission by an individual such as Berman is likely to have a more lasting impact than the multiple voices from within forestry communities that have worked for years to send a similar message.

Third, and perhaps most importantly, the anecdote challenges each of us to revisit the classification schemes that define actions as "regressive" and "progressive." It is easy to dismiss the rhetoric and perspectives of women in forestry communities as born from fear, hate, and materialistic desire. Yet among the plain talk and the fear-laden rhetoric lies a truth about the relations between urban and rural, production and consumption, protection and exploitation, and masculinist and feminist institutions that demonstrates their mutual connections rather than their separations. Berman's admission challenges us all to reconsider our assumptions and presents an opportunity for dialogue between factions that have long held a distant and uneasy recognition of their differences and interests.

Environmental and community protection organizations, like other social movements, contain both progressive and regressive tendencies. Presumably, our task is to identify and advance the progressive tendencies and block the regressive ones. As a society, we will, in part, be judged on what kind of ecological legacy we leave for future generations. But we will also be judged on the compassion that we have for people in the present. The choices between the two are not easy or clear. Nor are they mutually exclusive. It is a challenge, therefore, for feminist studies and other contemporary discourses to figure out just which are the regressive and which are the progressive tendencies, let alone how to create the balance between society and nonhuman nature that we desire. This effort requires us to turn our analytical and theoretical gaze not only at people living in rural communities but also toward those who occupy the landscape outside these social and geographic locations – be they researchers, urban dwellers, policy analysts, or other stakeholders. The object of such scrutiny would be to marry inquiries about rural peoples and places with questions about our own conceptions, beliefs, and assumptions.

The contradictions associated with resource exploitation and love of nature, gender relations and logging lifestyle, and social cohesion and social strictures of forestry communities are writ large across the landscape of the coastal rainforest of British Columbia. As we try to reconfigure social relations among ourselves, and between ourselves and nature, we must try to understand both historical and contemporary relations embedded in the places where forestry has inscribed the landscape. My hope is that this book will help individuals and groups who currently oppose one another in a politics of segregation and conflict to begin new conversations in a renewed politics of engagement and resolution.

Epilogue

The contradictions and consistencies of forestry culture come to life in the following excerpt of a poem by Peter Trower, a former logger on Canada's West Coast. "The Last Spar-Tree" could well be the tree that is "scorned as timber," the image used to cover this book. His poem inspires in me both rage and wonder, and reminds me that I still have a great deal to learn about culture – his culture, my culture, and the culture of forestry-town women. It also reminds me how partial my gaze into the life of forestry and forestry communities has been. In my brief career, I have interpreted human interaction with the nonhuman environment differently at different times and in different situations. Cornfields and catastrophes may both be apt descriptions of our approaches to forestry. I, too, gaze at the forest and see the monuments and cathedrals of which he writes. But I cannot condemn logging or loggers. Like Trower, I remain convinced that logging is "larger than life."

The Last Spar-Tree on Elphinstone Mountain
For Al Purdy

The last spar-tree on Elphinstone mountain
through drunken sunday binoculars
pricks the blue bubble of the sky
on that final ridge where the scar tissue peters out
been four years quiet now on the battered mountain's back
except for shakecutters hunters and stray philosophers
The trucks are elsewhere some of the drivers dead
and the donkeys gone to barber another hill

I'm always shooting my mouth off about mountains
sometimes climbing them
and sometimes just distantly studying them like this

My eyes need no caulk boots
I can vault to that ridge in my mind
Stand at the foot of that tree, forlorn as a badly-used woman
Become merely landmark and raven perch
I can touch its bark sun-warm as flesh ...

It's either a cornfield or a catastrophe
Either a crop or a tithe or a privacy
has been taken from this place
What matter? it's done Beyond that ridge is a valley
I helped hack and alter ...

Logging's larger than life Keep your sailors and cowboys ...

Dream on in peace, old tree
perhaps you're a truer monument to man
than any rock-top crucifix in Rio De Janeiro

– Peter Trower[1]

Appendix: Describing and Reflecting on Research Methods

> If you're coming up here to point out all the errors of our ways, you better be careful because you're in a logging town.
>
> – Interviewee, 1997

These words, expressed during one of the early interviews, rang throughout my visits to the North Island. I was an outsider from the metropolis of Vancouver, a place that, according to many women whom I interviewed, contained the largest clear-cut in the province. I had a university education and job security. In fact, I knew that, the tougher it got economically for residents of the North Island, the more relevant and lucrative my research agenda would become. I had a three-year research grant from a controversial government agency that had failed miserably to deliver land-based and community-based programs in forestry. During the initial interviews, I was four to six months pregnant, obviously a mother in the paid workforce. Furthermore, as the mother of a preschool child, I felt guilty for every hour that I spent away from home. Each trip away from Vancouver entailed complex logistical arrangements and tugged at my heartstrings. To reduce my time away, I flew to and from the study area. During my flights into the region, I viewed the watersheds and valleys that had been logged. There were so many clear-cuts that scraped mountains and valleys that were not visible by road. A few sections remained untouched. Some had greened up, while others remained to be replanted. I knew that I was entering logging country.

The idea for this research project was conceived at approximately the same time as my first child. Both "projects" became intertwined in complex ways of which I was only partially aware. My entry into this study as a mother and an academic influenced my choice of research topic, research design, philosophical approach, entry point into the communities, and physical organization of my work schedule and tasks. My status separated me from some women, while it provided some common ground with others. It affected my acceptance by women who opened their lives to me, some of whom I now call, perhaps presumptuously, colleagues and friends. It certainly shaped my analysis, providing me with firsthand knowledge of some of the daily realities that these women faced rather than a polite, but distant, ignorance.

In this appendix, I document and reflect on my research methods in some detail. Since several texts have been written about participatory research more generally, my purpose is not to make general statements about research practices. Instead, I provide considerable detail of my own strategies in an explicit attempt to expose specific research choices and issues associated with this project. I organize the discussion into three parts: a detailed chronology, a reflection on how I situated myself within the methods that I used and within feminist research practices, and reflections on the changing social context for research more generally. Despite making me and the findings more vulnerable to challenge, this open discussion can be a pedagogical tool for scholars to address their own research methodologies and to destabilize conventional norms about relations between the researcher and the research subjects, the academy, and funding agencies. My hope is that with such details others who might seek to use similar methods will be forewarned of the commitments, challenges, strengths, and limitations of the methods and, in this case, the researcher herself. Such advance knowledge may assist future researchers to improve their own entries into research situations.

A Chronology of Research Methods

That we shape the results of our research by the tools or methods we employ is perhaps self-evident. The standard "best practices" approach to research begins with a research question, develops an appropriate theoretical framework, and then uses research methods judiciously to advance the theory. Occasionally, when methods and theory do not mesh, we discard the theory and start anew. However, participatory research is different in many ways. In it, it is equally true that methods shape theory. That is, although my theoretical conceptions guided the choice of tools for data gathering and analysis, the methods also served to challenge the theoretical underpinnings of the research itself. Nowhere is this more true than in my constant examination and interpretation of forestry-town women and loggers' wives.

Entering the North Island

In January 1996, I was fortunate to take six months away from most of my administrative duties at the university to take up a position as an in-house scholar at the Centre for Research in Women's Studies and Gender Relations at the University of British Columbia. I used the opportunity to redirect my previous research interests. I immersed myself in feminist theory, methodology, and empirical studies related to women in rural resource communities, environmentalism, activism, et cetera. I wrote a grant proposal for an ambitious, three-year research project to examine communities on the West Coast using data collection and analysis methods associated with conventional forms of policy analysis, in combination with participatory action research used by feminist scholars. I thought that I had dared the impossible. But later that year, I was awarded the grant.

The methodology combined what I initially described as participatory action research with more conventional forms of data collection and analysis. In the first component, considerable time was spent getting to know the region. In February 1997, my graduate students, research assistants, and I wrote letters to community leaders introducing the research, and then we took the time to meet with several of them personally.[1] We obtained names of women who were considered community leaders in the local area as well as women who had been or were currently employed in forestry occupations. We also compiled a list of women who were active in different organizations, serving on present or past planning committees, forestry advocacy organizations, and community-based organizations. As well, we obtained names of women employed in forestry companies and in the Ministry of Forests. We developed a profile of the region and individual communities with respect to social and economic characteristics (e.g., community evolution, demographics, type and location of employment) using data from a variety of sources. This effort required nonstructured interviews with representatives from the municipal government, the Chamber of Commerce, and the Ministry of Forests. We also drew information from council minutes, planning documents, Ministry of Forests profiles, consultants' reports, land use planning initiatives, and Census of Canada data for 1991 and 1996. In addition, we gathered information about stakeholder groups in each community. We then undertook socioeconomic and policy profiles for Vancouver Island and eventually posted them on the World Wide Web.

As an inventory of stakeholders involved in planning/management and advocacy was compiled, we began the process of informing individual women of the research and conducting interviews with them to learn more about their advocacy work, employment histories, and home lives. My interest in the complexities, consistencies, and contradictions in the political voices of women in forestry communities led me, first, to collect stories about the most obvious examples of women's political activism, the women-led forestry organizations. Here I began with the membership rolls of Canadian Women in Timber. Second, I obtained the names of women who acted as volunteers in the local SHARE organizations. I sought out women who were currently or had historically been employed in the industry. And third, upon recommendation of one of the reviewers of the proposal, I went beyond these women to include a more general sample of women who did not have the same direct connections to forestry. While I was initially annoyed that some outside reviewer had toyed with my rationale, the result was a richer data set from which comparisons were made possible. These initial interviews took place between June and August 1997. My student assistants and I conducted, in all, thirty-two interviews.

Initially, I followed closely the research design described by Julie-Katherine Gibson-Graham (1994). Like her, I "employed" a number of local "loggers' wives" as co-researchers. Women were selected on the basis of their interests and abilities as well as their stages in the life cycle, family formation, type of forestry dependence, and place of residence. Ten women were selected. In late August 1997, I held a two-day workshop to inform the participants about the research project, develop questions for future interviews, determine who should be interviewed next, and undergo training in interviewing techniques. I outlined the following objectives when I brought the women together:

- to identify the kinds of information needed to consider the impacts of land uses and economic conditions for women living on the North Island
- to identify the kinds of information needed to pinpoint opportunities and barriers for women to become involved in making changes in land use and community development
- to investigate women's situations in relation to family life, paid work, and community service
- to examine how women's contributions to community service and advocacy are connected to their situations.

More specifically, I hoped that by the end of the workshop we would have:

- discussed and possibly revised the nature and scope of the research project and the methods to be used
- devised interview questions
- identified women to interview
- learned about and practised interview skills and research ethics
- learned something more about ourselves and dimensions of this community.

It was an ambitious agenda. By the time we left one another, the women had an interview schedule and a tool kit of resources upon which to draw. I was in their hands now. Each woman was responsible for conducting and recording three interviews. The women received payment for their interviewing work, and all expenses associated with the interviews and workshops were covered by the research grant. Only seven women from the first workshop undertook interviews since personal circumstances took over their agendas. I had anticipated this fallout and consequently relied on some of the remaining women to pick up additional interviews. During the fall and winter months, twenty more interviews were conducted, tape-recorded, and transcribed verbatim. Two interviews had to be omitted because they were incomplete or unrecorded. By the end of this stage, I had fifty completed interviews to analyze.

Analysis of Results

By June 1998, I had completed a preliminary analysis and was anxious to get some feedback from the communities. I undertook two forms of analysis. First, I compiled demographic characteristics of respondents into a database and made some general comparisons between the characteristics of the respondents and those of the population of the communities at large (as provided by BC STATS and Statistics Canada [census]). There are some significant limitations in doing this. For example, BC STATS only has data for incorporated communities, and communities such as Sointula are not incorporated; therefore, disaggregated data were not available. In addition, the sample size for those interviewed was very small, and it was not statistically random, so any statistical comparison was not appropriate. However, a general comparison provided some indications about the characteristics of those interviewees. In addition to undertaking the demographic profiles, I compiled what I called "policy profiles." I identified important changes in public policy and pursued the documentation of a history of these changes, in particular how public policy initiatives affected the North Island.

Next I focused on the qualitative and participatory element – the interviews. I had read each of the transcripts over at least once, and some several times, to develop a series of narratives or stories from which I could identify several themes. The transcripts were then classified according to these themes. From this exercise, 400 pages of single-spaced text were generated. To refine these themes, I created four general scenarios: The Nature of Forestry, The Rites of Spring (Effects of Environmentalism),[2] Women in the Woods, and Women in Communities. These scenarios were created as composite sketches. A conservative estimate is that each interview required fifteen to twenty hours for interviewing, transcribing, and completing the preliminary analysis.

In April to May 1998, preparations were made for focus groups to be held in Port McNeill at the beginning of June. Three focus groups were established. Some women had been previously interviewed, while others had not. One group was composed of women employed in the forestry sector, a second was composed of women involved in the delivery of social services and/or environmental activism, and the third was composed of women who had been active in protecting logging jobs and whose partners were in forestry. For each group, we discussed the scenarios that I had created. In some cases, women identified errors of interpretation; in others, they reinforced the preliminary observations. The focus groups also served to update information based on new issues that had emerged since collection of the primary data.

After the focus groups, further analysis was undertaken to prepare for a three-day workshop with female researchers only. It was conducted on Vancouver Island in November 1998. At this workshop, women from northern Vancouver Island shared their ideas and research experiences with women from Squamish, a forestry community located on the BC mainland.

I had several purposes for the workshop. First, I provided feedback to the women about their interviewing techniques. Each woman received a personal letter accompanied by examples of her interviews in which the strengths of her interviewing style were identified and possible improvements for the future were noted. In addition, there was time the first evening to discuss and examine particular situations in which the women had done well. This format was selected so that women would feel encouraged by their successes and be able to talk to me about specific situations in which they had had more difficulty without feeling like they were being disciplined. Second, I used the profile information to develop a slide show and a profile of each place to introduce the places to all the women and generate a discussion of their similarities and differences. This icebreaker provided an opening for women to speak about their similarities and differences in a respectful and interesting way. While I had originally planned a one-way slide presentation for the first night, the show quickly became interactive. Each slide offered an entry point for women to talk about their place of origin and to raise questions about other locations. So while I identified the images, the discussion was rightly taken out of my domain.

On the second day, we focused on two main themes, "women and work" and "women and advocacy." These themes were discussed with the use of interview materials and census data provided in a written package made available to each woman. The women were reminded that the process of maintaining confidentiality was important and that excerpts from interviews should be discussed in general terms even if the women themselves knew the respondents (e.g., possibly because they had conducted the interviews). We discussed the work that women do in their communities, the barriers that they face in employment, and the potential opportunities that could be pursued. We discussed differences and similarities within and between communities.

In addition, we identified activities that could extend the findings beyond standard academic papers and reporting mechanisms. Women suggested how the research could be used to inform other community organizations and government agencies. This was an important part of the funding requirement under this particular research grant as well as a cornerstone of participatory action research. We also included a section dealing with "women and activism," which discussed how women are active in their communities and the kinds of capacity-building activities that could be done to empower women. Several activities were identified in order to return the results to the communities in a format that they could appreciate and use.

One tool that I created was a booklet that used extensive quotations, figures, and cartoons to highlight issues that the women had documented. Part of the workshop was devoted to who would receive the booklet. The list became long, illustrating how women connected their issues to broad elements across their communities. This list also attested to the strong *social* component that women associated with changes in forestry. Those who received the booklet included:

- school boards
- principal of each public school in the region
- major forest companies
- Ministry of Forests
- Forest Renewal BC (FRBC)
- Human Resources Development Canada
- Community Futures
- Economic Development Commission
- North Island Women
- mayor of each municipality
- regional districts
- local (federal) Member of Parliament, local (provincial) Member of the Legislative Assembly
- public libraries
- local newspapers
- Inner Coast Natural Resource Centre
- North Island Citizens for Shared Resources
- chambers of commerce
- regional health boards
- Ministry of Women's Equality
- Employment and Family Assistance Plan
- Ministry of Social Services

In April 1999, I also presented the results at two community forums on the North Island. One community researcher received training in Web-based design and posted results on both my Web page at the university and the community Web site. In addition to these "deliverables," I was required to write progress reports to FRBC semi-annually and to complete a statistical profile of the demographic characteristics of participants for BC STATS, another provincial government agency. In total, I wrote fourteen reports in three and a half years to these agencies alone. This heavy commitment sapped my energies for writing up the research results and carrying out further extension activities that I might otherwise have undertaken within the communities themselves. By July 1999, I had completed the community presentation and all the reports to FRBC. I felt released from my technical reporting obligations but remained haunted by, and responsible for, other commitments that I thought were still unmet. It is to a broader reflection on these concerns that I now turn.

Reflections on Method

The Funding Context

The research grant was under the auspices of a recently created and short-lived Crown corporation, Forest Renewal BC (FRBC). This institution was funded by royalty and stumpage rates with the express purpose of returning money back into land- and community-based programs that relied on forestry. While the bulk of the funding was established for activities such as enhanced silviculture, watershed restoration, and wildlife inventories, a small portion was reserved for applied research. Within the overall budget of the research program, a tiny portion was allocated to social science research and, within that allocation, to research about forestry communities.

Yet to social scientists standing at the trough (me among them), this funding was like receiving gold coins from heaven. The allowances for assistants and other technical supports were approximately three times larger than for an individual researcher who might apply to the national social science granting agency, the Social Sciences and Humanities Research Council (SSHRC). Consequently, the grant provided sufficient funds to hire graduate students throughout the entire grant period. It also allowed me to pay the community researchers generous honoraria to take part in each workshop as well as to conduct the interviews. I attempted to ensure that the women received "good wages" for their work so that they would value their own contributions and know that I did so as well. In addition, I was the first person at my university to argue successfully that *community researchers and interviewees* should be reimbursed for expenses incurred for the child care required to carry out the research. These were benefits that have yet to be allowed under standard research grants.

Situating the Research and the Researcher

To anchor this research unequivocally in the realm of feminist research epistemology or methodology is to wade into a long-standing debate (McDowell 1992; Moss et al. 1993; Reinharz 1992). Early feminist research was inspired by "notions of doing research 'with' or 'for' rather than 'about women'" (McDowell 1992, 407). Methods that would break down unequal power relations between a researcher and her informants were advocated. While feminist researchers now agree that scholarship is not defined solely by method, most feminist research practices still attempt to establish mechanisms of collaboration, wherein relations between researcher and researched are characterized by engagement rather than separation. In addition, there is a recognition that, regardless of how the data are collected, the researcher is not assumed to be objective, value free, or distant from her subjects (McDowell 1992; Warrington 1997).

Feminist researchers also recognize the potential for differences in social status, power, and resources between interviewers and their subjects (Feldman and Welsh 1995; Haraway 1991; Sachs 1994; Whatmore, Marsden, and Lowe 1994). Some feminists advocated interpretive methods as a means to reduce the distance between the researcher and subjects. Yet Judith Stacey (1988, cited in McDowell 1992, 408) found that, in her detailed ethnographic fieldwork, she was more likely to become bound to her informants in a network of exploitative relationships, abandonment, and betrayal than in her earlier work: "Precisely because ethnographic research depends on human relationship, engagement and attachment, it places research subjects at grave risk of manipulation and betrayal by the ethnographer." Similarly, Daphne Patai suggested that "feminist researchers are unconsciously seductive towards their research subjects, raising their expectations and inducing dependency" (1991, 143). Linda McDowell argued that "women doing gender research ... are quite likely to find themselves in circumstances where they are more powerful, more affluent and with greater access to a range of resources than their subjects. It is too easy inadvertently to generate expectations of positive intervention on behalf of the women being studied and this sometimes leads, as Stacey warned, to feelings of disappointment or even betrayal" (1992, 408). These misgivings led McDowell to conclude that feminist scholars cannot, "nor should we aim to, empower our participants" (413). What, then, should be our purpose?

Of course, if women's lives are situated, partial, and open to a range of possible social actions, this includes the lives and strategies of women researchers. As Sandra Harding pointed out, "All scientific knowledge is always, in every respect socially situated ... We should think of the social location of our own research – the place in race, gender and class relations from which it originates and from which it receives empirical support – as part of the implicit or explicit evidence for our best claims as well as our worst ones" (1991, 11-12). In keeping with this understanding, I attempted to make clear my own social and geographical locations as I undertook and wrote up the research.

Throughout the research, I was self-conscious of my status as an outsider. From a solid, white, middle-class family in which education was given high importance, I had obviously attained some measure of success on this criterion. I knew (at least superficially) how to operate within a male-dominated institution (the academy) and a male-dominated discipline (geography). I was part of a dynamic department in which good theory was the hallmark of good scholarship.[3] Thus, I had to stake my tenure and promotion on whether or not I could "compete" (or at least survive) in the realm of theory. Applied or policy-based research was a sullied sister by comparison.

I was also a mother. I was a mother who had made choices about having children and working. These parts of my life were not hidden from my interviewees. As a result, they provided points of engagement and points of separation. For example, I had long discussions with some women about the trials and tribulations of motherhood, and we shared some discussion about separation anxieties and personal rewards of employment aside from income. But with some women, I received a rather cool reception. They had "never used day care," nor had they parted from their preschool children to engage in paid employment. My situation as a mother also shaped my research approach since I was reluctant to be away from home and child for long periods. Thus, I developed multiple strategies – going up island for a few days at a time and/or dragging my partner and the children with me. I also relied on my research assistants to a much greater extent than I had in any previous research. They performed most of the initial interviews. I do not know what the cumulative effects of these strategies have been on my results; I do know that they shaped my interpretive lens.

Perhaps the most challenging task of situating my work came at the first workshop. I recall the nervousness I felt upon meeting some of the women for the first time. I had listened to all of their voices on tape; I knew that many of them were strong women. I was worried that I would come across as an uppity, urban environmentalist out to "catch" them off guard. I knew that some women who had been interviewed did not want to participate in the research because they had already been researched to death or did not want another outsider to make them look bad. Maybe the women at the workshop were equally skeptical. In addition, I was familiar with the work of consultants who wrote reports on relevant topics of women and land use planning, women and work on the North Island, et cetera. None of these reports had gone far. I was an academic with a strong academic orientation. What could I do to serve these women if others before me had failed?

My positioning in the first workshop, therefore, was critical. Here is an excerpt from the workbook that each woman received before the workshop. I reiterated these themes in our first meeting:

> The research explores how changes in land use and economic development affect the lives of women who live in B.C. forestry communities. We will explore how women experience and interpret these changes, and how these experiences/interpretations shape their life choices – at home, at work, and as participants in their communities.
>
> In the past, my research has focused on the impacts of changes in environmental policy and land use on resource-dependent communities and identified the opportunities and constraints faced by local residents who work with provincial government agencies to tailor policies to meet their needs. I have spent considerable time thinking about what "sustainable development" and "sustainability" mean in the context of Canadian resource-dependent towns. While I have no conclusions yet, my sense is that there has been considerable effort made to bring the themes of environment and economy together in consideration of new policy options. However, the theme of social sustainability has somehow received much less attention.
>
> Also, I believe that women's voices and concerns have been under-represented in these discussions; hence, the focus on women in my current study. Previous research about women living in resource towns has tended to talk about "women's experience" as if all women shared the same opportunities and constraints. Yet, in looking at a region such as the North Island, one might suggest that the effects may differ according to differences in home life, social backgrounds and expectations, dependencies on forestry, and stages in the life course ... At this stage, I don't really know enough about these potential differences among women to make any general statements. I would like to uncover how women are affected by the changes in forestry and land use practices as well as how they are moved to act within their individual choices, work, families and communities (communities of affiliation and geographic communities), through community service organizations, and through political activities around environmental policy and land use. My objective is *not* to state that some women are right, while others are wrong; rather, it is to uncover the points of diversity and similarity among women.
>
> With such information, I seek to contribute to discussions about the social issues that accompany environmental policy and land use change. I also want to encourage sensitivity to the diversity of women's perspectives and experiences. In addition, as there has been criticism in the recent past that women have been excluded from the policy debates, I hope that this research will help to identify ways and means to include women in these discussions more directly.

I also wanted to situate and validate the importance of the work to be undertaken by the community researchers. In this regard, both the workbook and I told them:

> Each of you has a valuable contribution to make to the research effort. Some of you are long-time residents of the North Island, others are relative newcomers. Some of you have young children, others have grown children, some have no children at all. Some of you are directly affected by changes in forestry and land use policy; you rely on ongoing extraction. Others rely on forestry to provide you with jobs in restoration work. Some rely on both. For others, the forestry industry does not affect your income or employment prospects. As a group, you have variable life experiences, which you have kindly shared with my research assistants and myself. You may choose to share some of these over the course of this research project or you may choose to retain them for yourself.

From Participatory Action Research to Interactive Applied Research

In my desire to be seen as relevant and progressive, I clutched at the term "participatory action research" to describe my methodology to my community researchers. The participatory part of the research gets people who are active in the communities of study involved in the research process. Participatory research assumes that the primary researcher has a lot to learn from people in the community, and it is meant to give something back to the community(ies) in which it is done. One way that it does this is to increase the understanding of local issues. It is also an opportunity for community members to work together, to learn about each other, and potentially to strengthen their connections with each other. The process of participating, therefore, can build skills, confidence, and knowledge among all participants. At least this is what I told my community researchers.

When preparing for the first workshop, I identified seven potential benefits for community researchers, including getting to know others, learning about and contributing to research and community development, and developing skills in communication and critical thinking. But the flow of benefits was undeniably greater in one direction, back to me, the researcher. My status as an academic had increased since I attained the research grant (and such a sizable one), and I was able to provide graduate student support. As I began to write academic papers, I drew attention to my work and became more "authoritative" on gender and environmental policy issues. During the research, I was granted both tenure and promotion. Professionally and personally, I had achieved some tangible "success." I could not come close to offering such benefits to the women who participated.

This conclusion led me to question the label "action" research. The action part of the research relies on methods in which *"researching one's own situation* with others *who are similarly situated* is designed to have the effect of raising consciousness of shared conditions and oppression. This method of research relies upon an identification between researcher and researched and the discovery of a shared subject position from which political intervention can be discussed and enacted" (Gibson-Graham 1994, 215; emphasis added). Clearly, I was not "similarly situated" with these women. How could I presume to raise "our" consciousness when I was barely aware of the daily problems of social and geographic isolation, lack of formal education, limited job opportunities, fear for the safety of my partner on the job, et cetera? Gibson-Graham also questioned her own motivations and methods: "Without an assumed basis of unity between women could these research methods still be employed?" (1994, 215). She concluded that "action research need not focus upon the uncovering or construction of a unified consciousness upon which later interventions will be based. Action research can be a means by which we 'develop political conversations(s) among a complex and diverse "we"'" (220; citing Brown 1991, 81). This justification allowed me to continue to believe that I was going to make a difference in these women's lives. It did not, however, overcome the basic issue of how unevenly the benefits of the research would be distributed.

Given the benefits that I would attain from successful completion of the project, my motivations were strong. However, these motivations were appropriately questioned by interviewees. Three types of questions were raised relating to my motivations for the study or my opinions on particular issues. These were legitimate questions and required thoughtful and careful responses. This is one example of the questions raised by the interviewees about the project:

Q: You were really helpful. Do you have any questions that you'd like to ask?
A: Yes. There's just one; I have to know this, you're not with any environmental group?
Q: With UBC [University of British Columbia].
A: Just with UBC, it's not Greenpeace or ... ?
Q: No.
A: Okay. That's the only thing.
Q: No. If you read the –
A: I read it. I read it, but I just had to. I read it twice. But I just had to ask that.
Q: No. We're just looking at women and the challenges facing women, like when they're in a resource town and the forest industry is –

A: And it's funded by FRBC [Forest Renewal BC] too, isn't it?
Q: That's right. Yes.
A: That's good. That's really good.

I was asked more than once "Are you an environmentalist?" Because the research was funded by FRBC, a Crown corporation, some respondents wondered if I was an apologist for government policy. These issues were tricky. It was important to answer as honestly as possible while at the same time ensure that the respondent felt welcome to hold views different from our own.

As I read through the interviews conducted by community researchers, however, I found subtle, yet important, benefits from their involvement. One benefit was to connect women who might be interested in similar issues. For example, one woman identified some strong environmental sentiments. The interviewer indicated that the comments were not the first that she had heard. The interviewee was grateful to hear that she was not alone in the community. In another case, the interviewee identified other women who were coming together to address mutual financial concerns that had been raised during the interview. In this case, the interviewee was able to meet with women who shared similar concerns. Thus, an important benefit came in helping women to make connections with one another, where previously they had felt isolated. But for me, the greatest benefit came with the sense of self-worth among community researchers.

One of the community researchers had been active in several local struggles, including trying to establish the women's centre. During a follow-up workshop, she commented that "I think everyone has different agendas. They have different reasons for doing what they do. *And I think I have a role, and the people in the community have a role too – just as we were doing in this research project – that we need to stand up and speak and keep speaking until we're listened to.*" For me, the excitement came with the realization that she was taking responsibility for undertaking follow-up in her community. The researcher viewed the project as a means to develop awareness and to open discussions with other women, even if they had different viewpoints. While this was not necessarily the key to empowerment, the comment marked a genuine interest and desire to be enabled within the community. Ultimately, as I withdrew from the project and the region, I hoped that the sense of becoming enabled would be both contagious and long-lasting.

In reviewing my own work as well as that of others, I have come to conclude that the terminology of "interaction methodology" (Kleiber and Light 1978; Stanley and Wise 1983) is a more accurate reflection of my approach and intent. In interactive research, those researched become a greater part of the research process, helping to refine the instruments (in this case, the interview schedule), sharing information, and checking and rechecking interpretations. It also makes a much more modest claim for understanding others' positions and for empowering participants. Thus, it provides a more accurate reflection of the intentions and successes of this project. In the next section, I set the research into a broader context of research funding and of undertaking policy-relevant research.

A Changing Research Context

> Thank you Maureen. Your concern is felt.
>
> – Inscription on a gift to me from the nongovernmental organization North Island Women, after I presented a keynote address to a celebration that they organized in 1999

I face this inscription with considerable ambivalence. I am ambivalent because I still feel inadequate for the task of undertaking a scholarly work with a feminist orientation intended to provide results for public policy related to forestry and land use. This was my first project with an explicit feminist orientation, one of only two that would be funded by this short-lived, multi-million-dollar research program in British Columbia. This combination – a public policy focus of the research, my lack of prior experience in feminist research, the presumed dubious relevance of feminist research to the aims of the funding agency, and my desire to "make a difference" both theoretically and in the lives of my research subjects – created for me a near-impossible challenge in assessing the outcomes of the project. Hence my ambivalence. I was most disturbed by the challenge of meeting the dual needs of academic scholarship and public policy. I believe that this quandary is likely to be reproduced again and again as the terms of funding for social science research increasingly seek researchers who can combine theoretical rigour with public relevance.

However, it is not just the issue of being *socially* relevant that poses a challenge; to be successfully funded, feminist research must also be *policy* relevant. This demand widens the range of adjudicators and shapes research expectations for *our* projects. These interconnections exist at all phases of the research process, from the formulation of a problem through to the generation of research questions, from the selection of methods and entry into the "field" through to the analysis of results and their articulation and circulation in both academic and policy forums. I view this as somewhat of a Faustian bargain – by accepting funding from agencies with such high public policy demands, which compromises might I have had to make with respect to my own scholarly integrity and feminist intentions? As the previous section documents, feminist researchers have examined their own positionings in relation to their research subjects (e.g., related to similarities or differences of gender, class, sexuality, or ethnicity). Yet they have been less attentive to positionings in relation to the dynamics of the context of the research. Tensions arise between different expectations by the academy and the funding agencies; how these relationships are played out influences the setting of priorities for research and the criteria for evaluating the results.

Setting Research Priorities and Practices

New research priorities are beginning to shape our research questions and methods. For example, the major publicly funded social science funding agency in Canada, SSHRC, historically has provided research grants that have not required a public policy focus as a criterion of relevance. But times are changing. For individual researchers, SSHRC grant applications now *require* applicants to identify how results will be distributed and made relevant outside the academy. For larger, collaborative proposals, applicants are required to establish partnerships outside academia and to demonstrate how academics will contribute to the aims of their "lay" or "community" partners. Increasingly, and not surprisingly, Canadian researchers are seeking funding outside SSHRC. Funding may be obtained through a variety of agencies such as government departments or ministries and Crown corporations as well as nongovernmental organizations such as credit unions, private industry, or advocacy organizations. All of these agencies demand that their own policy priorities be reflected in the proposals if they are to be successfully funded, and this requirement quickly becomes problematic. These agencies may predefine key topic areas for research. They may pose direct questions for academics to answer. They may accept some methodologies, reject some, and appropriate still others.

Since my research was funded by FRBC, I had to demonstrate how my study would improve the well-being of forestry communities overall. My initial proposal was accepted, pending my agreement to revise its objectives according to the demands of a single reviewer. This reviewer requested that I expand the group of women beyond "protesters" to include a sample of women from a broader political and economic base. Thus, my compromise was to carry on with my own interests and "append" those of the reviewer in order to satisfy the granting agency. But it did not stop there: I had to make this compromise every time I made a report about the project (I made fourteen in total), hampering my abilities to stay true to my own research interests and questions.

The funding from FRBC also raised the expectations and hackles of residents from forestry communities themselves. The provincial government told residents that money from this corporation would be used to support local development of forest resources and communities. They were hopeful about but also wary of research, concerned that funding for research would supersede their needs for assistance during times of massive economic restructuring. Although FRBC administered two separate programs – a research program and a land management program (e.g., involving activities such as tree planting and watershed restoration) – in the minds of many community residents the objectives of the separate programs were blurred by the pressing concerns about the survival of local livelihood, community, and culture within a reforming forestry economy.

Notwithstanding these limits, there were some important benefits of going this route. The research grant from FRBC was about three times larger than what I could have secured through SSHRC. As David Demeritt (2000) points out, the amount of grant funding is an increasingly important currency in measuring the value of an academic. My relatively large grant greatly increased my average income to the department and the university. While large grants are valued, few individual feminist research projects can claim such advantage. And, as I noted before, I was able to pay generous honoraria and expenses to all who participated. In my mind, these were small but important successes. The honoraria and other dispersals were part of my contribution in redistributing the wealth provided through this grant.

Judging the Result: Expanding Assessment Criteria and Critics

> Always, I am amazed at what we tell,
>   how much faith we put in it.
> Never really knowing who is listening,
>   how they're going to take it, *where*.
>
> – Bronwen Wallace, cited by Stuart McLean (1992; emphasis added)

A movement into the realm of public policy research also expands the networks of relevant actors who judge the research effort – from the point of application, through to its implementation, and ultimately upon its completion. For example, usually only the most obscure research proposals funded by the government get cited in the newspaper each year in public jests about academic irrelevance. In contrast, the explicit public policy orientation of the FRBC project expanded the range of interests, relevant criteria, and potential critics pertinent to assessing its methods and results. This research was set within a policy environment in which forestry was a major provincial industry undergoing economic restructuring and in which government agencies were looking for research with policy relevance to help make government decisions. For some community research participants, accountability and research relevance were measured by the power of the academic to generate positive change in their lives. Yet, at the same time, expectations and prospects for failure were undeservedly high. This was brought home to me when I listened to one of the transcripts involving the community researchers:

> A: Is that what's going to happen with this [research ... be put on a shelf and ignored]? ... I'm just curious.
>
> Q: I think Maureen has a personal interest, not a vested interest, but a personal interest in the results. I believe, from meeting her, that she has a real interest in this sort of thing, and she has an incredible amount of valuable knowledge, and I do believe that she's got, in her position as being professor at ... [the University of British Columbia], she's probably got a high, a tremendous, amount of respect too ... It's been my experience that people who are in educational institutions have credibility and knowledge, and knowledge is power, so, you know. Hopefully, and as I say, she does have a personal interest in it, from the heart, not from –
>
> A: Perfect, that'll be good.

The interviewer appears to have had a much inflated view of my power to change policy. She translates my "concern" into a measure of success. Yet from the perspective of the most important criterion of this public policy context – jobs – the project was an utter failure: no jobs were created! In another interview, "Betty" remarked, "It's all a bit peculiar that this was going on, and for so long [three years], and money going to this [research] when it's, it's been cut for the men working who could maybe use the money."

This quotation continues to haunt me. It haunts me not because I intended my research to generate or supplant job opportunities but because this public expectation permeated the project despite my assertions to the contrary. This expectation was entirely reasonable because the agency that funded the research had also made such a strong commitment to job creation. The fact that the research program was separate from other FRBC programs was not relevant to those living in the communities. If I ignored this point, then I only highlighted my difference and my distance from my research subjects – that of a detached, urban, privileged, useless, *yet employed* academic. If I embraced it, then I set myself up for failure. My research simply did not create jobs. Perhaps Betty was right.

A New Context for Feminist Scholarship

In keeping with other feminist scholars (e.g., Rose 1997), I acknowledge that the power to define the parameters and to impose measures of success is not mine alone. Presumably, the granting agency can use the reports and findings in ways that I had not intended. I have not monitored the follow-up of all the reporting requirements. Meeting the requirements was draining enough. Importantly, the research subjects themselves can shape the criteria for success, apply them, and announce them in unexpected ways. This acceptance of others' power within the research process is consistent with the observations of feminist scholars who point out that researchers are situated subjects who have only partial knowledge and power to inscribe the research agenda. Gillian Rose described the power relations between researched and researcher as "fluid, marked by fragmented understandings, uncertainty, and risk" throughout research and dissemination practices (1997, 317). She suggested that "the research process is dangerous ... The risks of research are impossible to know" (317).

In contrast to Rose's more negative assessment, Demeritt argued that, as identities of, and relations among, researchers, partners, and publics are changing, the processes of "trust building, mutual understanding, and social learning involved in doing research can be as important for participants as the substantive results" (2000, 326). I agree that these intangible effects are often discounted. The fact that my concern was "felt" suggests that I built positive relations within the communities I studied. The invitation to be the keynote speaker at an inaugural celebration of "Women of Influence" on northern Vancouver Island suggests that, during my research, I attained a level of local trust and support. Yet I am acutely aware that mutual understanding and concern do not feed a family. And when research does not feed a family in a public policy context in which communities believe that they are threatened by actual or imminent (nutritional or political) starvation, processes of trust building erode. So does the perceived public value of the research project.

I write up these reflections because I believe that my experience has wider application. Academics are now encouraged by university administrations to apply to nonconventional funding sources that may have strings attached to public policy objectives. Even conventional sources such as SSHRC have new requirements for researchers to express their relevance to society. Feminist scholars, who try to uncover and undo real-world inequities, and who have focused scholarly attention on power relations, should be at the core of debates about funding. Importantly, with respect to the interpretation of our results, our successes will be determined in very public and uncontrolled arenas of policy debates and study locations. More fundamentally, these arenas shape the basic premises of the research itself. Sometimes they do so overtly, such as in preestablishing questions for research programs; sometimes these arenas shape research more subtly through ongoing renegotiations of the research project through its various stages. As feminist scholars, we need to discuss the implications of this emergent research context fully and openly among ourselves, policy makers, and research subjects.

Notes

Preface
1 Old nursery rhyme, provenance unknown.

Chapter 1: Introduction
1 The importance of Clayoquot Sound in highlighting and honing political strategies for the environmental preservation of Canada's West Coast cannot be underestimated. ENGOs have now moved beyond Clayoquot Sound to include most of the West Coast temperate rainforests as part of a carefully organized, well-financed, international campaign to protect wilderness. Communities throughout the West Coast are now being targeted by ENGOs to engage in partnerships for protection. These strategies are discussed in more detail in Chapter 2.
2 Yellow ribbons have become a signifier of the pro-logging movement. Beginning in the United States, organizations that formed to protect loggers and the industry illustrated their solidarity with and support for "forestry workers, families, and communities" by displaying yellow ribbons on lapels, in shop windows, on car bumpers, and at public rallies and protests. When I entered my study region, a large yellow banner hung from one of the hangars at the Port Hardy airport (see page 158).
3 I bear the burden of this criticism, but I will continue to use the term "community." I believe that the idea of community continues to resonate not only in academic circles but also, more importantly, with the rural people among whom I undertook this research.
4 Here I do not restrict myself to forestry towns but include in this discussion women from mining communities. The label "workers' wives" reflects this more inclusive discussion.
5 Alison Gill (1990) contributed an interesting corrective, suggesting that women have recently emerged in local politics because they are less constrained by shift-work schedules that characterize men's employment in resource industries.
6 The victims/victors dichotomy was presented by Julie-Katherine Gibson-Graham (1994).
7 Alternative family forms outside the nuclear family were rarely discussed, although there has been some recent effort to redress this imbalance (e.g., Brown 1995; Cloke and Little 1997).
8 According to Maria Garcia-Guadilla (1995), there is a class dimension to this hierarchy. For example, when mobilized actors are low-income women, they will receive even less attention from the media than would women from the middle or upper classes. However, she also argues that there is a general disadvantage for women since they are less likely to draw media attention than men of any class.
9 For a sociological discussion of these links in the context of Western European countries, see Littig (2001).
10 In public policy analysis, there is a long history of examining both decisions and non-decisions, the latter being situations in which conscious choices are made to do nothing, to thwart demands for change, or to adopt plans that are imperfectly implemented (Bachrach and Baratz 1971; Debman 1975; Rees 1990; Wolfinger 1971).

11 In local jargon, "the North Island" refers to the northern portion of Vancouver Island. It sometimes includes Woss and sometimes does not. Women who participated in the study argued strongly that Woss exhibited all the characteristics of a northern town and should be included in any description. All population figures are from the Census of Canada 1996 and are provided where available.
12 The region experiences wet, windy winters and mild summers. The "rainy season" can last for months at a time. Residents argued that tourists did not want to come in the rain to visit. However, this region has similar climatic conditions to Clayoquot Sound, which attracts a large, and growing, number of visitors all year. The North Island, however, does not have nearly the same level of hospitality and visitor services found to the south.
13 Here I would like to acknowledge the assistance of Janice May and Mary Pullen, my research assistants for data collection.
14 In forestry, the industry may shut down on a seasonal basis due to fire hazard in the woods or snow conditions. Temporary shutdowns may also take place when prices are low and/or there is sufficient product in stock to meet current demands. Women expressed concerns that shutdowns were being used on a more regular basis to effect changes in prices and/or worker demands, leading to a more structural character of these reduced work schedules.
15 Among the interviewees, five identified themselves as First Nations. I have not highlighted First Nations women because some women asked not to discuss their ethnicity, leaving numbers too small to retain anonymity.

Chapter 2: Transition and Social Marginalization of Forestry Communities
1 Industry uses the term "fall-down" to refer to lower volumes available when large, older trees have been harvested and replaced by younger trees with smaller volumes of wood. Fall-down is also sometimes used to refer to the decline in timber harvests resulting from harvesting trees at rates that exceeded their ability to reproduce within reasonable investment time frames (Clapp 1998).
2 In this sense, trajectories of "transition" share characteristics of environmental management. Environmental management has been characterized by change, uncertainty, complexity, and conflict (Mitchell 1995, 1997; Reed 1999a), whereby local and nonlocal conditions may be identified but their specific interactions are not likely to be fully understood, appreciated, or predicted in advance.
3 This notion of forests as productive places is prevalent in the writings of neoclassical and Marxist economists alike. For discussion, see Smith (1984).
4 These processes include disease transmission, forced resettlement, formal and informal violation of property rights, and outright exclusion from the benefits of resource use practices.
5 I chose this date to correspond to the report of the Royal Commission on Forest Tenure (Pearse 1976). At that time, several challenges were made by public interest groups against the outlook and objectives of the state in forest management. Increasing use of computer technology, conflicts with environmental organizations and First Nations, and ad hoc initiatives to allocate lands for wilderness emerged after this time. Arguably, however, the "management" philosophy and the policy primacy of the Ministry of Forests were not demonstrably altered until the 1990s, when several policy initiatives and regulatory requirements were more clearly articulated.
6 Resource managers had previously operated in departments that undertook sectoral approaches to management in which specific resources, such as forests, water, wildlife, and minerals, were managed or regulated in isolation from each other. Integrated resource management attempted to establish mechanisms of coordination and cooperation among agencies in an effort to allocate and manage resources more effectively (Mitchell 1989; Mitchell and Sewell 1981).
7 For example, the Ministry of Health gained some profile in water quality issues, and the Ministry of Environment was to be "consulted" in forest management planning. Admittedly, these agencies were not as powerful as the industry-oriented Ministries of Industry and Trade as well as Forests, but their interests would gain influence over time.

8   For example, in the mid-1980s, several disputes erupted on Vancouver Island. The first was opposition to logging on Meares Island. This island was visible from the village of Tofino, on Clayoquot Sound, which was building its economic base on ecotourism. An international protest of logging took place, and in 1985 a court-ordered injunction prevented the timber company, MacMillan Bloedel, from continuing its operations on the island pending the resolution of Aboriginal land claims. Further inland, MacMillan Bloedel was restricted from cutting on part of its timber licence in the Carmanah watershed because of its old-growth status. The government attempted to resolve the dispute by designating a park for the lower portion of the watershed to protect the giant spruces. Shortly thereafter, yet another dispute over the potential elimination of old-growth forests emerged over the next watershed to the south, the Walbran. Farther north, in Haida Gwaii (Queen Charlotte Islands), the provincial and federal governments agreed to establish a national park in 1987 after a fifteen-year public campaign to protect its ecological and cultural values. On the mainland coastal areas, several other watersheds and ecosystems also came under protest (e.g., Randy Stoltman Reserve near Squamish).
9   Also referred to as the "Great Bear Rainforest."
10 One paragraph hardly does justice to a long and detailed debate. I have noted here only a few authors who are geographers or who have influenced geographic thought on the "gendered nature of Nature." The point that people belong in understandings of nature and the environment has also been raised by those working on issues of environmental justice (see Di Chiro 1995).
11 There is a parallel here between how rural residents themselves view differences between urban and rural, where values of "good" and "clean" are attributed to rural places, whereas values of "evil" and "dirty" are attributed to urban environments. This dichotomy and its contradiction are aptly discussed by Fitchen (1991).
12 There is considerable variation in income for men and women across different job types. As noted in Chapter 4, workers in government forestry jobs do not draw nearly the income that industry workers do. Women in industry are often slotted into jobs that are even more economically marginal than men in either industry or government.
13 Since the early 1980s, union members have had to accept wage rollbacks and contracting out and other packages. However, for those who remain in the industry, wages remain higher than the Canadian average, and basic elements of the social safety net remain despite an increased unevenness of application.
14 For fictionalized accounts of logging life in the 1950s, read the trilogy by former logger Peter Trower (1993, 1996, 2000). The book *Dead Man's Ticket: A Novel of the Streets and the Woods* focuses on the mean streets of Vancouver, where many loggers of this era spent their "retirement."
15 This distinction between distribution of material benefits and other forms of oppression is similar to that made by Graham Room (1995) and Michael Samers (1998) between poverty and social exclusion.
16 My framework draws liberally and adapts extensively from Iris Young's (1990) theory of the five faces of oppression. After careful consideration, I chose the term "social marginalization" to refer to the concept of "oppression" explained by Young. She uses "marginalization" to describe the "face" that I call "social exclusion." I use her ideas with gratitude and apologize for errors of interpretation that this adaptation may demonstrate.
17 This brief summary does not do justice to the thesis of staples theory and uneven development. For a more extensive discussion, see Barnes (1993) and Hayter (2000).
18 These countries were important in the development of the staples economy in British Columbia. After the Second World War, Japan emerged as an important metropolitan player to which many staple products (wood, coal) were imported from British Columbia.
19 Gibson and Graham wrote separately until the mid-1990s, when they formally combined their names (Gibson-Graham) for the purpose of joint publication. Further reference to this duo will be made in the singular, as per Gibson-Graham's preference.
20 Although, as noted earlier, this potential is now part of the academic and environmentalist agenda (see Binkley 1997; Burda, Gale, and M'Gonigle 1998; Wilson 1997).
21 For example, Greenpeace expanded between 1970 and 1995 from twelve Vancouver-based

members to 2.9 million members located in 158 countries. In 1995, Greenpeace received donations of $152 million to support its activities and offices in thirty-two countries (Austin 1996).

22 Even within the forestry sector, environmental campaigns to protect the coastal forests have been far stronger than campaigns to protect the interior forests of British Columbia or the boreal forests in other parts of the country. Some may argue that environmental organizations follow the trajectory of economic exploitation, with the coastal region having been exploited before and more extensively than the interior region. Yet, if this explanation were the complete one, environmental organizations would be most active in eastern and central Canada, where settlement and resource exploitation took place long before they did in British Columbia.

23 There are some notable exceptions. For example, on the BC coast, the Tin Wis consortium was established in the early 1990s in an effort to bring together environmentalists, resource communities and workers, and First Nations in a common front to demand policy change (Pinkerton 1993). Its active phase was short-lived, however. More recently, bridges have been built by the David Suzuki Foundation and Ecotrust Canada (see Reed 1999b). The creation of Isaak, a joint business venture between the Nuu-Cha-Nulth First Nation and MacMillan Bloedel (now Weyerhaeuser) gained official support from Greenpeace. Yet, while these initiatives have begun to build local support and trust, ongoing efforts by most mainstream environmental organizations to protect the "Great Bear Rainforest" through international markets campaigns, promotion of a conservation area design drafted by environmental organizations, and joint negotiations involving only environmental organizations and private companies continue to exclude rural communities from participating meaningfully in the agenda for transition in forestry and contribute to their mistrust of others.

Chapter 3: Policy and Structural Change in Rural British Columbia

1 Sustainable development was first made popular with the report of the World Commission on Environment and Development published in 1987 (the Brundtland report). In British Columbia and elsewhere, the terminology of "sustainable development" first emerged in government documents to be replaced by the 1990s with the idea of "sustainability." Sustainable development lost favour because it maintained a position that economic growth in both "industrialized" and "developing" countries would be required to maintain economic, social, and environmental systems. Sustainability, originally with an environmental focus, came to adopt the three-part framework of sustainable development. It was favoured by public interest groups and government agencies alike because it sidestepped the issue of continuous economic growth. I have placed emphasis here on sustainability since it has been the more enduring term used in British Columbia.

2 Clayoquot Sound remained outside the purview of CORE. After several failed attempts to reach consensus using public advisory groups and multistakeholder negotiations, the government turned the "problem" of land allocation and management of Clayoquot Sound over to an independent scientific panel rather than to another, more public, process.

3 The original intention was to protect 12 percent of *representative* ecosystems in the province in accordance with a recommendation of the Brundtland Commission in 1987 to protect lands worldwide. To protect this proportion of representative ecosystems, the province would have to be divided according to ecological/climatic zones, and then 12 percent of each zone would have to be placed under some measure of protection. Due to the current status of land use in the province, this effort would result in protecting more than 12 percent of the land base overall. This proportion was disputed by both environmental and worker organizations because it was a ballpark estimate that lacked scientific credibility. Consequently, environmental organizations saw the proportion as a minimum, while worker organizations saw it as a maximum. In many individual disputes, the government refused to budge on this proportion, creating a stalemate among negotiating

parties. Over time, however, this goal of protecting 12 percent of representative ecosystems was quietly dropped, leaving room for more flexibility in resolving land allocation disputes. As a result, the provincial government was able to declare success in reaching its 12 percent target by November 2000.
4 The allowable annual cut (AAC) is determined by the chief forester of the Ministry of Forests. This is the volume permitted to be harvested within a given forest area on an annual basis. The chief forester determines this amount based on the number of trees, their ages, and other physical factors. Increasingly, the chief forester is also required to account for socioeconomic effects of his or her determinations.
5 After the provincial election in 2001, FRBC was formally shut down.
6 These changes took effect on 1 April 1996 under the Federal-Provincial Arrangements Act, which applies to health and social transfers. This act replaced the Canada Health and Social Transfer Act that had been repealed.
7 For discussion of the report and the ENGOs that used it, see Reed (1999b).

Chapter 4: Women and Woods Work
1 Caulk boots are pronounced "cork boots" in the local vernacular.
2 Although even this interpretation of "traditional" gender roles is questionable. Julie-Katherine Gibson-Graham (1994) poses an interesting question about whether or not "traditional" denotes long-standing and prevalent gender roles or ones that are relatively recently instituted or locally naturalized as hegemonic. This is an important political question for feminist researchers since labels such as "traditional" have been used by feminists (and nonfeminists) to denote inferior forms of relations. Here, however, I use the term "traditional" to denote ideas associated with women's "rightful" place in the home and men's "rightful" place in paid work outside the home to generate and sustain "the family wage." I leave it to others to debate the origins of these ideas.
3 This calculation is based on the women interviewed individually, not on the women involved in focus groups.
4 Although this term remains in common use, the association of nature with "resources" made valuable through economic production processes is highly contested by environmental organizations, ecofeminists, and philosophers of nature.
5 During the course of this study, the federal government changed the terminology of worker insurance from "unemployment insurance" (UI) to "employment insurance" (EI). This program is managed by the federal government but is paid by employers and employees. Upon job loss (temporary or permanent), insurance benefits are generally available only to those workers who receive income from an employer. This plan omits many self-employed and/or contract workers.
6 Some women were single, and others had previously been married to loggers. There was no known lesbian in the sample.
7 It appears that Canfor is the only company operating in the study region that retains its own scalers. In 2001 eight of ten scalers were women. Other companies contracted out this job. Althought total numbers are small (working in teams of five to ten), women typically compose 20 to 30 percent of contract scalers.
8 The woman discussed in this interview was eventually successful in her claim raised with the Labour Relations Board. Although financial compensation was minimal, she was later employed and, over time, was joined on the finishing floor by other women.
9 Public sector unions typically have higher proportions of women than do private sector unions and have worked systematically to promote parity in income and to obtain benefits that might be more congenial to women in the labour force, such as extended maternity benefits and flexible work hours.
10 Here WOBBLY refers to International Workers of the World, an attempt to unionize all waged workers. The International Woodworkers of America (IWA), the dominant union in the forest industry, may have once affiliated with this effort. It is in this context that the interviewee identified the IWW with this international labour movement.

Chapter 5: Women's Lives, Husbands' Wives

1 Tree planting is not the sole purview of women from forestry communities. Ironically, it is often done by university students who become the environmentalists who are the object of fear and scorn of many forestry-town women (see Chapter 6).
2 I deliberately say some workers because typically the high wages are provided to union workers in the woods and the mills as well as managers of companies. Women have been excluded from many of these job classifications. In addition, women and men in government positions rarely match the salaries of workers in the industry. Typically, unionized workers earn two to three times the average salaries of government regulators; women in clerical and administrative positions within companies earn "less than the men pay in taxes" (Interviewee).
3 In a pithy expression of the challenges faced by theorizing and acting out a women's politics of resistance, Sara Ruddick stated that "mothers and feminists cannot leave each other alone" (1989, 236).
4 I deliberately use the term "gender/development planning" to embrace the broadest literature in gender and development studies. In so doing, I hope to avoid conflating the broad literature with specific approaches, such as gender and development (GAD) or gender, environment, and development (GED).
5 Although I have classified this work under environmental justice, I recognize that many people involved in the movement and in recording it would classify these efforts under the rubric of "social justice." Many activists would resist being classified with other environmentalists, even in a contrasting position (see Di Chiro 1995, 2000).
6 While domestic violence is a criminal offence, it often goes unreported. Women on the North Island reported that RCMP officers were located too far away to be of much use during crisis (the local detachment was located in Port Hardy), and they believed that officers often went off duty at 8 p.m. Interviews with social service workers also documented the lack or recent reduction of services available in communities on the North Island related to basic provisions for health, physical therapy, employment insurance, income assistance, training, and basic education in both public and postsecondary institutions.
7 In the dynamics of these debates, the most colourful exchanges have been between individual workers and environmentalists, although companies and governments have provided other supports for the industry.
8 MOF is also referred to as the Forest Service.
9 This classification is explained in Chapter 4.
10 In developing these profiles, I either quoted directly or paraphrased the women's words and reserved most commentary for the following section.
11 All names have been changed.
12 To develop rapport during the interview, I opened a discussion about children and the challenges of mixing paid work with raising a family. While we both had children, our choices for child care had differed. In discussing these choices, she ensured that she established a position of superiority between us, a position that allowed her to continue to subject herself to the gaze and inquiry of an obvious outsider.
13 In this study, most women had had their first child when they were in their late teens or early twenties. By their mid-forties, their children had grown and left the family home.
14 Knowledge Network is a nonprofit organization dedicated to distributed learning or distance education. In addition to other venues, it provides public education programs available on cable television.

Chapter 6: Communities Confront Outsiders

1 Of all the localities in the study, only Port Hardy had traffic lights within the town. In fact, it had one.
2 During the 1990s, environmental organizations working to protect coastal rainforests successfully directed attention to the buyers of forest products, encouraging them to boycott wood products obtained from old-growth forests where clear-cutting was still practised. Environmental organizations were successful in getting large corporate buyers such

as Hallmark and Home Depot to boycott old-growth forest products. Germany was one of the first countries where this campaign was successful.
3 Although I do not equate the specific issues of concern, I note that Giovanna Di Chiro (2000) also discusses "the tour" (in her case, the toxic tour) as a political strategy to raise awareness and invite concrete actions against environmental injustices.
4 Stumpy was a name given to a large cedar stump removed from Clayoquot Sound by environmental organizations. The stump was taken across Canada and Europe to draw attention to clear-cut logging practices.

Chapter 7: Fitting In

1 The commission defined shared/consensus decision making to mean that, "on a certain set of issues for a defined period of time, those with the authority to make a decision and those who will be affected by that decision are empowered jointly to seek an outcome that accommodates rather than compromises the interests of all concerned" (CORE 1992, 25).
2 Nonetheless, in the late 1990s, the region was caught up in a similar planning process, the Central Coast Land and Coastal Resources Management Plan (CCLCRMP). This initiative was facilitated by CORE's successor, the Land Use Co-ordination Office (see Chapter 3). This particular planning process was extremely complex due to the large number of stakeholders, the contentious character of stakeholder groups focused in the region, and the attempt of the process to address both land and coastal zone issues. The process made headline news in 2000 when environmental organizations and six major forest companies opted to sign a memorandum of understanding related to logging in the region. The memorandum excluded independent loggers, the government, First Nations, tourism representatives, and others. While it did not come into practice, this memorandum was decried by excluded groups but added impetus to the planning process.
3 The plan stated that, with other assumptions regarding market conditions for pulp, these levels could go as high as 930 direct and 540 indirect person years of employment respectively (CORE 1994a).
4 The argument goes beyond the numeric representation of women in the planning processes to identify how the potential material realities for women in rural resource communities were considered in the crafting of the transition strategy that emerged. While it may be possible to examine the ways in which the planning process incorporated the *physical participation* of women, this tack is not developed here.
5 Although several social problems associated with the land use allocation were identified, CORE itself talked about estimating the scope of "the problem" in the singular.
6 I acknowledge Ann Rowan for use of this term.
7 Recall from Chapter 4 that reliable employment counts by resource sector, location, and gender in combination are not routinely collected by Statistics Canada, other government agencies, researchers, or industrial employers. By using CORE's estimate that 95 percent of resource workers (not limited to forestry) on Vancouver Island were male, one might estimate that approximately 18,750 resource workers on the island were men, while 938 were women.
8 In addition, 331 jobs (37 percent) would be lost in direct harvesting, and 237 (26 percent) would be lost in direct processing.
9 The authors attempted to reach out to women associated with a variety of aspects of local life by hosting meetings at different times and places, advertising, and using word of mouth; however, their stay in the communities was short. The report does not provide specific details about each participant, and a direct comparison against census data is beyond the scope of this chapter. From the limited demographic information provided in the report, and from previous research in public involvement, it is likely that middle-aged women of middle-class backgrounds were overrepresented.
10 Although an arguable distinction, I identify bargaining power with effective participation during a participatory land use process and attribute influence to some groups over others on the basis of final plan decisions and outcomes.
11 This model can also be criticized for how uneven power relations might operate within

and among mainstream groups (e.g., how some forestry companies or environmental organizations may dominate others). My interest here, however, lies in how it reinforces gender bias by stereotyping the roles and relations of residents of forestry communities.
12 These are Canadians of East Indian descent, not First Nations.
13 The Charter states, "Our ability to sustain a quality environment depends upon our ability to foster a strong and sustainable economy" (CORE 1994b, n. pag.).

Chapter 8: Social Sustainability and the Renewal of Research Agendas
1 As noted later, I do not attest to the accuracy of this claim. These social issues pervade society beyond local forestry cultures. Instead, I use this example to illustrate how women simultaneously spoke out about serious problems that *they* attributed to forestry culture while they continued to support forestry in public land use debates.
2 For an interesting discussion of the effects of this polarization on a researcher's positioning, see Proctor (1995).

Epilogue
1 In Trower 1999 (100-1). Reproduced by permission of the publisher, Ekstasis Editions Canada.

Appendix: Describing and Reflecting on Research Methods
1 At the outset, I describe the research efforts in the plural to acknowledge the assistance of my graduate research assistants at that time, Janice May and Mary Pullen. Later in the appendix, I use the singular form to claim full responsibility for the interpretive portion of the study.
2 This title came out of one of the interviews, in which the interviewee commented that environmentalists come out every spring to protest logging. She called this "the rites of spring."
3 At the time of the research, I was employed by the University of British Columbia (UBC). The Department of Geography there has an international reputation for the strength of its theorists in human geography.

References

Agarwal, B. 1992. The gender and environment debate: Lessons from India. *Feminist Studies* 18: 119-58.
Ali, M. 1986. The coals war: Women's struggle during the miners' strike. In *Caught Up in Conflict: Women's Responses to Political Strife,* ed. R. Ridd and H. Callaway, 84-105. London: Macmillan.
Auditor General of BC. 1999/2000. *Report 6: Forest Renewal BC.* Victoria: Auditor General of BC.
Austin, I. 1996. Greenpeace: It all started here: Environmental colossus is 25 today. *Province* 15 September: A26.
Bachrach, P., and M.S. Baratz. 1971. *Power and Poverty: Theory and Practice.* Oxford: Oxford University Press.
Barnes, T.J. 1993. Innis and the geography of communications and empire. *Canadian Geographer* 37: 357-59.
Barnes, T.J., and R. Hayter. 1992. The little town that could: Flexible accumulation and community change in Chemainus, B.C. *Regional Studies* 26: 647-63.
–. 1994. Economic restructuring, local development, and resource towns: Forest communities in coastal British Columbia. *Canadian Journal of Regional Science* 17, 3: 289-310.
–, eds. 1997. *Troubles in the Rainforest: British Columbia's Forest Economy in Transition.* Canadian Western Geographical Series No. 33. Victoria: Western Geographical Press.
Bauman, Z. 1973. *Culture as Praxis.* London and Boston: Routledge and Kegan Paul.
BCRTEE [British Columbia Round Table on the Environment and the Economy]. 1991. *Reaching Agreement – Consensus Processes in British Columbia.* Vol. 1. Victoria: BCRTEE.
–. 1993. *Strategic Directions for Community Sustainability: British Columbia and the Environment.* Victoria: BCRTEE.
BC Treaty Commission. 1998. *Annual Report.* Victoria: BC Treaty Commission.
Beckley, T.M. 1995. Community stability and the relationship between economic and social well-being in forest-dependent communities. *Society and Natural Resources* 8: 261-66.
Beder, S. 1997. *Global Spin: The Corporate Assault on Environmentalism.* Devon and Vermont: Green Books and Chelsea Green Publishing Company.
Bell, S. 1993. Ecofeminists run "peace camp" at Clayoquot Sound. *Vancouver Sun* 19 August: B1.
Bender, T. 1978. *Community and Social Change in America.* New Brunswick, NJ: Rutgers University Press.
Bengston, D. 1994. Changing forest values and ecosystem management. *Society and Natural Resources* 7: 515-33.
Berkes, F. 1999. *Sacred Ecology: Traditional Ecological Knowledge and Resource Management.* Philadelphia: Taylor and Francis.
Berman, T., G. Ingram, M. Gibbons, R. Hatch, L. Maignon, and C. Hatch. 1994. *Clayoquot and Dissent.* Vancouver: Ronsdale Press.

Binkley, C.S. 1997. A crossroad in the forest: The path to a sustainable forest sector in British Columbia. In *Troubles in the Rainforest: British Columbia's Forest Economy in Transition,* ed. T.J. Barnes and R. Hayter, 16-35. Canadian Western Geographical Series No. 33. Victoria: Western Geographical Press.

Birkeland, J. 1993. Towards a new system of environmental governance. *Environmentalist* 13: 19-32.

Bossin, B. 1999. Nature made it, women saved it: Five women pull off one of the world's great environmental victories. *Homemakers*: 54 -70.

Boucher, P. 1994. Women in the shadows of the industrial forest: Silences, tensions, and contradictions. Paper presented at *Women and the Canadian Environment Conference,* organized by M. MacDonald, M. Hessing, and R. Raglon. University of British Columbia, Vancouver.

–. 1998. Ecology, Feminism, and Planning: Lessons from Women's Environmental Activism in Clayoquot Sound. PhD diss., University of British Columbia.

Boulding, E. 1981. Women as integrators and stabilizers. In *Women and the Social Costs of Economic Development: Two Colorado Case Studies,* ed. E. Moen, E. Boulding, J. Lillydahl, and R. Palm, 119-50. Boulder, CO: Westview Press.

Bowen, W., M. Salling, K. Haynes, and E. Cyran. 1995. Toward environmental justice: Spatial equity in Ohio and Cleveland. *Annals of the Association of American Geographers* 85: 641-63.

Bradbury, J. 1988. Living with boom and bust cycles: New towns on the resource frontier in Canada, 1945-1986. In *Resource Communities: Settlement and Workforce Issues,* ed. T.B. Brealey, C.C. Neil, and P.W. Newton, 3-20. Canberra: Commonwealth Scientific and Industrial Research Organization.

Braun, B. 1998. Review of *Seeing the Ocean through the Trees: A Conservation-Based Development Strategy for Clayoquot Sound. BC Studies* 118: 126-30.

–. 2002. *The Intemperate Rainforest: Nature, Culture, and Power on Canada's West Coast.* Minneapolis: University of Minnesota Press.

Briassoulis, H. 1989. Theoretical orientations in environmental planning: An inquiry into alternative approaches. *Environmental Management* 13: 381-92.

Brown, B.A. 1995. *In Timber Country: Working People's Stories of Environmental Conflict and Urban Flight.* Philadelphia: Temple University Press.

Brown, D. 1996. *Strategic Land Use Planning Source Book.* Victoria: Commission on Resources and Environment.

Brown, W. 1991. Feminist hesitations, postmodern exposures. *Differences* 3: 63-84.

Brownhill, S., and S. Halford. 1990. Understanding women's involvement in local politics: How useful is a formal/informal dichotomy? *Political Geography Quarterly* 9: 396-414.

Bryant, B., and P. Mohai, eds. 1992. *Race and the Incidence of Environmental Hazards.* Boulder, CO: Westview Press.

Bryant, C.R., and A.E. Joseph. 2001. Canada's rural population: Trends in space and implications in place. *Canadian Geographer* 45: 132-37.

Bullard, R. 1990. *Dumping in Dixie: Race, Class, and Environmental Quality.* Boulder, CO: Westview Press.

–, ed. 1994. *Unequal Protection: Environmental Justice and Communities of Color.* San Francisco: Sierra Club Books.

Burda, C., F. Gale, and M. M'Gonigle. 1998. Eco-forestry versus the state(us) quo. *BC Studies* 119: 45-72.

Buttel, F. 1992. Environmentalization: Origins, processes, and implications for rural social change. *Rural Sociology* 57: 1-27.

Byron, R.N. 1978. Community stability and forest policy in British Columbia. *Canadian Journal of Forestry Research* 8: 61-66.

Caragata, L. 1999. The privileged public: Who is permitted citizenship? *Community Development Journal* 34: 270-86.

Carroll, M.S. 1995. *Community and the Northwestern Logger.* Boulder, CO: University of Colorado Press.

Carroll, M.S., and S.E. Daniels. 1992. Public land management and three decades of social change: Thoughts on the future of public lands and public demands. In *Multiple Use and Sustained Yield: Changing Philosophies for Federal Land Management*, ed. Committee on Interior and Insular Affairs, US House of Representatives, 45-86. Committee Print No. 11. Washington, DC: US Government Printing Office, Congressional Research Service, Library of Congress.

Carroll, M.S., S.E. Daniels, and J. Kusel. 2000. Employment and displacement among northwestern forest products workers. *Society and Natural Resources* 13: 151-56.

Cashore, B., G. Hoberg, M. Howlett, J. Rayner, and J. Wilson. 2001. *In Search of Sustainability: British Columbia Forest Policy in the 1990s*. Vancouver: UBC Press.

Caudill, H.M. 1962. *Night Comes to the Cumberlands: A Biography of a Depressed Area*. Boston: Little, Brown and Company.

Clapp, A.R. 1998. The resource cycle in forestry and fishing. *Canadian Geographer* 42: 129-44.

Cloke, P., and J. Little. 1990. *The Rural State? Limits to Planning in Rural Society*. Oxford: Clarendon Press.

Cloke, P., and J. Little, eds. 1997. *Contested Countryside Cultures: Otherness, Marginalization, and Rurality*. London and New York: Routledge.

Collins, P.H. 1990. *Black Feminist Thought: Knowledge, Consciousness, and the Politics of Empowerment*. Boston: Unwin Hyman.

Conger, R.D., and G.H. Elder Jr. (in collaboration with F.O. Lorenz, R.L. Simons, and L.B. Whitbeck). 1994. *Families in Troubled Times: Adapting to Change in Rural America*. New York: Aldine de Gruyter.

CORE [Commission on Resources and Environment]. 1992. *Report on a Land Use Strategy for British Columbia*. Victoria: CORE.

–. 1994a. *Vancouver Island Land Use Plan, Volume I*. Victoria: CORE.

–. 1994b. *Vancouver Island Land Use Plan, Volume III: Vancouver Island Table Report*. Victoria: CORE.

Cortner, H.J., and M.A. Moote. 1999. *The Politics of Ecosystem Management*. Washington, DC, and Covelo, CA: Island Press.

Cortner, H.J., M.A. Shannon, M.G. Wallace, S. Burke, and M.A. Moote. 1996. *Institutional Barriers and Incentives for Ecosystem Management: A Problem Analysis*. General Technical Report PNW-GTR-354. Portland: Pacific Northwest Research Station, Forest Service, United States Department of Agriculture.

Cronon, W. 1995. The trouble with wilderness; Or, getting back to the wrong nature. In *Uncommon Ground: Toward Reinventing Nature*, ed. W. Cronon, 69-90. New York and London: W.W. Norton and Company.

Crowe, G., and G. Allan. 1994. *Community Life: An Introduction to Local Social Relations*. New York: Harvester Wheatsheaf.

CS/RESORS Consulting Limited. 1997. *Women and the Forest Industry. Report to the Policy Development Division, Ministry of Employment and Investment*. Victoria: Ministry of Employment and Investment.

Daniels, S.E., C.L. Gobeli, and A.J. Findley. 2000. Reemployment programs for dislocated timber workers: Lessons from Oregon. *Society and Natural Resources* 13: 135-50.

Daniels, S.E., and G.B. Walker. 1996. Collaborative learning: Improving public deliberation in ecosystem-based management. *Environmental Impact Assessment Review* 16: 71-102.

David Suzuki Foundation. 1999. New measures needed for crises in coastal communities. News release 28 January. Available at <http://www.davidsuzuki.org> (20 February 2003).

Davis, D.L. and J. Nadel-Klein. 1991. Gender, culture, and the sea: Contemporary theoretical approaches. *Society and Natural Resources* 5: 135-47.

Davis, H.C., and T.A. Hutton. 1989. The two economies of British Columbia. *BC Studies* 82: 3-15.

Dearden, P., and B. Mitchell. 1997. *Environmental Change and Challenge: A Canadian Perspective*. Toronto: Oxford University Press.

Debman, G. 1975. Nondecisions and power. *American Political Science Review* 69: 889-904.

De Bruin, A., and A. Dupuis. 1999. Towards a synthesis of transaction cost economics and a feminist oriented network analysis: An application to women's street commerce. *American Journal of Economics and Sociology* 58: 807-27.

Demeritt, D. 2000. The new social contract for science: Accountability, relevance, and value in US and UK science and research policy. *Antipode* 32: 308-29.

Di Chiro, G. 1995. Nature as community: The convergence of environment and social justice. In *Uncommon Ground: Toward Reinventing Nature*, ed. W. Cronon, 288-320. New York and London: W.W. Norton and Company.

–. 1997. Local actions, global visions: Remaking environmental expertise. *Frontiers* 18: 203-31.

–. 1998. Environmental justice from the grassroots: Reflections on history, gender, and expertise. In *The Struggle for Ecological Democracy: Environmental Justice Movements in the United States*, ed. D. Faber, 104-36. New York: Guilford.

–. 2000. Bearing witness or taking action? Toxic tourism and environmental justice. In *Reclaiming the Environmental Debate: The Politics of Health in a Toxic Culture*, ed. R. Hofichter, 275-99. Cambridge: MIT Press.

Dietrich, W. 1992. *The Final Forest: The Battle for the Last Great Trees of the Pacific Northwest*. New York: Simon and Schuster.

Doeringer, P., and M. Piore. 1971. *Internal Labour Markets and Manpower Analysis*. Lexington: D.C. Heath.

Doherty, B., and M. deGeus, eds. 1996. *Democracy and Green Political Thought: Sustainability, Rights, and Citizenship*. London and New York: Routledge.

Draper, D. 1998. *Our Environment: A Canadian Perspective*. Scarborough: Nelson.

Drushka, K. 1985. *Stumped: The Forest Industry in Transition*. Vancouver: Douglas and McIntyre.

Drushka, K., B. Nixon, and R. Travers, eds. 1993. *Touch Wood: BC Forests at the Crossroads*. Madeira Park, BC: Harbour Publishing.

Dunk, T. 1991. *It's a Working Man's Town: Male Working-Class Culture in Northwestern Ontario*. Montreal and Kingston: McGill-Queen's University Press.

–. 1994. Talking about trees: Environment and society in forest workers' culture. *Canadian Review of Sociology and Anthropology* 31: 14-34.

Durbin, K. 1996. *Tree Huggers: Victoria, Defeat, and Renewal in the Northwest Ancient Forest Campaign*. Seattle: Mountaineers.

Dye, T.R. 1986. Community power and public policy. In *Community Power Directions for Future Research*, ed. R.J. Waste, 29-51. Beverly Hills: Sage Publications.

Eckersley, R. 1992. *Environmentalism and Political Theory: Toward an Ecocentric Approach*. New York: State University of New York Press.

Ecotrust Canada. 1997. *Seeing the Ocean through the Trees: A Conservation-Based Development Strategy for Clayoquot Sound*. Vancouver: Ecotrust Canada.

Egan, B., and S. Klausen. 1998. Female in a forest town: The marginalization of women in Port Alberni's economy. *BC Studies* 118: 5-40.

Eichler, M. 1995. Designing eco-city in North America. In *Change of Plans: Towards a Non-Sexist Sustainable City*, ed. M. Eichler, 1-24. Toronto: Garamond Press.

Elliott, J. 1999. *An Introduction to Sustainable Development*. 2nd ed. London: Routledge.

England, K. 1993. Suburban pink collar ghettos: The spatial entrapment of women? *Annals of the Association of American Geographers* 83: 225-42.

–. 1994. Getting personal: Reflexivity, positionality, and feminist research. *Professional Geographer* 46: 80-89.

Ettlinger, N. 1990. Worker displacement and corporate restructuring: A policy-conscious appraisal. *Economic Geography* 66, 1: 67-82.

Evans, P.M., and Wekerle, G.R. 1997. The shifting terrain of women's welfare: Theory, discourse, and activism. In *Women and the Canadian Welfare State: Challenges and Change*, ed. P.M. Evans and G.R. Wekerle, 3-27. Toronto: University of Toronto Press.

Eyerman, R., and A. Jamison. 1991. *Social Movements: A Cognitive Approach*. Cambridge, UK: Polity Press, in association with Basil Blackwell.

Feldman, S., and R. Welsh. 1995. Feminist knowledge claims, local knowledge, and gender divisions of agricultural labor: Constructing a successor science. *Rural Sociology* 60: 23-43.

Fincher, R., and J. Jacobs, eds. 1998. *Cities of Difference*. New York and London: Guilford Press.
Fitchen, J. 1981. *Poverty in Rural America: A Case Study*. Boulder, CO: Westview Press.
–. 1991. *Endangered Spaces, Enduring Places: Change, Identity, and Survival in Rural America*. Boulder, CO: Westview Press.
Fitzsimmons, M. 1989. The matter of nature. *Antipode* 21: 106-20.
Fitzsimmons, M., and R. Gottlieb. 1988. A new environmental politics. In *Reshaping the US Left: Popular Struggles in the 1980s*, ed. M. Davis and M. Sprinker, 114-30. London: Verso.
Forgacs, O. 1997. The British Columbia forest industry: Transition or decline? In *Troubles in the Rainforest: British Columbia's Forest Economy in Transition*, ed. T.J. Barnes and R. Hayter, 167-80. Canadian Western Geographical Series No. 33. Victoria: Western Geographical Press.
Frank, A.G. 1967. *Capitalism and Underdevelopment in Latin America*. New York: Monthly Review Press.
Fraser, N. 1997. *Justice Interruptus: Critical Reflections on the "Postsocialist" Condition*. London: Routledge.
Freudenberg, W.R. 1992. Addictive economies: Extractive industries and vulnerable localities in a changing world economy. *Rural Sociology* 57: 305-32.
Friedmann, J. 1966. *Regional Development Policy: A Case Study of Venezuela*. Cambridge: MIT Press.
–. 1987. *Planning in the Public Domain: From Knowledge to Action*. Princeton: Princeton University Press.
Friedmann, J., and H. Rangan. 1993. *In Defense of Livelihood: Comparative Studies on Environmental Action*. West Hartford, CT: Kumarian Press.
Furney, G. 1994. Our forests, our future. Editorial. *Vancouver Sun* 26 March: A23.
Garcia-Guadilla, M.P. 1995. Gender, Environment, and Empowerment in Venezuela. In *Engendering Wealth and Well-Being: Empowerment for Global Change*, ed. R.L. Blumberg, C.A. Rakowski, I. Tinker, and M. Monteón, 213-37. Boulder, CO: Westview Press.
Garner, J. 1999. *Never under Table: A Story of British Columbia's Forests and Government Mismanagement*. Nanaimo: Cinnabar Press.
Gibson, K. 1992. Hewers of cake and drawers of tea: Women, industrial restructuring, and class processes on the coalfields of central Queensland. *Rethinking Marxism* 5, 4: 29-56.
Gibson-Graham, J.-K. 1994. Stuffed if I know! Reflections on post-modern feminist social research. *Gender, Place, and Culture* 1: 205-24.
–. 1995. Beyond patriarchy and capitalism: Reflections on political subjectivity. In *Transitions: New Australian Feminisms*, ed. B. Caine and R. Pringle, 172-83. Sydney, Australia: Allen and Unwin.
–. 1996. *The End of Capitalism (as We Knew It): A Feminist Critique of Political Economy*. Oxford: Blackwell.
Gill, A.M. 1990. Women in isolated resource towns: An examination of gender differences in cognitive structures. *Geoforum* 21, 3: 347-58.
Government of British Columbia. 1994. *The Vancouver Island Land Use Plan*. Victoria: Government of British Columbia.
Government of British Columbia, Land Reserve Commission. 2001. *Annual Report 2000-2001: Working Farms, Working Forests*. Victoria: British Columbia, Land Reserve Commission.
Granovetter, M. 1985. Economic action and social structure: The problem of embeddedness. *American Journal of Sociology* 91: 481-510.
Grass, E. 1987. Employment Changes during Recession: The Case of the British Columbia Forest Products Manufacturing Industries. MA thesis, Simon Fraser University.
Grass, E., and R. Hayter. 1989. Employment change during recession: The experience of forest product manufacturing plants in British Columbia, 1981-1985. *Canadian Geographer* 33, 3: 240-52.
Greenpeace Canada. 1998. *British Columbia Communities at the Crossroads: Towards Ecological and Economic Sustainability*. Vancouver: Greenpeace Canada.
Griffin Cohen, M. 1997. From the welfare state to vampire capitalism. In *Women and the*

Canadian Welfare State: Challenges and Change, ed. P.M. Evans and G.R. Wekerle, 28-70. Toronto: University of Toronto Press.
Grumbine, R.E. 1994. What is ecosystem management? *Conservation Biology* 8: 27-38.
Guha, R. 1989. Radical American environmentalism and wilderness preservation: A Third World critique. *Environmental Ethics* 11: 71-83.
Gunderson, L.H., C.S. Holling, and S. Light, eds. 1995. *Barriers and Bridges to the Renewal of Ecosystems and Institutions.* New York: Columbia University Press.
Haley, D., and M. Luckert. 1995. Policy instruments for sustainable development in the British Columbia forestry sector. In *Managing Natural Resources in British Columbia: Market, Regulations, and Sustainable Development,* ed. A. Scott, J. Robinson, and D. Cohen, 54-79. Vancouver: UBC Press.
Hall, J. 1986. Disorderly women: Gender and labour militancy in the Appalachian South. *Journal of American History* 73: 354-82.
Halseth, G. 1999. We came for the work: Situating employment migration in BC's small, resource-based communities. *Canadian Geographer* 43: 363-81.
-. 2002. Gender at work and gender at home: The mediating role of the household economy in resource dependent towns in northern British Columbia. Paper presented to the Annual Meeting of the Canadian Association of Geographers, May 2002, Toronto.
Hammond, H. 1991. *Seeing the Forest among the Trees.* Winlaw, BC: Polestar Press.
Hanson, S., and I. Johnston. 1985. Gender differences in work-trip length: Explanation and implications. *Urban Geography* 6: 193-219.
Hanson, S., and G. Pratt. 1995. *Gender, Work, and Space.* London and New York: Routledge.
Haraway, D. 1991. *Simians, Cyborgs, and Women: The Reinvention of Nature.* New York: Routledge.
Harding, S. 1991. *Whose Science? Whose Knowledge? Thinking from Women's Lives.* Ithaca: Cornell University Press.
Harrison, K. 1996. Environmental protection in British Columbia: Postmaterial values, organized interests, and party politics. In *Politics, Policy, and Government in British Columbia,* ed. R.K. Carty, 290-309. Vancouver: UBC Press.
Hawkins, L.J. 1999. Open and Sectoral Models of Public Participation: Does Model Type Make a Difference in Land Use Planning? MSc thesis, University of Northern British Columbia.
Hay, E. 1993. Recession and Restructuring in Port Alberni: Corporate, Household, and Community Coping Strategies. MA thesis, Simon Fraser University.
Hayter, R. 2000. *Flexible Crossroads: The Restructuring of British Columbia's Forest Economy.* Vancouver: UBC Press.
Hayter, R., and T.J. Barnes. 1992. Labour market segmentation, flexibility, and recession: A British Columbian case study. *Environment and Planning C* 10: 333-53.
-, eds. 1997. *Troubles in the Rainforest: British Columbia's Forest Economy in Transition.* Canadian Western Geographical Series No. 33. Victoria: Western Geographical Press.
Hayter, R., T.J. Barnes, and E. Grass. 1993. *Single Industry Towns and Local Development: Three Coastal British Columbia Forest Product Communities.* Lakehead University Centre for Northern Studies, Research Report No. 34, ISSN 0843-9885. Thunder Bay: Lakehead University Centre for Northern Studies.
Henderson, M. 1993. Letter to the editor. *Chilliwack Times* February 23: 9.
Hessing, M., and M. Howlett. 1997. *Canadian Natural Resource and Environmental Policy: Political Economy and Public Policy.* Vancouver: UBC Press.
Hollinshead, K. 1990. The powers behind play: The political environments for recreation and tourism. *Australia Journal of Park and Recreation Administration* 8: 35-50.
hooks, b. 1984. *Feminist Theory: From Margin to Center.* Boston: South End Press.
-. 1990. *Yearning: Race, Gender, and Cultural Politics.* Boston: South End Press.
Horne, G. 1999. *British Columbia Local Area Economic Dependencies and Impact Ratios 1996.* Victoria: Business and Economic Statistics.
Hughes, A. 1997. Rurality and "cultures of womanhood": Domestic identities and moral order in village life. In *Contested Countryside Cultures: Otherness, Marginalization, and Rurality,* ed. P. Cloke and J. Little, 123-37. London and New York: Routledge.
Innis, H. 1933. *Problems of Staple Production in Canada.* Toronto: Ryerson.

International Union for the Conservation of Nature and Natural Resources (IUCN). 1980. *World Conservation Strategy: Living Resource Conservation for Sustainable Development.* Gland, Switzerland: International Union for Conservation of Nature and Natural Resources.
Jakes, P., and D. Anderson. 2000. Introduction: Diverse perspectives on community. *Society and Natural Resources* 13: 395-97.
Jamal, T.B., and D. Getz. 1995. Collaboration theory and community tourism planning. *Annals of Tourism Research* 22: 186-204.
Jamison, A., R. Eyerman, and J. Cramer. 1990. *The Making of the New Environmental Consciousness: A Comparative Study of the Environmental Movement in Sweden, Denmark, and the Netherlands.* Edinburgh: Edinburgh University Press.
Jennissen, T. 1997. Implications for women: The Canada health and social transfer. In *The Welfare State in Canada: Past, Present, and Future,* ed. R.B. Blake, P.E. Bryden, and J.F. Strain, 219-29. Toronto: Irwin Publishing.
Jordan, D. 1989. Negotiating salmon management on the Klamath River. In *Co-operative Management of Local Fisheries: New Directions for Improvement Management and Community Development,* ed. E. Pinkerton, 73-81. Vancouver: UBC Press.
Kellert, S.R., J.N. Mehta, S.A. Ebbin, and L.L. Lichtenfield. 2000. Community natural resource management: Promise, rhetoric, and reality. *Society and Natural Resources* 13: 705-15.
Kelly, R.A., and D.K. Alper. 1995. *Transforming British Columbia's War in the Woods: An Assessment of the Vancouver Island Regional Negotiation Process of the Commission on Resources and Environment.* Victoria: University of Victoria, Institute for Dispute Resolution.
Kettle, B. 1995. Gender and environments: Lessons from WEDNET. In *Engendering Wealth and Well-Being: Empowerment for Global Change,* ed. R.L. Blumberg, C.A. Rakowski, I. Tinker, and M. Monteón, 239-59. Boulder, CO: Westview Press.
King, Y. 1990. Healing the wounds: Feminism, ecology, and the nature/culture dualism. In *Reweaving the World: The Emergence of Ecofeminism,* ed. I. Diamond and G. Orenstein, 128-54. San Francisco: Sierra Club Books.
Kleiber, N., and L. Light. 1978. *Caring for Ourselves.* Vancouver: UBC Press.
Knox, P., and S. Marston. 2001. *Places and Regions in Global Context: Human Geography.* 2nd ed. Upper Saddle River, NJ: Prentice-Hall.
Kofman, E., and L. Peake. 1990. Into the 1990s: A gendered agenda for political geography. *Political Geography Quarterly* 9: 313-36.
Kruger, L.E., and M.A. Shannon. 2000. Getting to know ourselves and our places through participation in civic social assessment. *Society and Natural Resources* 13: 461-78.
Kusel, J. 1996. Well-being in forest-dependent communities, part 1: A new approach. In *Sierra Nevada Ecosystem Project Final Report to Congress.* Vol. 2: *Assessments and Scientific Basis for Management Options,* 361-74. Davis, CA: University of California, Centers for Water and Wildland Resources.
Kusel, J., S. Kocher, J. London, L. Buttolph, and E. Schuster. 2000. Effects of displacement and outsourcing on woods workers and their families. *Society and Natural Resources* 13: 115-34.
Langer, V. 2000. Personal communication. Friends of Clayoquot Sound.
Leach, B. 1993. Flexible work, precarious future: Some lessons from the Canadian clothing industry. *Canadian Review of Sociology and Anthropology* 30: 64-81.
Lee, K. N. 1993. *Compass and Gyroscope.* Washington: Island Press.
–. 1999. Appraising adaptive management. *Conservation Ecology* 3, 2. Available at <http://www.consecol.org/vol3/iss2/art3> (13 January 2003).
Liepins, R. 1998. "Women of broad vision": Nature and gender in the environmental activism of Australia's "Women in Agriculture" movement. *Environment and Planning A* 30, 7: 1179-96.
Littig, B. 2001. *Feminist Perspectives on Environment and Society.* Essex: Pearson.
Little, J. 1986. Feminist perspectives in rural geography: An introduction. *Journal of Rural Studies* 2: 1-8.
–. 1987. Gender relations in rural areas: The importance of women's domestic role. *Journal of Rural Studies* 3: 335-42.
–. 1994. *Gender, Planning, and the Policy Process.* Oxford: Pergamon.

–. 1997. Employment marginality and women's self-identity. In *Contested Countryside Cultures: Otherness, Marginalization, and Rurality*, ed. P. Cloke and J. Little, 138-57. London and New York: Routledge.

Little, J., and P. Austin. 1996. Women and the rural idyll. *Journal of Rural Studies* 12: 101-11.

Mackenzie, S. 1986. Women's responses to economic restructuring: Changing gender, changing space. In *The Politics of Diversity, Feminism, Marxism, and Nationalism*, ed. R. Hamilton and M. Barrett, 81-100. London: Verso.

–. 1987. Neglected spaces in peripheral places: Homeworkers and the creation of a new economic centre. *Cahiers de géographie du Québec* 31: 247-60.

MacGregor, S. 1995. Deconstructing the man-made city: Feminist critiques of planning thought and action. In *Change of Plans: Towards a Non-Sexist Sustainable City*, ed. M. Eichler, 25-50. Toronto: Garamond Press.

Maggard, S.W. 1990. Gender contested: Women's participation in the Brookside coal strike. In *Women and Social Protest*, ed. G. West and R.L. Blumberg, 75-98. New York: Oxford University Press.

Marchak, P. 1983. *Green Gold: The Forest Industry in British Columbia*. Vancouver: UBC Press.

–. 1991. For whom the tree falls: Restructuring in the global forest industry. *BC Studies* 90: 3-24.

Marchak, M.P., S.L. Aycock, and D.M. Herbert. 1999. *Falldown: Forest Policy in British Columbia*. Vancouver: David Suzuki Foundation and Ecotrust Canada.

Marchand, M.H., and J.L. Parpart, eds. 1995a. *Feminism/Postmodernism/Development*. London and New York: Routledge.

Marchand, M.H., and J.L. Parpart. 1995b. Part 1: Exploding the canon: An introduction/conclusion. In *Feminism/Postmodernism/Development*, ed. M.H. Marchand and J.L. Parpart, 1-23. London and New York: Routledge.

Maroney, H., and M. Luxton. 1997. Gender at work: Canadian feminist political economy since 1988. In *Understanding Canada: Building on the New Canadian Political Economy*, ed. W. Clement. Montreal and Kingston: McGill-Queen's University Press.

Marshall, T.H. 1964. *Class, Citizenship, and Social Development*. Garden City, NY: Doubleday.

Marston, S. 1990. Who are the "people"? Gender, citizenship, and the making of the American nation. *Environment and Planning D: Society and Space* 8: 449-58.

–. 2000. The social construction of scale. *Progress in Human Geography* 24: 219-42.

Marston, S., and L. Staeheli. 1994. Citizenship, struggle, and political and economic restructuring. *Environment and Planning A* 26: 840-48.

Martopo, S., and B. Mitchell, eds. 1995. *Bali: Balancing Environment, Economy, and Culture*. Department of Geography Publication Series No. 44. Waterloo, ON: University of Waterloo, Department of Geography.

Massey, D. 1994. *Space, Place, and Gender*. Cambridge and Oxford: Polity Press.

Matthews, R. 1983. *The Creation of Regional Dependency*. Toronto: University of Toronto Press.

McCann, L.D., ed. 1987. *Heartland and Hinterland: A Geography of Canada*. 2nd ed. Scarborough: Prentice-Hall Canada.

McDowell, L. 1992. Doing gender: Feminism, feminists, and research methods in human geography. *Transactions, Institute of British Geographers* 17: 399-416.

–. 1993a. Space, place, and gender relations: Part 1: Feminist empiricism and the geography of social relations. *Progress in Human Geography* 17: 157-79.

–. 1993b. Space, place, and gender relations: Part 2: Identity, difference, feminist geometries, and geographies. *Progress in Human Geography* 17: 305-18.

–. 1997. Women/gender/feminisms: Doing feminist geography. *Journal of Geography in Higher Education* 97: 381-400.

McDowell, L., and J.P. Sharpe. 1999. *A Feminist Glossary of Human Geography*. London and New York: Arnold.

McLain, R.J. 1993. *Compass and Gyroscope: Integrating Science and Politics for the Environment*. Washington, DC; Covelo, CA: Island Press.

McLain, R.J., and R.G. Lee. 1996. Adaptive management: Promises and pitfalls. *Environmental Management* 20: 437-48.

McLean, S. 1992. *Welcome Home: Travels in Smalltown Canada*. Toronto: Penguin Books.

Mellor, M. 1997. *Feminism and Ecology.* Cambridge: Polity Press in association with Blackwell.
Merchant, C. 1980. *The Death of Nature: Women, Ecology, and the Scientific Revolution.* San Francisco: Harper and Row.
–. 1995. *Earthcare: Women and the Environment.* London and New York: Routledge.
M'Gonigle, M. 1997. Reinventing British Columbia: Towards a new political economy in the forest. In *Troubles in the Rainforest: British Columbia's Forest Economy in Transition,* ed. T.J. Barnes and R. Hayter, 15-35. Canadian Western Geographical Series No. 33. Victoria: Western Geographical Press.
M'Gonigle, M., and B. Parfitt. 1994. *Forestopia: A Practical Guide to the New Forest Economy.* Madeira Park, BC: Harbour Publishing.
Mies, M. 1986. *Patriarchy and Accumulation on a World Scale: Women in the International Division of Labour.* London: Zed Press.
Ministry of Forests, Port McNeill District. 1998. Personal communication.
Ministry of Industry. 2000. *Income in Canada 1998.* Ottawa: Statistics Canada.
Mitchell, B. 1989. *Geography and Resource Analysis.* 2nd ed. New York: Longman.
–. 1995. *Resource and Environmental Management in Canada.* Toronto: Oxford University Press.
–. 1997. *Resource and Environmental Management.* Essex, UK: Addison Wesley Longman.
Mitchell, B., and W.R.D. Sewell, eds. 1981. *Canadian Resource Policies: Problems and Prospects.* Toronto: Methuen.
Molyneux, M. 1985. Mobilization without emancipation? Women's interests, the state, and revolution in Nicaragua. *Feminist Studies* 11: 227-54.
Moote, M., B. Brown, E. Kingley, S. Lee, D. Voth, and G. Walker. 2001. Process: Redefining relationships. In *Understanding Community-Based Forest Ecosystem Management,* ed. G. Gray, M.J. Enzer, and J. Kusel, 99-116. New York: Food Products Press.
Morris, L. 1990. *The Workings of the Household.* Cambridge: Polity Press.
Moser, C.O.N. 1993. *Gender Planning and Development: Theory, Practice, and Training.* London: Routledge.
Moss, P., J. Eyles, I. Dyck, and D. Rose. 1993. Focus: Feminism as method. *Canadian Geographer* 37: 48-61.
Murray, K. 1995. Women's political strategies in a logging town. In *Living on the Edge: The Great Northern Peninsula of Newfoundland,* ed. L.F. Felt and P.R. Sinclair, 164-84. St. John's: Institute of Social and Economic Research.
National Film Board. 1979. *No Life for a Woman.* Video. Ottawa: National Film Board.
Neal, D.M., and B.C. Phillips. 1990. Female-dominated local social movement organizations in disaster-threat situations. In *Women and Social Protest,* ed. G. West and R.L. Blumberg, 243-55. Oxford: Oxford University Press.
Nesmith, C., and P. Wright. 1995. Gender, resources, and environmental management. In *Resource Management and Development: Addressing Conflict and Uncertainty,* 2nd ed., ed. B. Mitchell, 80-98. Toronto: Oxford University Press.
Ness, K.A. 1992. *Community Resources Boards as a Public Participation Technique for Sub-Regional Resource Planning.* Report for the Resource Planning Section, Integrated Resources Branch, British Columbia Ministry of Forests. Victoria: British Columbia Ministry of Forests.
Neumann, R., and R. Schroeder. 1995. Manifest ecological destinies: Local rights and global environmental agendas. *Antipode* 28: 321-24.
New Lexicon Webster's Dictionary of the English Language. 1990. New York: Lexicon Publications.
Ontario Ministry of Labour. n.d. *The Displaced Workers of Ontario: How Do They Fare?* Report prepared by Ontario Ministry of Labour. In *Vancouver Island Land Use Plan.* Vol. 2: *Appendices.* Victoria: Commission on Resources and Environment.
Oregon Economic Development Commission. 1995-97. Biennial Report. Salem: Oregon Economic Development Commision.
O'Riordan, T. 1976. *Environmentalism.* London: Pion.
Owen, S. 1994. Our forests, our future. Editorial. *Vancouver Sun* 26 March: A23.
Paehlke, R. 1992. Eco-history: Two waves in the evolution of environmentalism. *Alternatives* 19: 18-23.

Painter, M. 1991. Participation and power. In *Citizen Participation in Government*, ed. M. Munro-Clark, 21-36. Sidney, NSW: Hale and Iremonger.
Parr, J. 1990. *The Gender of Breadwinners: Women, Men, and Change in Two Industrial Towns: 1880-1950*. Toronto: University of Toronto Press.
Patai, D. 1991. US academics and Third World women: Is ethical research possible? In *Women's Words: The Feminist Practice of Oral History*, ed. S.B. Gluck and D. Patai, 137-53. London: Routledge.
Pearse, P.H. 1976. *Timber Rights and Forests Policy in British Columbia: Report of the Royal Commission on Forest Resources*. Victoria: Queen's Printer.
Peet, R., and M. Watts. 1993. Introduction: Development theory and environment in an age of market triumphalism. *Economic Geography* 69: 227-53.
Philo, C. 1992. Neglected rural geographies. *Journal of Rural Studies* 8, 2: 193-207.
Pinkerton, E., ed. 1989. *Co-operative Management of Local Fisheries: New Directions for Improvement Management and Community Development*. Vancouver: UBC Press.
–. 1993. Co-management efforts as social movements: The Tin Wis Coalition and the drive for forest practices legislation in British Columbia. *Alternatives* 19: 33-38.
Plumwood, V. 1991. Nature, self, and gender: Feminism, environmental philosophy, and the critique of rationalism. *Hypatia* 6: 3-27.
–. 1993. *Feminism and the Mastery of Nature*. London and New York: Routledge.
Porter, M. 1985. "She was skipper of the shore-crew": Notes on the history of the sexual division of labour in Newfoundland. *Labour/Le Travailleur* 15: 105-23.
–. 1987. Peripheral women: Toward a feminist analysis of the Atlantic region. *Studies in Political economy* 23: 41-73.
Power, T., ed. 1996. *Economic Well-Being and Environmental Protection in the Pacific Northwest: A Consensus Report by Pacific Northwest Economists*. Missoula: University of Montana, Department of Economics.
Pratt, G. 1996. Editorial: Trashing and its alternatives. *Environment and Planning D: Society and Space* 14: 253-56.
Pratt, G., and S. Hanson. 1994. Geography and the Construction of Difference. *Gender, Place, and Culture* 1: 5-29.
Pred, A. 1991. Vega symposium introduction: Everyday articulations of modernity. *Geografiska Annaler* 73B: 3-5.
Preston, V., D. Rose, G. Norcliffe, and J. Holmes. 2000. Shifts and the division of labour in childcare and domestic labour in three paper mill communities. *Gender, Place, and Culture* 7: 5-19.
Price Waterhouse. 1995. *Analysis of Recent British Columbia Government Forest Policy and Land Use Initiatives: Report to the Forest Alliance of British Columbia*. Vancouver: Price Waterhouse.
Prince, M.J. 1996. At the edge of Canada's welfare state: Social policy-making in British Columbia. In *Politics, Policy, and Government in British Columbia*, ed. R.K. Carty, 236-71. Vancouver: UBC Press.
Prior, D., J. Stewart, K. Walsh. 1995. *Citizenship: Rights, Community, and Participation*. London: Pitman Publishing.
Proctor, J. 1995. Whose nature? The contested moral terrain of ancient forests. In *Uncommon Ground: Toward Reinventing Nature*, ed. W. Cronon, 269-97. New York and London: W.W. Norton and Company.
Prudham, S., and M. Reed. 2001. Looking to Oregon: Comparative challenges to forest policy reform and sustainability in British Columbia and the US Pacific Northwest. *BC Studies* 130: 5-40.
Pulido, L. 1996. *Environmentalism and Economic Justice: Two Chicano Struggles in the Southwest*. Tucson: University of Arizona Press.
–. 2000. Rethinking environmental racism: White privilege and urban development in southern California. *Annals of the Association of American Geographers* 90: 12-40.
Randall, J.E., and R.G. Ironside. 1996. Communities on the edge: An economic geography of resource-dependent communities in Canada. *Canadian Geographer* 40: 17-35.

Redclift, M. 1987. *Sustainable Development: Exploring the Contradictions.* London and New York: Methuen.
Reed, M. 1995. Co-operative management of environmental resources: An application from northern Ontario, Canada. *Economic Geography* 71, 2: 132-49.
–. 1997a. Seeing trees: Engendering environmental and land use planning. *Canadian Geographer* 14: 398-414.
–. 1997b. The provision of environmental goods and services by local non-governmental organizations: An illustration from the Squamish Forest District, Canada. *Journal of Rural Studies* 13, 2: 177-96.
–. 1999a. Collaborative tourism planning as adaptive experiments in emergent tourism settings. *Journal of Sustainable Tourism* 7, 3-4: 331-55.
–. 1999b. "Jobs talk": Retreating from the social sustainability of forestry communities. *Journal of Forestry* 75: 755-63.
–. 2000. Taking stands: A feminist perspective on "other" women's activism in forestry communities of northern Vancouver Island. *Gender, Place, and Culture* 7, 4: 363-87.
Rees, J. 1990. *Natural Resources: Allocation, Economics, and Policy.* 2nd ed. London: Routledge.
Reinharz, S. 1992. *Feminist Methods in Social Research.* New York and Oxford: Oxford University Press.
Resnick, S., and R. Wolff. 1987. *Knowledge and Class: A Marxian Critique of Political Economy.* Chicago: University of Chicago Press.
Roberts, R., and J. Emel. 1992. Uneven development and the tragedy of the commons: Competing images for nature society analysis. *Economic Geography* 68: 249-71.
Robinson, J., G. Francis, R. Legge, and S. Lerner. 1990. Defining a sustainable society: Values, principles, and definitions. *Alternatives* 17: 36-46.
Rocheleau, D., B. Thomas-Slayter, and E. Wangari. 1996. *Feminist Political Ecology: Global Issues and Local Experiences.* London and New York: Routledge.
Room, G. 1995. Poverty and social exclusion: The new European agenda for policy and research. In *Beyond the Threshold: The Measurement and Analysis of Social Exclusion,* ed. G. Room, 1-9. Bristol: Policy Press.
Rose, G. 1993. *Feminism and Geography.* Minneapolis: University of Minnesota Press.
–. 1997. Situating knowledges: Positionality, reflexivities, and other tactics. *Progress in Human Geography* 21: 305-20.
Roseland, M. 1999. Natural capital and social capital: Implications for sustainable community development. In *Communities, Development, and Sustainability across Canada,* ed. J. Pierce and A. Dale, 190-207. Vancouver: UBC Press.
Rowell, A. 1996. *Green Backlash: Global Subversion of the Environmental Movement.* London: Routledge.
Ruddick, S. 1989. *Maternal Thinking: Towards a Politics of Peace.* Boston: Beacon Press.
Rural Sociological Society of America. 1993. *Persistent Poverty in Rural America: Rural Sociological Society Task Force on Persistent Rural Poverty.* Rural studies series of the Rural Sociological Society. Boulder, CO: Westview Press.
Sachs, C. 1994. Rural women's environmental activism in the USA. In *Gender and Rurality,* ed. S. Whatmore, T. Marsden, and P. Lowe, 117-35. London: David Fulton.
–. 1996. *Gendered Fields: Rural Women, Agriculture, and Environment.* Boulder, CO: Westview Press.
Sacks, K.B. 1989. Toward a unified theory of class, race, and gender. *American Ethnologist* 16: 534-50.
Safa, H. 1990. Women's social movements in Latin America. *Gender and Society* 4: 354-69.
Salleh, A. 1984. Deeper than deep ecology: The ecofeminist connection. *Environmental Ethics* 6: 339-45.
Samers, M. 1998. Immigration, "ethnic minorities," and "social exclusion" in the European Union: A critical perspective. *Geoforum* 29, 2: 124-44.
Satterfield, T. 2002. *Anatomy of a Conflict: Identity, Knowledge, and Emotion in Old-Growth Forests.* Vancouver: UBC Press.
Schoonmaker, P.K., B. von Hagen, and E.C. Wolf, eds. 1997. *The Rain Forests of Home:*

Profile of a Bioregion. Washington, DC, and Covelo, CA: Island Press with Ecotrust/Interrain Pacific.

Schrecker, T. 1994. Environmentalism and the politics of invisibility. *Alternatives* 20: 32-37.

Scientific Panel for Sustainable Forest Practices in Clayoquot Sound (BC), and F.L. Bunnell. 1995. *Report of the Scientific Panel for Sustainable Forest Practices in Clayoquot Sound*. Victoria: Clayoquot Scientific Panel.

Seager, J. 1993. *Earth Follies: Coming to Terms with the Global Environmental Crisis*. New York: Routledge.

–. 1996. "Hysterical housewives" and other mad women: Grassroots environmental organizing in the United States. In *Feminist Political Ecology: Global Issues and Local Experience*, ed. D. Rocheleau, B. Thomas-Slayter, and E. Wangari, 271-86. London and New York: Routledge.

Seitz, V.R. 1995. *Women, Development, and Communities for Empowerment in Appalachia*. Albany: State University of New York Press.

–. 1998. Gender, class and resistance in the Appalachia Coal Fields. In *Community Activism and Feminist Politics: Organizing Across Race, Class and Gender*, ed. N. Naples. 213-36. London and New York: Routledge.

Sewell, W.R.D., P. Dearden, and J. Dumbrell. 1989. Wilderness decisionmaking and the role of environmental interest groups. *Natural Resources Journal* 29: 146-69.

Shiva, V. 1989. *Staying Alive: Women, Ecology, and Development*. Delhi/London: Kali for Women/Zed Press.

Sibley, D. 1998. The problematic nature of exclusion. *Geoforum* 29, 2: 119-21.

Sierra Club of British Columbia. 1997. *Mid-Coast Cut and Run*. Victoria: Sierra Club of British Columbia.

Sloan Commission. 1945. *Report of the Commissioner Relating to the Forest Resources of British Columbia*. Victoria: King's Printer.

–. 1956. *Forest Resources of British Columbia: Report of the Commissioner*. Vols. 1 and 2. Victoria: Queen's Printer.

Smith, N. 1984. *Uneven Development: Nature, Capital, and the Production of Space*. Oxford: Basil Blackwell.

Smith, S. 2000. Citizenship. In *Dictionary of Human Geography*, 4th ed., ed. R.J. Johnston, D. Gregory, G. Pratt, and M. Watts, 83-84. Oxford and Malden, MA: Blackwell.

Smith, Y. 1997. The household, women's employment, and social exclusion. *Urban Studies* 34, 8: 1159-78.

Snow, D. 1992. *Inside the Environmental Movement: Meeting the Leadership Challenge*. Washington, DC: Island Press.

Sommers, P. 1996. Consensus report denies economy's complexity. In *Changing Northwest* [newsletter of Northwest Policy Center]. Seattle: University of Washington. Available from author.

Stacey, J. 1988. Can there be a feminist ethnography? *Women's Studies International Forum* 11: 21-7.

Staeheli, L. 1996. Publicity, privacy, and women's political action. *Environment and Planning D: Society and Space* 14, 5: 601-19.

Stanley, L., and S. Wise. 1983. Back into "the personal": Or, our attempt to construct "feminist research." In *Theories of Women's Studies*, ed. G. Bowles and R.D. Klein, 192-209. Boston: Routledge and Kegan Paul.

Stanton, M. 1989. Social and Economic Restructuring in the Forest Products Industry: A Case Study of Chemainus. MA thesis, University of British Columbia.

Statistics Canada. 1999. *Profile of Census Divisions and Subdivisions*. 1996 Census of Canada, Catalogue number 95-191-XPB. Ottawa: Industry Canada.

Stone, C. 1986. Power and social complexity. In *Community Power Directions for Future Research*, ed. R. Waste, 77-113. Beverly Hills: Sage Publications.

Sturgeon, N. 1997. *Ecofeminist Natures: Race, Gender, Feminist Theory, and Political Action*. New York and London: Routledge.

Sundberg, J. 1999. Conservation Encounters: NGOs, Local People, and Changing Cultural Landscapes. PhD diss., University of Texas.

Susskind, L., and J. Cruikshank. 1987. *Breaking the Impasse: Consensual Approaches to Resolving Public Disputes.* New York: Basic Books.

Suzuki, D. 1987. A park is won, wilderness fight goes on. *Globe and Mail* 11 July: D4.

Switzer, J. 1996. Women and wise use: The other side of environmental activism. Paper presented at the Western Political Science Association annual meeting, 14-16 March, San Francisco.

–. 1997. *Green Backlash: The History and Politics of Environmental Opposition in the U.S.* Boulder, CO: Lynne Rienner.

Taylor, D. 1992. Disagreeing on the basics: Environmental debates reflect competing world views. *Alternatives* 18: 26-33.

Teather, E. 1996. Farm women in Canada, New Zealand, and Australia redefine their rurality. *Journal of Rural Studies* 12: 1-14.

–. 1997. Voluntary organizations as agents in the becoming of place. *Canadian Geographer* 41: 226-34.

Tennant, P. 1990. *Aboriginal People and Politics: The Indian Land Question in British Columbia, 1849-1989.* Vancouver: UBC Press.

Tigges, L.M., A. Ziebarth, and J. Farnham. 1998. Social relationships in locality and livelihood: The embeddedness of rural economic restructuring. *Journal of Rural Studies* 14: 203-19.

Trower, P. 1993. *Grogan's Café: A Novel of the BC Woods.* Madeira Park, BC: Harbour Publishing.

–. 1996. *Dead Man's Ticket: A Novel of the Streets and the Woods.* Madeira Park, BC: Harbour Publishing.

–. 1999. *Chainsaws in the Cathedral: Collected Woods Poems 1964-1998.* Victoria: Ekstasis Editions Canada.

–. 2000. *The Judas Hills: A Novel of the BC Woods.* Madeira Park, BC: Harbour Publishing.

United Nations Development Program. 1999. *Human Development Report 1999.* Oxford and New York: Oxford University Press.

Valentine, G. 1997. Making space: Lesbian separatist communities in the United States. In *Contested Countryside Cultures: Otherness, Marginalization, and Rurality*, ed. P. Cloke and J. Little, 109-22. London and New York: Routledge.

Vosko, L.F., and L. Bueckert. 1994. *Women in Port McNeill and the Vancouver Island Land Use Plan.* Report prepared for the Ministry of Employment and Investment. Victoria: Ministry of Employment and Investment.

Warren, K.J. 1987. Feminism and ecology: Making connections. *Environmental Ethics* 9: 3-21.

–. 1990. The power and promise of ecological feminism. *Environmental Ethics* 12: 125-46.

–. 1992. Role-Making and Coping Strategies among Women in Timber-Dependent Communities. MSc thesis, University of Washington.

Warrington M. 1997. Reflections on a recently completed PhD. *Journal of Geography in Higher Education* 21: 401-10.

Watkins, M. 1984. A staple theory of economic growth. In *Approaches to Canadian Economic History*, ed. W.T. Easterbrook and M.H. Watkins, 49-73. Ottawa: Carleton University Press.

Weller, G.R. 1977. Hinterland politics: The case of northwestern Ontario. *Canadian Journal of Political Science* 10: 727-54.

West, G., and R.L. Blumberg. 1990. Introduction. In *Women and Social Protest,* ed. G. West and R.L. Blumberg, 3-36. New York: Oxford University Press.

West, P.C. 1994. Natural resources and the persistence of rural poverty in America: A Weberian perspective on the role of power, domination, and natural resource bureaucracy. *Society and Natural Resources* 7: 415-27.

Wharf Higgins, J. 1999. Citizenship and empowerment: A remedy for citizen participation in health reform. *Community Development Journal* 34: 287-307.

Whatmore, S. 1991. *Farming Women: Gender, Work, and Family Enterprise.* London: Macmillan.

Whatmore, S., R. Marsden, and P. Lowe. 1994. Feminist perspectives in rural studies. In *Gender and Rurality,* ed. S. Whatmore, T. Marsden, and P. Lowe, 1-10. London: David Fulton.

White, R. 1995. "Are you an environmentalist or do you work for a living?": Work and nature. In *Uncommon Ground: Toward Reinventing Nature*, ed. W. Cronon, 171-85. New York and London: W.W. Norton and Company.

Widenor, M. 1995. Diverging patterns: Labor in the Pacific Northwest wood products industry. *Industrial Relations* 34, 3: 441-63.

Willems-Braun, B. 1997a. Buried epistemologies: The politics of nature in "post" colonial British Columbia. *Annals of the Association of American Geographers* 87: 3-31.

–. 1997b. Colonial vestiges: Representing forest landscapes on Canada's West Coast. In *Troubles in the Rainforest: British Columbia's Forest Economy in Transition*, ed. T.J. Barnes and R. Hayter, 99-127. Canadian Western Geographical Series No. 33. Victoria: Western Geographical Press.

Williston, E., and B. Keller. 1997. *Forests, Power, and Policy: The Legacy of Ray Williston*. Prince George, BC: Caitlin Press.

Wilson, J. 1997. Implementing forest policy change in British Columbia: Comparing the experiences of the NDP governments of 1972-75 and 1991-? In *Troubles in the Rainforest: British Columbia's Forest Economy in Transition*, ed. T.J. Barnes and R. Hayter, 75-97. Canadian Western Geographical Series No. 33. Victoria: Western Geographical Press.

Wine, S. 1998. *Fury for the Sound: The Women at Clayoquot*. Video. Vancouver: Telltale Productions.

Wolfinger, R. 1971. Nondecisions and the study of local politics. *American Political Science Review* 65: 1063-80.

World Commission on Environment and Development (WCED). 1987. *Our Common Future*. Oxford: Oxford University Press.

Wright, M. 2001. Women in the Newfoundland fishery. In *Framing Our Past: Canadian Women's History in the Twentieth Century*, ed. S.A. Cook, L.R. McLean, and K. O'Rourke, 343-46. Toronto: Oxford University Press.

Young, I.M. 1990. *Justice and Politics of Difference*. Princeton: Princeton University Press.

Index

Aboriginal peoples. *See* First Nations
activism, 14-15; appropriateness and, 126-27; around practical-domestic concerns, 218-19; choices in, 223; within community culture, 153-54; content vs location, 222; and dependence, 11-12; embeddedness of, 13, 15-16, 222-23; environmental, 152-53; gendered aspects, 14; gendered division of labour and, 126; income sources and, 135; international, 36; location of, 13, 15, 47, 223; multiplicity of forms, 155-56, 221, 222, 225-26; policy changes and, 127; progressive vs conservative, 16; repressive/progressive, 229-30; social contexts, 13, 15-16, 222-23; social services and, 126; space and, 16; status quo retention in, 15, 119; withdrawal from, 170-71
advocacy, 14
African American women, 121
Agarwal, Bina, 12-13
Agricultural Land Reserve, 62
agriculture, and forestry, 173-74
Allan, Graham, 8, 9
anti-environmentalism, 132; citizenship and, 48; environmentalism and, 14, 47-52, 222, 226; forestry protection as, 218; wilderness preservation and, 220, 226, 229; wise use movement and, 49
aquaculture, 18. *See also* fish hatcheries
attachment; community of, 8; to forestry, 80, 114, 222; to forestry communities, 161-62; to place, 121-22
attitudes, 112-13

bargaining power, 202, 206-7
barge incident, 159-60
Barnes, Trevor, 27

Bauman, Zygmunt, 53
BC STATS, 237
Beaver Cove, 102
beliefs, 112. *See also* values
Berman, Tzeporah, 229
Binkley, Clark, 38
Birkeland, Janis, 211, 212
boom-and-bust cycles, 27, 45, 69
boundaries; of communities, 9, 162-3; rural/urban, 179; solidarity and, 162
Brown, Beverly, 76
Brundtland report on sustainable development, 27-28
Bryant, Bunyan, 225
Bryant, Christopher, 224
Bueckert, Lynn, 199-201
Buttel, Frederick, 25, 48-49

Canadian Institute of Forestry, 135
Canadian Pacific Railway, 32
Canadian Women in Timber (CWIT), 50, 136-37, 151, 159, 167, 171, 229, 235
Carroll, Matthew, 8, 30-31, 218
caulk boots, 79
Central Coast plan, 19, 212
child care, 94, 97, 200
children, in protests, 175-76
Chinese immigrants, 32
Chipko movement (India), 154
citizen participation, 227; participatory citizenship vs, 211-12, 213, 228
citizenship; anti-environmentalism and, 48; marginality and, 39, 40; participatory, 211-13
class, 46-47
Clayoquot Sound Peace Camp, 3-4, 154-55, 163-66
Clayoquot Sound protests, 3, 19, 52, 59, 64, 159, 186

clear-cutting, 65-66
Coalition for Shared Resources on Northern Vancouver Island, 140
Cody, Linda, 229
command power, 202, 203-6
Commission on Resources and the Environment (CORE), 19, 190, 191; achievements, 60, 61-62, 192-93; consensus decision making and, 193; consensus decision making under, 193; creation of, 59; employment under, 194-95; focus on jobs, 195, 199, 210; gender stereotypes under, 193; harvest reduction under, 194; job losses under, 87, 198; land use charter, 60, 192; land use plan, 4, 29, 66; land use planning, 59-60, 192-94; mandate, 59; power relations structure and, 192; protected areas under, 18-19, 194; rally against, 166-68; sectoral interests under, 193; social impacts for women, 190; and societal inequalities, 193; stress and, 106, 107; sustainability and, 195; transition strategy, 195; and women's employment, 87, 197-98; and women's roles, 195-97; zoning system, 61
communities: of attachment, 8; boundaries in, 9, 162-63; cracks in consensus, 182-85; effects of employment losses, 210; forestry (see forestry communities); home and, 118; insider/outsider divisions, 9, 186, 187; interest, 8; occupational, 8; rural (see rural resource communities); social groups vs, 8-9; territorial, 7. See also forestry communities; rural resource communities
community development activities, 117, 120-21, 129-36, 137-38, 154
compliance: employment in, 103, 168, 169-70; stress and, 109
computers, 109. See also Internet
cone picking, 100-1, 138-39
conflict: and planning process, 191; in wilderness protests, 59
conservatism: community work and, 16; home and, 119; progressive activism vs, 16; of social mothering, 119
consumption, 117, 153, 220
core-periphery framework, for economies, 45
corporate interests, in VICORE, 203-4, 205
Crowe, Graham, 8, 9
Crown land, 58
cultural imperialism, 43

culture: defined, 53; of forestry (see forestry culture); rural vs urban, 53-54; worker, 54

danger, in forestry occupations, 105-6, 107, 113, 132
Daniels, Steven, 218
day care. See child care
deindustrialization, 74
Demeritt, David, 249, 251
demographic structure of North Island, 88
developing countries, 35-36, 227
Di Chiro, Giovanna, 121
dichotomies, 6, 229-30; anti- vs pro-environmentalism, 14, 47, 222, 226 (see also anti-environmentalism; environmentalism); of masculinity/femininity, 6, 11, 119; preservation/use, 6; progressive/conservative, 16, 229; regressive/progressive, 229-30; rural/urban, 6; us/them, 175, 186, 187
difference: in feminist theory, 6; focus on, 6; recognition of, 228
discursive exclusions, 40
diversification, economic, 45, 75, 195
division of labour, 45-47. See also gendered division of labour
Doeringer, Peter, 83
dominant society, 43-44
drop-in centres, 123-24
Dunk, Thomas, 179

East Indian settlers, 32
ecofeminism, 3, 5, 12, 154, 218
economic dislocation, stress from, 196-97
economic restructuring, 25-26, 69-70, 73-74; community management work in, 120; stress from, 196-97
economic sustainability, 28, 208
economic transition, 69-70, 73-74, 87
ecosystems: forest, 58; management, 71
ecotourism, 110-11
education: common-sense vs, 54; employment and, 95, 110
Egan, Brian, 86
embeddedness, 222-23; of activism, 13, 15-16; of environmental perspectives/positions, 13-14; within forestry culture, 114; within place, 15-16; social, 13-14, 15-16, 81, 122; of transition strategies, 15-16; of women's work, 114
employment: disparity in opportunities, 81-82; drops in, 38-39, 69-70 (see also job losses); education and, 95, 110;

effect of restructuring upon community/household economies, 227; family considerations and, 95-97; forestry culture and, 97-98; future of, 110; gender differences during restructuring, 38-39; lack of opportunities, 75; mobility and, 95; power relations and, 96-97; production uncoupled from, 69; reductions under CORE, 194; social sustainability and, 197-99; transportation and, 94-95; volunteer work and, 134-35. *See also* women's employment

employment insurance, 68, 87

enforcement, 71; employment in, 103, 109

environmental nongovernmental organizations (ENGOs), 3, 32; as enemy, 187; and forest ecosystems, 58; internationalization and, 30; as mainstream, 51; social implications and, 5, 28, 70; and sustainability, 65; sustainability and, 28; wilderness preservation and, 26, 33, 36

environmental quality, spatial differences for, 121

environmental sustainability, 28-29, 208

environmentalism, 71, 225, 226; anti-environmentalism and, 14, 47-52, 222, 226; defined, 48; evolution of, 229; feminist (*see* feminist environmentalism); feminist theory and, 5; as mainstream, 51; and marginalization of forestry communities, 41, 217; northern/southern divide, 179-80; as religion, 176; resource extraction and, 161; rhetoric about, 176-77; rural/urban divide, 179; and social justice, 5, 55; in universities, 180-81; wise use movement and, 49; women and, 12-13

environmentalists: perceptions of, 165-66; stereotyping of, 181-82; and work in nature, 34

environmentalization, 48-49, 55

ethnic communities, 32, 34, 205

exclusions: discursive, 40; material, 40; moral, 43, 160-63, 224; social, 38, 42, 68

exploitation, 41-42, 224

families: employment and, 95-97; extended, 94; in protests, 175; separated, 95-96; type of activities and, 135. *See also* home

Farnham, Jennifer, 81

femininity/masculinity, 6, 11, 34, 119

feminism: planning and, 190-91; poststructuralist, 155

feminist environmentalism, 5, 12-13, 14

feminist politics vs women's politics, 118

feminist theory, 5, 6-7

First Nations, 26, 32; cultural activities, 18; government and, 67; land claims, 34, 63; and land tenure, 63-64; poverty among, 205; and wilderness, 34

fish hatcheries, 171-72

fishing, 18

Fitchen, Janet, 8, 9

food banks, 127

foreigners, protestors as, 163, 165, 174. *See also* Germany

Forest Alliance, 50, 184

Forest Jobs Commission, 66-67

Forest Land Reserve Act, 62

forest management practices, 64-66, 132, 133

Forest Practices Code, 65-66, 102, 103-4, 108-9, 109-10, 168-70, 178, 184

Forest Renewal BC (FRBC), 8, 67, 240, 246, 248-50

Forest Renewal Plan (FRP), 67

forested landscapes: as resource landscapes, 31-33; as wilderness landscapes, 31, 33-35

forestry: attachment of women to, 80, 114, 220; future of, 110; management practices, 151, 153; new definition of, 67; as primary industry, 87; volume-based vs value-intensive, 28; women's employment in, 84-87, 98-99

forestry communities: boundaries and openings in, 162-63; challenges for women, 151; and changes in forestry practices, 151; Clayoquot Sound Peace Camp and, 163 (*see also* Clayoquot Sound Peace Camp); community identity within, 185-87; defined, 7, 9-10, 82; economic well-being, 37-38, 45; globalization and, 27; identity within, 52-53; and international environmentalism, 52; lifestyle, 220; marginalization, 36, 40-41, 161, 217; MOF employment and, 168-69; rhetoric of, 183-85; social infrastructure, 38; solidarity within, 127-29, 162; students from, 180-81; sustainability and, 27; sustained yield policies and, 58; transition and, 26, 27, 30-31; women's attachments to, 117, 161-62. *See also* communities; rural resource communities

forestry culture, 83, 225; containment of women in, 97-98; danger and, 106, 113; employment and, 97-98; hard

work/hard play in, 106, 113; as male-dominated, 141, 153; masculine identity and, 112, 113; moral exclusion and, 160; negative aspects, 125, 139, 149-50, 152, 221; opposition to changes, 186; positive formations of, 162; shared, 53, 186-87; traditions, 185
forestry days, 153, 162
forestry employees, women, 98-99
forestry tours, 174-75
forestry-town women, 4, 5-6, 10, 11, 79, 87, 219
forestry workers: CORE emphasis on, 199; displacement of, 46; economic circumstances of, 35; as nature lovers, 177-78; unions and, 38. *See also* loggers
Friends of Clayoquot Sound, 163, 229
Fury for the Sound, 163

Garcia-Guadilla, Marcia, 14, 117, 199
gender: environment and, 12-13; and environmental activism, 14; exploitation, 41-42; identities, 12, 16, 117, 122-23; ideology, 124; interests, 14; job losses and, 85, 198; landscape interpretation and, 34; and political participation, 120; relationship with nature and, 12, 155; roles/relations, 10-12; and transition strategies, 189-90, 197; and Vancouver Island Land Use Plan, 194, 195-97; wages and, 89, 93-94, 103, 113
gendered division of labour, 82, 85-86, 88, 113-14, 126, 197
Germany, influence on Canadian forestry, 165-66
Gibson, Katherine, 46-47
Gibson-Graham, Julie-Katherine, 6, 21, 47, 236, 245, 255n19
globalization, 27, 44, 52, 63
government: and land use planning, 202; in planning process (CORE), 209; responsibility for lands, 58; role in forest land, 32-33, 33-34. *See also* policy; regulation(s)
government-industry cooperation, 71
grading, 102
Granovetter, Mark, 81
Grass, Eric, 38-39, 85
Great Bear Rainforest, 19, 33, 65
Great Bear Wilderness, 33
Green Gold (Marchak), 5, 86
Green parties, 166
Greenbelt movement (Kenya), 154
Greenham Common (England), 154
greening, 48-49

Greenpeace, 51, 148, 159-60, 163, 165, 166, 175, 229
Griffin Cohen, Marjorie, 74
groups: identification of, 8-9; marginalized, 6, 37; as "other," 43, 49; pluralism and, 191-92; selection for participation in VICORE, 203-4; social, 8-9. *See also* communities

habitat protection, 135
Hanson, Susan, 15, 83
Harding, Sandra, 218, 241
harvest reductions under CORE, 194
harvesting methods, 70, 132
Hayter, Roger, 27, 38-39, 44, 83, 85
health services, 68, 201, 224-25
helicopter logging, 70, 107, 108
Hessing, Melody, 30
highgrading, 45
home, 219; community and, 118; conservatism and, 119; isolation within, 123. *See also* families; public/private domains
Homemaker, 163
home/work separation, 82
hooks, bell, 223
Howlett, Michael, 30

identity, -ies: formation of collective, 53; gender (*see under* gender); multiple, 6, 187, 226; rural, 52, 53; shared, 53
identity politics, 224
ideology: gender, 124; and women's employment, 104
income: activism and, 135; levels, 92(t); part-time, 89; sources of, 88, 135; women's, 88-89, 92(t), 93-94, 103, 113, 135, 150-51, 153. *See also* consumption; wages
Indo-Canadians, 205
influence, in planning process, 202-3, 206-8
Innis, Harold, 44
insider/outsider divisions, 9, 37, 186, 187
integrated resource management, 33, 133, 134
interest communities, 8
International Union for the Conservation of Nature and Natural Resources (IUCN), 27-28
internationalization, 30, 69-70
Internet, 30, 52
Island Copper Mine, 18
isolation, 75, 123

job losses, 132; community effects, 38, 210; under CORE, 61, 87; Forest Jobs

Commission and, 66; gender differences in, 85, 198; seniority and, 108; social exclusion and, 42; for women, 209
job segregation, 82, 88-89
jobs: classification, 86; CORE emphasis on, 195, 199, 210, 227; Forest Practices Code, 109-10; manufacturing, 102-3; new, 67, 110-11, 168
Jobs and Timber Accord, 67
Joseph, Alun, 224

Kennedy, Robert Jr., 52
Kennedy Lake Division, 164
kinship networks, 185
Klausen, Suzanne, 86
Kusel, Jonathan, 218

labour market, and infrastructure development, 68
labour segmentation, 82-84
labour studies theory, 218
labour unions. *See* unions
land: Aboriginal claims, 34, 63; allocation, 59-64; CORE definition of, 192; tenure, 58, 62-63; zoning, 61
land and resource management plans (LRMPs), 19, 66
Land Use Charter (CORE), 60, 192, 207-8
land use planning: agenda in, 206; CORE's definition of, 192; funding of representation, 206-7; power relations in, 202-3; public policies, 58-59, 132; sectoral coalition model, 193, 205-6; the state and, 202. *See also* Vancouver Island Land Use Plan
layoffs, 74, 85. *See also* job losses
Lee, Kai, 213, 217
Liepins, Ruth, 155
life chances, diminishment of, 224
livelihood, protection of, 35-36, 52, 54, 150, 224
loan programs, 201
log scaling, 102
logger sports, 53, 221
loggers, 10, 176; female, 98; rhetoric about, 177-79
loggers' wives, 4, 10, 98, 219
logging, 105-6, 107, 138, 225
Lower Mainland, 25

MacGregor, Sherilyn, 190-91
MacMillan Bloedel. *See* Weyerhaeuser
mainstream environmental organizations, 51
manufacturing jobs, 102-3, 107

Marchak, Patricia, 83-84; Green Gold, 5, 86
marginality: citizenship and, 39, 40; defined, 37; of rural residents, 226-27; of women, 99
marginalization: and economic relations, 37; of forestry communities, 36, 40-41; four-part framework, 41-44, 217-18, 224; of groups, 6, 37; liberal ideas, 37; Marxist ideas, 37; of women, 11, 204-5, 221
marriage breakdown, 205
Marshall, Thomas, 39
Marston, Sallie, 82, 118
masculine identity: and changes in forestry practices, 151; in forestry culture, 112, 113
masculinity/femininity, traditional conceptions of, 11, 119
masculinity/femininity dichotomy, 6
Massey, Dorren, 121
material exclusions, 40
McDowell, Linda, 21, 37, 241
McLain, Rebecca, 213
Mellor, M., 15
middle-aged, new jobs for, 110-11
Mifflin Plan, 170
mining, 18
Ministry of Forests (MOF), 32-33, 109-10, 132-33; employment in, 103-4, 168-69
mobile communications, 109
mobility, 9, 95, 123. *See also* transportation
Mohai, Paul, 225
Molyneux, Maxine, 120
moral exclusion, 43, 160-63, 224
Moser, Caroline, 120
Mount Waddington Community Resources Board, 19
Mount Waddington Regional District (MWRD), 17, 22, 82, 89; industrial participation rates, 90-91(t)
Mountain Equipment Co-op, 179
multinational firms, 63
multiplicity, 6, 13, 155-56; in forms of activism, 221, 222, 225-26; of identities, 6, 187, 226; in layering of marginality, 205; of rural positions, 47; and social relations, 121
Murray, Kathleen, 119-20

nature: identity, and relationship with, 12, 155. *See also* wilderness
networking, 123
Nevada Nuclear Test Site, 155
New Democratic Party (NDP), 57, 68, 73

Nisga'a Agreement, 64
noncompliance, 71
North Island, 17-21
North Island Women, 139, 143
Nuu-Cha-Nulth First Nation, 229
Nuu-Cha-Nulth Tribal Council, 64-65

occupational community, 8
oppositional politics, 53
Oregon, 75-76
"other," groups as, 43, 49. *See also* us/them dichotomy
out-migration, 74, 197, 210-11, 224, 225
Owen, Stephen, 4, 190
ownership, of forest lands, 58

Paehlke, Robert, 48
paid employment. *See* employment; jobs; women's employment
participatory citizenship, 211-13, 228
part-time income, 89
Patai, Daphne, 241
paternalism, of companies, 185-86
patriarchal structures, and political participation, 119-20
Pearse, Peter, 58-59
pesticides, 182
Piore, Michael, 83
place, attachments to, 121-22
planning processes, 202; agencies, as neutral, 191-92; conflict and, 191; CORE's definition of, 192; feminism and, 190-91; participatory, 202; as political process, 191; power relations and, 209, 228; scale of, 212; values-based vs interest-based, 212
policy: changes, and activism, 127; changes in, 29, 38, 57; economic, 73; initiatives, 59-60; land use, 58-59; role of, 71; social, 72-73; sustained yield and, 58; in transition, 27. *See also* government; regulation(s)
political participation: domesticity and, 120-21; opportunities, 205; within patriarchal structures, 119-20
Port Alberni, 27, 86
Port Alice, 88, 107
Port Hardy, 93
Port McNeill, 88, 93, 127, 173
positionality, 36
poststructuralist feminism, 155
poverty, 73, 74, 205
power relations: among groups, 191-92; and employment, 96-97; within household, 96-97; and planning process, 202-3, 209, 228

powerlessness, 42-43, 224
Pratt, Geraldine, 15, 83, 222-23
praxis, 53
Pred, Allan, 122
preservation, of wilderness, 6, 26, 36, 44, 229
Prince, Michael, 72
Prince George, 85
Prior, David, 211
private property rights, 50, 63
production: uncoupled from employment, 69; volume-based vs value-intensive, 28
Protected Areas Strategy (PAS), 19, 62, 207, 208
protests: Clayoquot Sound (*see* Clayoquot Sound protests); against CORE, 61, 167-68; families in, 175-76; fears regarding participation, 177; and us/them dichotomy, 186, 187; women in, 3-4. *See also* activism
Provincial Land Use Strategy, 59
public/private domains, 7, 13, 14, 118, 217
Pulido, Laura, 36, 51, 53, 54-55, 224

quality of life, and environmental issues, 224

rainforests: as focal point of activism, 52; in tropical areas, 35
recession, economic, of 1980s, 73
recreation, 18
reforestation, 58
regulation(s), 132; environmental, 71-72
Reinharz, Shulamit, 21
restructuring, 27; economic, 25-26, 69-70, 73-74, 120, 196-97; of employment, 38-39, 227; social, 73-76; women portrayed in, 11
retirement age, 88
retraining, 66, 68, 112-13, 200. *See also* training
rhetoric: about environmentalism, 176-77; of forestry communities, 183-85; about loggers, 177-79; stereotyping, 177
ribbon campaigns, 53
right, political, 73, 209
roads, 94-95
Rose, Gillian, 251
Rowell, Andrew, 49
Ruddick, Sara, 118, 220
rural identity, 52, 53, 221
rural lifestyle, 150, 161, 225
rural resource communities, 8, 225; in

boom-and-bust cycles, 27, 45, 69; effects of social restructuring, 74-76; gender relations in, 10-11; isolation and, 123; marginalization, 226-27; sustainability and, 29; traditional conceptions of masculinity/femininity in, 11, 119. *See also* communities; forestry communities
Rural Sociological Society of America, 43, 160-61
rural women's organizations, 122
rural/urban divide, 6, 179-82, 224

Sacks, Karen, 46
Safa, Helen, 120-21
salaries. *See* income; wages
salmonid production, 135, 171
Samers, Michael, 40
Satterfield, Terre, 80, 146, 154
SSHRC, 248, 251
Seager, Joni, 155
Seitz, Virginia, 37, 120
self-help programs, 127
sexism, 99-101, 104-5, 114, 126
SHARE movement, 49, 140, 142, 151, 164, 229
Sharpe, Joanne, 37
shutdowns, 108
Sierra Club, 163
Skills Now, 68
Sloan Commission, 58
small businesses, 201
Social Credit government, 73
social dislocation, 52, 175, 176, 204
social exclusion, 39-40, 42, 224
social group vs community, 8-9
social infrastructure, 38, 68
social issues, and structural biases, 205
social justice, 5, 41, 55
social loss, 75
social mothering, 118, 119, 135, 219-20
social policy, 72-73
social relations: activism embedded in, 13, 15-16, 222-23; multiplicity shaping, 121; socioeconomic restructuring and, 75
social restructuring, 73-76
social services: changes in, 68-69, 125-26, 201; and CORE, 209; employment in, 197; future of, 224-25; regionalization, 68-69; unemployment and, 201
social sustainability, 29-30, 195-97, 204, 207-8, 217, 227
social transactions, 202
social transition, 29-30, 68
socioeconomic status, 112

solidarity: CORE rally and, 168; within forestry communities, 127-29, 162; through Clayoquot Sound Peace Camp, 163
Sommers, Paul, 46, 76
spatial entrapment, 94
Stacey, Judith, 241
Staeheli, Lynn, 16, 221-22
staple thesis, 44-45
state, the. *See* government
status quo, retention of, 15, 119
stereotyping, 43; CORE and, 193; of environmentalists, 181-82; exclusion and, 161; rhetoric and, 177
Stewart, John, 211
stigma, social, 75
stream restoration, 135, 144, 152, 153, 182
stress: changes and, 106-7; from Clayoquot Sound protest, 164; from due diligence, 109; from economic dislocation, 196-97; Forest Practices Code and, 108-9
surveillance: employment in, 133, 168
sustainability: CORE and, 60; definitions of, 27-28; economic component (*see* economic sustainability); environmental component (*see* environmental sustainability); rural vs urban ideals, 26; social dimension of (*see* social sustainability); transition and, 30-31. *See also* economic sustainability; environmental sustainability; social sustainability
sustainable development, 57-58
sustained yield, 57

Taylor, Duncan, 48
Teather, Elizabeth, 15, 121-22
technological changes, 69, 71, 107-8, 132
territorial communities, 7
Tigges, Leann, 81
timber extraction, 32
Toastmasters, 143
tourism, 18, 110-11, 113
trade disputes, with US, 74
training, 95-96, 103, 195, 200, 201. *See also* retraining
transfer payments, federal-provincial, 73
transition, 26; defined, 26; economic, 29; forestry communities and, 30-31; government measures, 66-69; in interpretation of forested landscape, 31-35; job opportunities and, 98; programs, 29; public policy debate in, 27; social, 29-30, 68; sustainability and,

30-31; from volume-based to value-intensive production, 28
transition strategies: for community needs, 200-1; embeddedness of, 15-16; gendered aspects, 189-90, 197; paid employment in, 190, 201; proposed by CORE, 195; socioeconomic, 209; targeting of jobs, 227; for women, 200-1; women's contributions and, 227
transportation, 94-95, 123, 201
treaties with Aboriginal peoples, 63-64
tree planting, 117
Trower, Peter, 231

uneven development, 44-45, 47, 54, 224
unions, 38, 204
United Nations Development Conference, Rio de Janeiro, 1992, 148
universities, environmentalism in, 180-81
urban areas, environmental degradation in, 36
urbanites, 165, 172-73, 220-21
us/them dichotomy, 175, 186, 187. *See also* "other," groups as

values, 112; changes in, 29; identification of shared, 212-13; moral exclusion and, 160; shared, 186-87
values-based vs interest-based model, of participatory planning, 212
Vancouver Island CORE (VICORE), 193, 203
Vancouver Island CORE regional plan, 60-61
Vancouver Island Land Use Plan, 4, 19, 67, 147, 159, 166, 194, 195-97, 199-201
volunteer work, 119, 120, 134-35, 136, 209
Vosko, Leah, 199-201

wages, 106, 107, 111; family, 42, 110; gender difference in, 89, 93-94, 102-3, 113; in office jobs, 103
Walsh, Kieron, 211
welfare provisions, 68
welfare state, 72, 73-74, 209
Western Canada Wilderness Committee, 180
Weyerhaeuser, 65, 229
White, Richard, 34
wilderness; forested landscape as, 31, 33-35; gender and, 34; preservation of,

6, 26, 36, 44, 229; resource landscapes and, 35; urbanites and, 172-73; working forest vs, 172
wise use movement, 49, 175, 176
women: dependent on forestry, 99 (*see also* forestry-town women); disempowerment of, 42-43; in forested landscape, 32; income, 88-89, 92(t), 93-94, 103, 113, 135, 150-51, 153; in industrial disputes, 11; isolation of, 123; job losses for, 209; marginalization of, 11, 204-5, 221; perspectives on land use planning, 200; planning and, 190-91, 198-99; rural organizations, 122; socioeconomic restructuring and, 73-74; transition strategies for, 200-1; voices muted, 223-24
women in forestry communities, 98
women in forestry families, 98
Women in Timber, 50, 136
women's centres, 127
women's employment, 113; classification of, 83-84, 86, 87; and CORE, 87, 197-99; disengagement from, 97-98; domestic work and, 124-25; embeddedness and, 81; lack of opportunities, 75, 93, 221; limitations on, 89, 93-96; marginality in, 99; percentages in forestry, 81; traditional vs nontraditional, 84; transition and, 98
women's identities, 10, 156, 219, 222, 226
women's interests: collectivity vs differences, 228
women's issues: marginalization of, 204-5
women's politics: feminist politics, vs, 118
worker culture, 54. *See also* forestry culture; loggers
workers' wives, 10, 11, 79
workforce participation rates, 88, 90-91(t)
work/home separation, 82. *See also* public/private domains
working forest, 32, 171-74
workingman's culture, 83
World Wide Web, 71-72

yellow ribbon campaigns, 53, 132
Young, Iris Marion, 8-9, 41, 42

Ziebarth, Ann, 81